LOCATING CONSCIOUSNESS

ADVANCES IN CONSCIOUSNESS RESEARCH

ADVANCES IN CONSCIOUSNESS RESEARCH provides a forum for scholars from different scientific disciplines and fields of knowledge who study consciousness in its multifaceted aspects. Thus the Series will include (but not be limited to) the various areas of cognitive science, including cognitive psychology, linguistics, brain science and philosophy. The orientation of the Series is toward developing new interdisciplinary and integrative approaches for the investigation, description and theory of consciousness, as well as the practical consequences of this research for the individual and society.

Volume 4

Valerie Gray Hardcastle

Locating Consciousness

LOCATING
CONSCIOUSNESS

VALERIE GRAY HARDCASTLE
Virginia Polytechnic Institute and State University

JOHN BENJAMINS PUBLISHING COMPANY
AMSTERDAM/PHILADELPHIA

The paper used in this publication meets the minimum requirements of American National Standard for Information Sciences — Permanence of Paper for Printed Library Materials, ANSI Z39.48-1984.

Library of Congress Cataloging-in-Publication Data

Hardcastle, Valerie Gray.
   Locating consciousness / Valerie Gray Hardcastle.
     p.   cm. -- (Advances in consciousness research, ISSN 1381-589X ; v. 4)
   Includes bibliographical references and index.
     1. Consciousness. 2. Philosophy of mind. 3. Human information processing. I. Title. II.
Series.
BF311.H338   1995
128'.2--dc20   95-31971
ISBN 90 272 5124 X (Eur.) / 1-55619-184-7 (US) (Pb; alk. paper)   CIP

John Benjamins Publishing Co. • P.O.Box 75577 • 1070 AN Amsterdam • The Netherlands
John Benjamins North America • P.O.Box 27519 • Philadelphia PA 19118-0519 • USA

FOR MY PARENTS

Table of Contents

List of Tables and Figures

Preface

In my (albeit limited) experience in these matters, I have discovered that there are two sorts of people engaged in the study of consciousness. There are those who are committed naturalists; they believe that consciousness is part of the natural world, just as kings and queens and sealing wax are. It is completely nonmysterious (though it is poorly understood). They have total and absolute faith that science will someday explain this as it has explained the other so-called mysteries of our age.

Other are not as convinced. They might believe that consciousness is part of the natural world, but surely it is completely mysterious. Thus far, science has had little to say about conscious experience because it has made absolutely no progress in explaining *why* we are conscious in the first place. Different folk draw different morals from this observation. Some conclude that a scientific theory of consciousness is well-nigh impossible; others believe that it is possible, but do not expect anything of value to be immediately forthcoming; still others remain confused and are not sure what to think.

I have also noticed that these two camps have had little to say to one another — their differences are deep and deeply entrenched. There are few useful conversations; there are even fewer converts. Nevertheless, they all can agree that consciousness presents us with a conundrum if we see the mind fundamentally as an information processing machine. For, if we understand the mind as a system that takes in bits of information via sensory transduction, transforms those bits according to some computational algorithm, and then outputs the transformed bits of information, presumably as some motor response, *consciousness disappears*. Consciousness has no impact on the structure of the input, the transformational algorithms, or the final form of the information.

Some conclude that insofar as consciousness plays no causal role in any mental processing, then the phenomena of consciousness have no place in theories about the mind. If we antecendently accept information-processing models of the mind, we relegate consciousness to a domain untouched — and maybe untouchable — by scientific inquiry.

However, by my lights, insofar as we want to maintain that we are sentient, simply ignoring the phenomena of consciousness is unacceptable. The mind is conscious. Somehow our mental processes give rise to this phenomenon. Moreover, I am a member of the naturalist camp. Hence, I hold that there is not any obvious *a priori* reason why consciousness cannot be studied and modeled scientifically.

Indeed, I believe absolutely and certainly that empirical investigation is the proper approach in explaining consciousness. What needs to be changed is our information processing approach to the mind. Changing the way we view the mind so that we give greater weight to the neurophysiological underpinnings opens the possibility that we can locate consciousness in the dynamical structure of the neural firing patterns. In this book, I examine what neuropsychology can tell philosophers about qualitative experience. And in proposing my own more "structural" theory of consciousness, I aim to remove the conundrum of consciousness from the cognitive sciences.

If you are interested in exploring what science tells us about conscious experience today, both with respect to developing an empirical theory and with respect to philosophical issues within the naturalist framework, I encourage you to read on. I am peddling two things here: a theoretical framework for understanding consciousness and a vision about how to understand the project in general. You can't buy one without the other; but beware: the vision isn't really for sale. You probably already have to buy into the basic tenets of materialism, mechanism, and naturalism before you can sincerely appreciate what follows.

And what follows are details. Naturalists are convinced that science can tell us something important about conscious experience. Well, what can it? And how does what we know answer the broader philosophical concerns? In particular, I focus on the three following questions and their relation to various skeptical challenges. (1) What are the appropriate properties of the mind and the brain to study in order to develop a theory of consciousness? (2) What informational role does consciousness play in our psychological life? (3) How does the underlying neurophysiological structure of consciousness relate to higher-level information processing descriptions of consciousness?

By answering these queries, I generate naturalist responses to the more recent and popular philosophical arguments against the possibility of any scientific theory of consciousness by spelling out how much we in fact already know about the phenomena of consciousness and how this information should be integrated into a theory proper. In what follows I sketch philosophical landscapes and illustrate how naturalists do and should think about them, given the data.

I see two motifs running through this work. First, under the rubric of philosophy of mind, I examine how best to unite the information processing theories in psychology with hypotheses based on neural network research and anatomical and physiological data from neuroscience. More specifically, I use my analysis of the empirical issues to focus on particular theoretical and conceptual difficulties associated with our modern version of the mind/body problem. For example, the computer metaphor, so rampant in cognitive psychology, has fundamentally misled our analysis of mentality for it strips computational theories of their connection with underlying physical interactions. A truly interdisciplinary perspective opens the possibility that consciousness is best understood as a "structural" phenomenon relative to our higher level informational processing capacities.

Second, in a purely empirical framework, I sketch recent data concerning multiple memory systems, which I believe is the most promising avenue for advancing a scientific theory of consciousness. This framework reflects work done by others as well as experiments I have carried out myself. By studying the different functional properties of each memory system, we can begin to understand the type of causal network that underwrites consciousness. As we quantify the interactions of our memory systems, we move ever closer to understanding the properties of consciousness.

I intend this book to function as an extended example of interdisciplinary research. I support my philosophical and speculative arguments using data drawn from cognitive and developmental psychology, AI programming, linguistics, clinical neurology, neurophysiology, and neuropsychology. In turn, I try to develop a perspective that all these fields should be able to use when considering the phenomena of consciousness, or defending themselves against well-meaning but skeptical philosophers.

Acknowledgments

Chapters 1, 2 and 3 draw on a previously published paper, "The Naturalists versus the Skeptics: The Debate Over a Scientific Theory of Consciousness," 1993, *Journal of Mind and Behavior* 14.27-50, copyright 1993, *The Journal of Mind and Behavior*. Chapter 6 is a revised and expanded version of the previously published article, "Psychology's Binding Problem and Possible Neurobiological Solutions," 1994, *Journal of Consciousness Studies* 1.66-90. I thank the editors for permission to use the material.

This research was funded in part by a research assistantship and a travel grant from the Philosophy Department at UCSD, two generous summer research fellowships from the McDonnell-Pew Foundation for Cognitive Neuroscience, a fellowship from the American Association of University Women, and a pilot project grant and a creative match grant from Virginia Polytechnic Institute and State University. I am grateful for this support.

I am also in debt to a great many individuals, without whom this book simply would not have occurred. Gary Cottrell, Jerry Doppelt, Charles Dupre, Owen Flanagan, Charles Gray, Dan Lloyd, George Mandler, Sandy Mitchell, Harlan Miller, Helen Neville, Vilayanur Ramachandran, Maxim Stamenov, and an anonymous referee read earlier drafts of this book and provided detailed comments. The final product is much better because of them. In addition, I must acknowledge Partricia Churchland for pointing me in the right direction and for sharing her amazing wealth of knowledge. Owen Flanagan gave detailed suggestions concerning the first three chapters and has supported me throughout this project. Dan Lloyd recommended I include chapter 5 and gave me a hard time with chapter 7 — both important moves. Walter Freeman, Charles Gray, and Ann Treisman were kind enough to discuss their research and their philosophical inclinations with me, and chapter 6 is much richer for it. Patricia Churchland and Patricia Kitcher commented on earlier versions of chapter 8.

Sharon Coffey, Debra Mills, Margaret Mitchell, John Polich, Twyla Saferty, Chris Weber-Fox, and most especially Helen Neville taught me the ins and outs of ERP research, which culminates here in chapter 9. Bertie Kaal, Joe Pitt, and Maxim Stamenov were endlessly patient and quite helpful my attempts in finding a home for this project.

I also owe tremendous thanks to my understanding husband, who knew who I was long before I did, and to my three well-behaved children, who have grown up believing mothers are permanently attached to word-processors. Finally, I must mention my parents, to whom this book is dedicated. I have been very lucky in having two parents who have always maintained that I was the best at everything — even when I quite clearly was not. This unflagging (and maybe irrational) support gave me the confidence to try my best anyway. I wrote this book to answer my own questions. However, I could not have done so without my parents literally and metaphorically watching over me.

VGH
Blacksburg, Virginia
May 1995

Naturalism about Subjective Experience
Chapter One

That we have minds is a wonderfully eerie fact about us. But minds are strange indeed, for they are conscious — at least in part. We have astoundingly vivid perceptions of the world. I go to the symphony and hear symbols crashing, flutes warbling, violins sighing, tubas booming. I see the conductor waving her hands, the musicians concentrating, patrons shifting in their seats, and the curtains gently and ever-so-slightly waving. I smell the perfume of the woman next to me, the damp must of the chairs, the ink on the program. What is a mind such that it has these amazing powers?

This book tries to answer this question. I want to know: What is consciousness? And how is it related to our understanding of the rest of ourselves? Of course, how we answer these questions depends upon what metaphysical status we accord the mind and consciousness. Needless to say, there are a multitude of different ways of conceiving them. I am a materialist and a naturalist. That is, I believe that there are only physical objects in this universe and that consciousness is part of this universe. Moreover, I believe that consciousness can be completely explained within the framework of natural science. I try to do this here. I am confident that I at least make a substantive start.

I also recognize though that laying my cards on the table at the beginning is not enough. I need to explain why materialism and naturalism are correct. The phenomena of consciousness are weird, no doubt about it. We can talk ourselves into quite scary situations if we contemplate our own phenomenological experiences too long. Some people think that this weirdness means that consciousness is beyond the pale of science. There is gap between conscious experience and scientific explanation that cannot be breached. In this chapter and the next one, I articulate why I don't find such sentiments persuasive. I complete my introduction in chapter 3 by arguing against various eliminativists who are materialists and naturalists, but who think that consciousness is not an appropriate subject matter for science nonetheless.

The real work then begins in chapter 4. I am interested in what science already knows about consciousness and whether we can fit this information into a tidy, digestible package. I think we can. Moreover, I think that the result is both surprising and interesting. But I am getting ahead of myself. Let us first meditate on the weirdness of consciousness and what that means for the possibility of scientific inquiry.

1.1. What the Mind Is Not

Most of us have dualist tendencies. In our common, everyday, nonreflective interactions, most of us act as though we believe that minds are not bodies. We talk about thoughts coming to us in a moment of inspiration, not about information processing among layers of neurons. We claim we walked to the refrigerator to get a beer because we were thirsty, not because of certain muscular contractions. But living in a linguistic community that implicitly assumes a division between the mind and body gives us little reason to believe that (some version of) dualism is true. Our linguistic practices arise and are maintained because they allow us to communicate with one another successfully. They are designed to get us what we want with a minimum of effort. What is actually the case, what science (for example) claims the world is like, is an entirely separate matter. Keeping our intuitions and our folk practices separate from what is reasonable to believe on other grounds will be a theme in this book. I acknowledge that most of the time we think as though we are dualists; however, I want to consider for a moment the more principled arguments for why one might want to be a dualist.

By far, the most popular defense of dualism today rests on an argument from irreducibility. The argument itself dates back to Descartes. He suggested that neither reason nor language — two paradigm mental capacities — were the sort of thing that one could implement in purely physical devices. The advent of artificial intelligence programming, however, suggests that Descartes is probably wrong. Though we don't (yet) have machines that reason as we do, nor do we have machines that successfully "speak" or interpret natural languages, we do have a rough idea how a machine might be built and programmed to do these things. In any event, the abilities to reason and to speak a language no longer mystify scientists such that they feel forced to postulate the existence of mental stuff as the only way to account for these capacities.

Nevertheless, even though reason and language appear might be explained or modeled in terms of some set of physical interactions, other properties of our mental states are not so clearly reducible. The qualitative character of perceptions and sensations is such a case. How could the blueness of a blue sky, the bitterness of foul-tasting salt peter, the clatter of a noisy train be merely the interactions of some physical components? It is fairly easy to understand how one might build a machine that would be able to differentiate blue skies from gray, salt peter from tuna sandwiches, or noisy trains from silent ones in terms of reflected wave triplets, chemical composition, or atmospheric compression waves. However, it seems beyond imagination how any machine would thereby *experience* these properties.

Notice that what is gripping in this argument are deep intuitions concerning mechanical interactions. We just can't picture what is necessary for consciousness; certainly no particular causal interactions seem to be (more on this point in chapter 7). Hence, we can't imagine consciousness as a purely physical process. What holds us in dualism's sway is a certain fundamental failure in imagination.

But the story does not end here. These sorts of intuition pumps — however satisfying in isolation — conflict radically with the materialist program of science. Materialism has a vast array of resources at its disposal. It can draw on all we know about the brain to gesture towards explaining consciousness. And we do know a great deal about our brains. Neuroanatomists have charted the general pattern of connectivity among and within brain areas. Neurophysiologists can characterize approximately what sorts of inputs the different areas process. With the help of mathematicians and computer scientists, they are also starting to understand the properties of the nonlinearly connected networks and circuits that comprise the various brain areas. In addition, we know quite a lot about the function of individual neurons — what makes them "fire"; which ions flow through their membranes; how neurotransmitters work. Though there is much work left to be done and much we still do not know, science does provide us with a scaffolding such that we can envision how the eventual complete story of the brain might run.

Moreover, this scaffolding also gives us a sense of how a materialist theory of the mind might go. Scientists have catalogued a number of interesting and specific correlations between some interference with the brain and a subsequent change in mental state. These include the connections between the hippocampus and memory, the frontal lobes and purposive actions, the lateral geniculate nuclei and vision, Wernicke's areas and linguistic abilities, cortical activation and arousal, as well as the ingestion of cocaine and euphoria, alcohol and disinhibition, ibuprophin and the cessation of pain, lysergic acid diethylamide and perception.[1] Though there are hugely important questions for which we have nothing even approaching an answer (why do we sleep? how do we regulate our levels of alertness?), we are nonetheless left with an impression of how some mental events result from purely physical interactions.

When we contrast this relatively rich predictive nexus with what dualists can tell us about the properties of mental substances, we quickly see that a dualist science of mind would not be nearly as advanced as our materialist mind/brain sciences. Dualists cannot tell us much about the nature of mental substances — are they composed of more fundamental elements? how do they come into existence? when do they go out of existence? what laws govern their operations? Dualists cannot tell us about types of interactions that mental substances engage in — can minds affect other minds directly? how do they "animate" a body? can bodies affect minds? Indeed, it is difficult to tell how they would even go about answering these questions from a scientific point of view. In sum, there is nothing that even approximates a dualist theory of mind. And without *some* sort of foundational principles, we can't conceptualize a serious program of dualism. Previous intuitions notwithstanding, dualism is a bust as an explanatory position.

Here we find the most basic difficulty with explaining consciousness. On the one hand, our intuitions are strongly dualistic. It is extremely difficulty to conceive what a satisfactory explanation of qualitative phenomena would look like in a materialist framework. On the other hand, the framework of science is materialist and it is extremely difficult to conceive how a dualistic explanatory scheme might work.

This tension motivates most dualists to retreat to a dualism about properties, while maintaining a monadism about substances. Property dualists concede that the materialist mind/brain sciences provide powerful explanatory schemes. However, they also notice that most theories concerning the brain leave untouched important aspects of the mind. For example, neurophysiological or neuropsychological theories might correlate brain events with certain changes in one's mental states, but they do not explain what these mental states *are*. A vast explanatory gulf exists between what we know about the brain and what we know about our own minds. Our best scientific theories exclude the phenomenal world systematically. Hence, mental phenomena must be non-reducible properties of brain events, untouched and untouchable by our best scientific theories.

This view comes in two flavors: *epiphenomenalism* and *interactive property dualism.* (To be fair, I should point out that not all epiphenomenalists are property dualists, but, at least in modern instances, their motivations for adopting this position are relevantly similar.) Epiphenomenalists believe that, contrary to appearances, some mental phenomena do not causally interact with anything physical. Consciousness "rides above" the physical, similar to the way steam rides above a train, or the hum rides above a machine. The brain might cause consciousness, but then once caused, consciousness does little more.

Consciousness then becomes a property of our minds, brought about by brain events, but whirling along without interference or interfering. If we examine the brain carefully, it is true that there does not seem to be anything in there that is mind-like. We find chemicals reacting, neurons firing, and patterns forming. We do not find my belief that Reno is west of San Diego, my desire to avoid skin cancer, my perception of Brush Mountain at sunset, the sensation of my tongue against my teeth — nor do we find anything that even resembles these things. Moreover, consciousness being epiphenomenal would certainly explain why the sciences omit the mental. Since scientists are primarily concerned with predicting and explaining causal interactions in this world, if consciousness does not causally interact, then trivially it would be beyond the scope of scientific reckoning.

This fact notwithstanding, a true epiphenomenalist position is not plausible. (As far as I know, no one actually publicly subscribes to being an epiphenomenalist either.[2]) Consider for a moment how we know about things in this world. We know about things by causally interacting with them (or representations of them). But any sort of causal theory of knowledge immediately rules out the possibility of knowing that we have minds or consciousness.[3] How would we know that we are conscious if we cannot causally interact with our consciousness in any way? If consciousness is epiphenomenal, we can't sense the products of its interaction (since it doesn't have any). But if it doesn't affect the body, then we have no way of verifying — even implicitly — that consciousness exists at all, including our own consciousness.

That is a crazy conclusion, of course. I know that I am conscious, even if I don't know what that is exactly. And I know this as a result of interacting with the world and my mind. My mind affects the world and the world affects my mind. I explain my actions as stemming from certain conscious perceptions or beliefs. I ducked because I saw a ball headed in my direction. I felt hungry, so I ate a Snickers bar. My conscious perceptions are prior to and necessary for my verbal reports of those perceptions. I say my dog appears shaggy to me because I sensed that my dog is shaggy. A property dualism epiphenomenalism has to be false.

One might respond that true epiphenomenalists don't believe I learn about my mind by causal interactions. I know about my conscious states in some other way. However, it is unclear to me how one could be a materialist and maintain that position cogently. Once we give up on dualism for independent reasons (perhaps for the considerations of simplicity, parsimony, and consiliance alluded to above), we are restricted to discussing only causal interactions in the world, for that is just what a materialist view of the world presumes. With materialism comes mechanism: things happen because of some interaction of forces or another.

Perhaps though one could claim that I learn about my qualitative experiences immediately, hence denying any distinction between the "raw feels" of experiences and our judgments concerning those experiences. Introspection would then be a special sense that would tell us how things are to us without any sort of (other) cognitive mediation. We just know how things seem to us because don't need to think about it. Judgments aren't required for experiences; we just have them. We distinguish introspection from our other senses by claiming that introspective access is direct and infallible (more on this below).

Our visual system tells us that grass is green and solid. However, contrary to appearances, we know that objects are in fact mostly empty space and that we perceive color in virtue of triplets of photons being reflected off lattices of molecules. Our auditory system tells us that B.B. King is playing the blues. However, contrary to appearances, we know that a sound is in fact a compression wave train in an atmosphere. Our somatosensory system tells us that the room is hot. However, contrary to appearances, we know that temperature is mean molecular kinetic energy. But being green does not look like reflected photons; being solid does not look like empty space; hearing a tune does not sound like a compression wave train; heat does not feel like mean molecular kinetic energy. As Locke held, our senses tell us that *something* is happening in our environment, but they do not give us insight into the real nature of things. We distinguish a thing's *appearance*, which is how it seems to us, from its *reality*, how it actually is. And no one expects our perceptual systems to give us a privileged access to reality.

Should we expect introspection to fare any differently? I maintain that when we introspect, we perceive some appearance and then make a judgment about that experience. Our introspective judgments could be wrong, just as our perceptions and judgments about the external world can be wrong.[4] Absent some argument (which, as far as I know, no epiphenominalist has given), we have no more reason to believe that introspection gives us insight into how things really are any more than other sense.

At first blush, it might seem perverse to think that we could be mistaken about what we are thinking or feeling — after all, who would know better than I how things seem to me? I might be mistaken about how things actually are in the world, but I can't be mistaken about how *I think* they are. There doesn't seem to be any appearance/reality distinction for the mind. I can understand that the table is mainly empty space and I can applaud the science that gives us that result. But if science were to develop a theory of consciousness such that one implication of the theory is that I am not conscious, I would not remark upon the sophistication of the science that could produce a that result. On the contrary, I would say that there has to be something wrong with the theory because I know that I am conscious. End of story.[5]

On the other hand, though, there are ways in which we might be mistaken about how things seem to us. To take an easy example, suppose that you have a pitcher of iced tea in the refrigerator, but you (mistakenly) believe the container is full of apple juice. Being thirsty, you quickly pour yourself a glass of the liquid and gulp some down. What is your initial reaction? My reaction, at least, is that I have just drunk some spoiled apple juice. It is only upon reflection that I realize I had consumed iced tea instead. Or let us take Paul Churchland's (1984) more macabre example. Suppose I am torturing you by applying small but painful electric shocks to the nape of your neck. After twenty or so of these shocks, now (unbeknownst to you) instead of jabbing you with an electrode, I touch you with an ice-cube. What is your reaction? Most likely, you would first react in pain and then only upon reflection realize that the last stimuli was cold, not painful.

Bottom line: We can be mistaken about how things seem to us; we can incorrectly judge the qualitative character of our experiences. Despite our intuitions, there is a coherent and robust appearance/reality distinction between our perceptions and our judgments of those perceptions. Hence, it makes sense to require an epiphenomenalist who wishes to deny a causal theory of knowledge to defend the claim that introspection is a special sense. And until done, the weight of the evidence (not our intuitions) suggest that knowledge of self works just knowledge of anything else; we learn by interacting and judging.[6]

Upon reflection, we can see that epiphenomenal properties would be very strange beasts anyway. Aside from the mind, there is nothing else in the universe that could stake a claim to being epiphenomenal. Even steam and hums interact with the world. Steam drives turbines and hums can shatter glass, if they are loud enough. Of course, steam might not causally interact with the train that produces it, just like hums might not interact with the machines that produce them. But that is very different from claiming that they don't interact with *anything at all*. The mind would truly be mysterious and anomalous if it were epiphenomenal.[7]

Again, programmatic considerations of parsimony, consiliance, and simplicity, as well as our basic mechanistic view of the world suggest that we should drop the claim to epiphenomenalism. Once again, dualists must retreat. We are left with the view that the mind somehow emerges from and interacts with the brain, but is not reducible to it. We are left with an interactive property dualism which holds that mental properties are things arising out of the very complexity of our brains' neuronal connections and firing patterns, but are more than a mere sum of that activity. Consciousness is greater than the sum of its parts, as it were.[8] We can't account for all mental phenomena just in terms of physical machinations; the mind is *from* the brain, but not *of* the brain.

Though admittedly vague, this sketch of a position suffers from an irresolvable tension between the mind being non-reducible and being a property of the physical. If something cannot be explained in terms of the physical, then it is unclear how it could be a physical property. Similarly, it is difficult to see how one might account for physical properties except by recounting physical events. Any other property which we take to emerge from underlying complexity — such as solidity, color, being alive — is explicable in terms of the underlying physical interactions. Of course, we didn't always believe in the reducibility of those properties, but as science progressed, we learned otherwise. We know now, e.g., that the "*elán vital*" is nothing more than a set of completely non-mysterious chemical reactions. Similarly, even though we have no actual reductions of consciousness available today, *prima facie* there is little reason to assume that they won't be forthcoming.

Considering the past success in these sorts of reductions and explanations in science, a case has to be made that somehow the mind is special such that, regardless of how science progresses, it will elude any sort of reduction to a physical science. Of course, the argument from irreducibility is supposed to do just that. It seems quite inconceivable that we could ever be able to account for the qualitative feel of our sensory impressions, memories, and so on in purely physical terms. Are these intuitive pushes on the explanatory gap telling?[9]

We have already seen that reason and language no longer appear as plausible candidates as something that cannot be reduced to mere physical interaction. Qualia though are a different story. In part, this book is designed to address this issue. For the moment, however, it looks as though this argument is a draw. Dualistically-minded skeptics are right when they claim that we do not have an account of how we might reduce or explain the qualitative character of experience in purely naturalistic terms. Many have tried; most have obviously failed; no one has succeeded yet.

But in order to run their argument, the skeptics have to claim something stronger. It is not enough to point out that the reduction hasn't occurred yet; they have to show that it *can't* be done. In order to use the argument from irreducibility to prove that consciousness cannot be reduced, then they have to claim that it is *impossible* to account for minds in terms of purely physical interactions. As far as I know, no one has done that either yet. At best, the skeptics can claim that they can't see how it could be done, but this is just the failure of imagination mentioned earlier. Not being able to imagine something is not the same thing as not being possible.[10] Dualists lacks a positive argument for their position as well.

The jury is still out. Materialists shouldn't claim that all aspects of the mind are reducible; dualists shouldn't claim the contrary. The best we can say is that we simply don't know yet. However, the argument from irreducibility does not work as an argument against materialism. Until we know more, it should not move us one way or the other. Nevertheless, just because we have not shown conclusively that consciousness is reducible to and explainable in materialist framework does not mean that we should be silent. Other factors should mitigate our intellectual bets. The weight of scientific evidence points to there only being one sort of stuff in the universe. That fact coupled with the lack of positive arguments for dualism implies that consciousness is not metaphysically special — there is nothing spooky or mysterious about it.

1.2.   The Naturalists Versus the Skeptics

However, if I set qualia on the table as *explananda*, I inevitably confront theorists such as Thomas Nagal (1974) who argue against any possibility of a naturalist theory of consciousness, regardless of consciousness's metaphysical status. How exactly am I to understand their complaints, given that we agree that consciousness is part of the material world and that science is in the business of explaining the different parts of that world? Here and in the next chapter, I address the question of what exactly we should be able to derive about the qualitative character of individual experiences from a completed theory of consciousness, taking seriously the idea that the properties of consciousness are non-mysterious. At the end of the discussion, I hope that it will be clear that the materialist position I adopt is completely uncontroversial. When we clarify what the naturalists and the skeptics are both claiming, we shall see that they do not actually disagree with one another in a serious way.

Here again is the difficulty: On the one hand, we know that brains somehow are conscious. On the other hand, we so thoroughly fail to understand this causal connection that *any* link between the two seems utterly mysterious, even eerie.   Neurotransmitters, neurons, neuronal firing patterns, neural networks — none of these seem to be the right stuff for being conscious. We want to explain how a change in the brain produces a change in phenomenology; we want to be able to point to a property of the brain that can account for the psychophysical link.   Having a solution to this mind-body problem means, among other things, removing the spookiness of the link between the brain and consciousness, notwithstanding intuitions about the impossibility of the project. More specifically, having a solution means explaining how the subjective aspects of experience depend upon the brain (and possibly its environment).

There is a fairly vague but deep sentiment that even if we could point to this natural attribute as the causal factor in question, something important would still be left out, *viz.*, the subjective aspects or the "first-personness" of consciousness.   Nagel articulates a distinction between the subjective and the objective such that there is conceptual division between (subjective) qualitative experience and the (objective) products of scientific investigation.   Subjective experiences, according to Nagel, are representations from the vantage point of a particular life form and from a particular position. In contrast, objective representation's defining features are "externality and detachment" (1979: 208). The contrast he sees is clear: science understands the world "from nowhere in particular and [from the point of view of] no form of life in particular at all" (p. 208); subjective experience, on the other hand, can only be grasped "from the vantage point of a special type of life and awareness" (p. 208). "Every subjective phenomena is essentially connected with a single point of view," therefore, "objective, physical theory [inevitably abandons]...that point of view" (1974: 166). Nagel concludes that a scientific theory of qualitative conscious states is oxymoronic: "if the facts of experience — facts about what it is like *for* the experiencing organism — are accessible only from one point of view," then "the true character of experiences" simply cannot be unveiled an mechanical account of the brain (p. 166).[11]

Some naturalists respond that this feeling of malaise results from misunderstanding what science actually does. In the final analysis, I agree with this sentiment — there is something profoundly wrong about letting our untutored intuitions govern *a priori* the possibilities of knowledge. However, there is labor involved before making this point. Let us examine what explaining consciousness scientifically would amount to.

The skeptics worry that any naturalistic or scientific explanation of consciousness, in virtue of being a third-person, "objective" account, necessarily fails to capture the true and fundamental character of personal subjective experience. Facts about experience, facts about what these experiences are like for an organism, are accessible only from particular first-person stances and any "scientistic" theory will ignore single points of view. If any naturalistic story cannot even adequately *describe* half of the psychophysical equation under question, then it stands to reason that whatever property of the brain we point to as the relevant causal factor would fail to capture consciousness adequately as well (except perhaps accidentally).

Following Owen Flanagan, we can see this worry as having two components: (1) any objective science will "fail to *capture* what consciousness is from a particular point of view," and (2) any completed scientific account will "fail to *exhaustively analyze* consciousness" (1985: 386, italics his). Naturalists argue that both components of the worry indicate that skeptics fundamentally misapprehend the abstract nature of scientific theory. They hold that while the first claim may be true, it is irrelevant, and that the second is simply false (*Cf.,*

Flanagan 1985, 1992; Rorty 1982; see also Dennett 1982). I discuss the first component in the remainder of this chapter, and the second in chapter 2.

Science is interested in uncovering general laws which govern the behavior of types, not tokens. Individual instances of phenomenological experience are not the *explananda* of theories. Instead, theories want to explain what is common to all experiencing creatures (Flanagan 1985, 1992). We should not expect any scientific theory of consciousness to tell us what it is like to be any single person at a particular time directly since science does not deal with particulars in that manner. For example, we would not expect to derive from the laws of planetary motion alone where Venus shall appear first in the sky tonight. Likewise, we should not expect to know from a theory of visual processing what color Bill Clinton is observing at this moment. Instead, science presents us with general rules that we can use to calculate a particular instance when conjoined with specified boundary and initial conditions. Skeptics can't complain that a theory of consciousness will not tell us directly what it would be like to be another person at this particular moment, for no theory does that for any phenomenon.

But perhaps I am begging the question against the skeptics here. I am suggesting that individual subjective experiences and first person reports of those experiences serve as the evidence for more encompassing scientific theories and that consequently the skeptics simply misunderstand where the first person point of view fits into the game of science.[12] But perhaps the skeptics intend that first person points of view are the *only way* to describe qualitative experiences adequately. If this is the case, then theory-building using third person perspectives cannot even begin, so whether any resultant theory is from no particular point of view is inconsequential. The skeptics' point would stronger than merely complaining that any completed theory will abandon individual instance, for any attempt to describe the *data* objectively must fail in the first place.

But if this is what the skeptics mean, then I think they still fail to understand how first person accounts are used in theory-building and the connection between our everyday, first person, "folk" descriptions of how the world seems to us and our objective, third person, scientific theories about the workings of that world. It is simply not the case that physical theories disregard first person points view. We know, for example, that objects which appear red to us do so because they reflect a certain wavelength triplet of electromagnetic radiation. We know that surfaces which seem warm to us do so because their mean molecular kinetic energy is above a certain level relative to the MMKE of our skin. And so on. Science regularly and nonproblematically redescribes the way the world seems to us from our first person point of view in third person objective terms.

This form of *concept translation* falls out of a broad and loose connection between two explanatory frameworks. We get a concept translation when we claim that the translating predicate in the new conceptual framework can be applied in (at least) all the cases in which the translated predicate was thought to have applied in the old conceptual framework. And we are licensed to make these identity statements in virtue of the preservation of the causal factors needed for explanation in the old conceptual framework.[13] By explicating the physical mechanisms in virtue of which qualitative events conform to some generalization, we can thereby exhibit first person generalizations as rough analogs of true scientific theories. In particular, a term *f* in the old conceptual framework translates to term *g* in some new theory just in case we can translate a description of the *causal powers* into the new scheme, and some sort of bridging regularity links *f* and *g*. Being an *f* translates to being a *g* if and only if the causal powers of being an *f* are a subset of the causal powers of being a *g* and *f* regularly co-occurs with *g*.[14] The point of the translations would be to explain the success of the generalizations of our folk conception of the world by translating those generalizations to a more rigorous and detailed scientific vocabulary.[15]

Skeptics who accept that any scientific account will fail to capture what consciousness is like believe that the entity denoted by *f* exists and co-occurs with some set of circumstances addressed by the new theory, but *f* cannot be translated to any term in the new theory. This will happen whenever the new theory does not have the wherewithal to define all the causal powers of being an *f*. Does this happen with the phenomena of consciousness and, say, neuroscience? To argue that it does, the skeptic must argue that (1) even if we know everything there is to know about the properties of brain states, (2) there still is something we don't know about the properties of sensations, namely, what it is like to have a sensation.[16]

However, Paul Churchland (1989) points out that that argument is a *non sequitur*, for it equivocates on "knows about."[17] This ambiguity turns on the distinction between "knowledge by description" and "knowledge by acquaintance" (*Cf.*, Bertrand Russell 1912). The former refers to propositional knowledge. We know things by description in virtue of understanding the appropriate sentences. The latter refers to having some experience or other — we know by acquaintance our own perceptions, regardless of how we later characterize them. Churchland describes it as "having a representation...in some prelinguistic or sublinguistic medium...for sensory variables, or...being able to *make* certain sensory discriminations, or something along these lines" (p. 62). So, to take Frank Jackson's (1986) famous example, color-blind Mary knows red by *description* since she is a super-scientist who understands all aspects of normal brain processing, but she does not and cannot know red by *acquaintance*, since the cones in her retina simply do not respond to the appropriate wavelengths. My daughter Kiah is only four and has barely heard of a brain, much less does she comprehend how it operates. She does not know red by description. However, she will happily point out all tokens of red when queried, indicating that she knows red by acquaintance. The difference between what Mary and Kiah know is not a difference in *thing*; *ex hypothesis* they both know red well. Rather, the difference resides in *how* they know it.

We can see this difference clearly if we rewrite the skeptic's arguments to remove its ambiguity: (1) even if we understand the complete set of true sentences about the properties of brain states (know mental states by description), (2) we still may not represent sensations prelinguistically or be able to make sensory discriminations (know mental states by acquaintance).[18] No naturalist would disagree. There are more ways of knowing than knowing by description. Concept translation does not precludes this. However, being acquainted with conscious states directly does not mean that we cannot have third-person accounts of consciousness; rather it means simply that we can represent the world to ourselves in a variety of ways.

If first person accounts and third person accounts are just different sorts of descriptions of the same events, then objective accounts should include all the causal powers of subjective accounts. This worry that scientific accounts of consciousness necessarily can't capture individual points of view adequately then must be unwarranted, for if both conceptual frameworks could describe the same causal interactions, albeit in different terms, then whatever we see from the first person point of view, we should be able to describe in the third.[19]

But perhaps I have again misunderstood the skeptics' position. Perhaps their complaint is not that first person perspectives can tell us things that a third person account could not specify *with respect to* a scientific theory. Rather, perhaps it is that any complete specification of the boundary and initial conditions end up being viciously circular in that they will always already assuming what it is like to be conscious instead of allowing us to predict the quality of such states. If we are going to predict the location of Venus, we not only need to know the laws of planetary motion and the location of the heavenly bodies at some previous time, but we also implicitly rely on general background knowledge about how our universe works. For example, we assume that the laws of gravitation will continue to hold in the future. We do not believe that the path of Venus will be disturbed by interstellar aliens. And so on, for an indefinite number of assumptions. This is information that normally we do not explicitly specify when performing the actual calculations or derivations in order to predict some future event. Nevertheless, a successful prediction depends upon this background knowledge in just the same way that it depends on the explicit specification of the more traditional boundary and initial conditions.

Let us now move closer to the issue at hand. We can read a description of the Civil War. In so doing, we can then imagine what it would be like to have been in the Civil War. How do we do this? Of course the description isn't the war; it is an abstract history of the events which details (perhaps) relevant psychological, economic, and sociological theories plus the initial conditions for the conflict. We then use our background knowledge of what it is like to fight, what it is like to be hungry, what it is like to be cold, what it is like to be scared, what it is like to hurt, and so on, to go from the abstract history to a detailed imaginative event.

Now this scenario does seem relevantly similar to the previous example of using the laws of planetary motion, specified boundary and initial conditions, plus relevant background information to make a specific prediction about where Venus will be tonight. However, there is one crucial difference. In predicting the location of a particular planet we do not need to have in our background knowledge or in the specification of the boundary and initial conditions information about what planets *are*. That is, as long as we can uniquely identify the heavenly body in terms of its orbital path, then its *planetness* does not enter our calculations. Hence, we can learn about properties of planets without already knowing them. This is just what scientific progress is. However, when we are imagining what it is like to fight in the Civil War, it seems that we carry in the background all the relevant knowledge of what it is like to be a soldier. The description tells us the rules for applying that knowledge in this particular case, but the only way we know what it is like to be a Civil War soldier is if we already know what it is like to be in certain states. We implicitly have in our background knowledge exactly what it is that a complete description of the Civil War should specify, namely, what it is like to be a soldier.

Here then is the question: Would applying a "theory" of mind be more similar to predicting the location of Venus or to reading a Civil War history? That is, can we predict what it is like to have a particular quale without already assuming what it is like to have it? If we were to remove our background knowledge of what it is like to have experiences, could we, purely on the basis of abstract theoretical relations and specified boundary and initial conditions, bootstrap our way into what the resultant qualitative experience would be like? Presumably the skeptics would answer no.

Let us consider a particular case. Suppose we wanted to know what it is like to be under the influence of lysergic acid diethylamide without taking the drug itself. Now suppose that whatever it is like to be under the influence of LSD, it is qualitatively different than any other experience. In this case, it seems we would have no background knowledge that would make predictions concerning LSD-experiences circular. Could we make this prediction? I think the answer is yes: If we know what effect LSD has on the brain, then all we have to do is force our brains into a similar configuration, perhaps through the use of other drugs. Of course, this would not be a *true* LSD-experience — it would only mimic one — but maybe it would come close enough. In this case, we could bootstrap our way into what a particular qualitative experience would be like.

We perform this sort of "derivation" all the time when we communicate with one another. Though we don't literally force our brains into alternative configurations, we do try to do arrange circumstances so that we can feel what it is like to feel something new. You might press the palms of your hands against your eyes to feel what it is like to see the stars you would see if you were hit over the head. We use third person language plus ostension to make our points: Press the palms of your hands into your eyes. *That* perception of stars is what I am talking about.

But these examples might be cheating. It may be true that we need not have LSD experiences to understand them, but we have had experiences of what it is like to be something. Is there some kind of knowledge about qualitative states, specifically, what it is like to have them, that cannot be had unless one already has qualia? Owen Flanagan finds this possibility completely unremarkable: The presumption that "the qualitative feel of some experience should reveal itself in a theoretical description" willfully ignores what scientific theories are (1992: 93). Of course, a complete account of the Civil War will not reproduce the war. But this remark is not quite to the point. Maybe what we need to know is whether we can make predictions about what it is like to have an experience without knowing what experiences are like at all.

Here, I think the discussion stops. Maybe a theory of consciousness would be fundamentally circular; maybe it would not. I submit that we have no clear intuitions about sophisticated cognizing creatures who are not conscious themselves but are trying to project what consciousness must be like. The thought experiments and intuition pumps the skeptics and the naturalists traditionally rely upon fail radically at this juncture because we can't conceptualize the possibilities adequately enough. I, for one, have no intuitions about what science-oriented nonconscious aliens could or could not know. That circumstance is so far beyond my usual realm of experience, I just don't know how to think about it.

Instead, let us grant the skeptic the circularity and turn to an easier question. Suppose it *were* the case that we could not devise a non-circular account of consciousness. Does this mean that the project itself should be abandoned or is hopeless? Is this then the something special about consciousness that makes it fundamentally beyond the reach of science? Of course, a language may not be able to express certain facts because of limitations in its expressive power. For example, the quantificational truths cannot be expressed in propositional calculus. However, we can extend propositional calculus to produce a quantificational calculus that can then express any quantificational truth. The supposition I am making is that no matter how a third person language is embellished or extended, it will fail to convey the knowledge of what it is like to have qualitative states to a subject who has never actually had them. Is consciousness special in that this feature is present only in the case of qualitative states?

Perhaps not. There seems to be an analogous situation with theories about time and temporal states. There are facts about the temporal aspects of objects, states, and events that we can know only by being at a certain moment in time which we cannot express from a third person perspective. For example, there is no text which expresses what time it is. A complete history of the world can convey the sequence of events, what follows after what, the date of each of event. But no book expresses which event in the series is happening *now*. Even if our objective language were extended to include not only terms for temporal locations (dates) and relations ("before," "after," "simultaneous with") but also the indexical "now," no text would capture, record, articulate, or express what time it is now. The sentence, "Now it is *t*," would not tell us that it is now *t unless* we were in time and at *t.* To *know* what time it is now, we have to *be* at that time.

Philosophers have disagreed about the significance of this feature of time. John McTaggart (1927) makes much of the thesis that times having tenses as well as dates is an essential feature of time and uses the "paradoxes" which plague the notion of tense to argue that there really is no such thing as time. David Mellor (1981) counters with an account of time as real but without being tensed. He argues that the knowledge we have when we know what time it is nothing more than knowledge about certain linguistic tokens (*viz.*, that certain tokens are true).

But regardless of where one comes down on this debate, what seems relevant about the analogy between time and qualia is this. Even if it is true that certain features about time cannot be expressed in a third person language, it does not follow that there cannot be a theory of time. We have one, thanks in part to Einstein. Moreover, science has discovered startling things about time — it is frame-relative; it is part of a space-time continuum; it may not be unidirectional. Therefore, even if it were true that certain features about qualia cannot be expressed in a third person language to those who have never been conscious, it need not follow that there can be no third person, objective, naturalist theory of conscious states that explains consciousness.

I conclude that the first component of the skeptics' worry, that objective science will fail to capture what consciousness is from a first person perspective, is unfounded. Science can redescribe first person accounts in third person language and preserve all relevant causal powers. Theoretically, we could use these third person accounts and our knowledge of what it is like to have qualitative experiences to "derive" what other experiences must be like by putting our brains in similar configurations. A combination of third person descriptions and ostension seems to be all we need. Finally, I acknowledge that any scientific account of consciousness might be circular in that it would only explain consciousness to creatures who are already consciousness, but a theory of consciousness would not be special if this were the case. Time appears to be subjective in a manner similar to consciousness and we have perfectly acceptable theories of time. This worry misses the mark.

So we have little reason to be a dualist, though we do have dualistic intuitions. *A priori* any identification of consciousness with something in the brain might seem far-fetched. But then again, maybe *a priori* most identifications seem far-fetched. Aside from Democritus, who would have believed that water was H_2O before we had molecular chemistry? Cognitive dissonance alone is not a reason to give up on science. Presumably in an appropriately rich framework, all (correct) identifications and explanations make sense. Thus far, those who are already committed to naturalism have little reason to change.

The Limits of Theory
Chapter Two

We should not think though that because a scientific description should be able to capture the first person perspective and that other theories grapple with the seemingly elusive aspects of our world that all is now roses for the naturalists. There are limits to theories. They only explain certain things and not others. We need to examine the other component of the skeptics' complaint and investigate whether a theory of consciousness will tell us what we want to know about qualitative experience. Here, I think, the skeptics might have a point.

2.1. Theory and Observation

The skeptics' second worry is that any completed scientific account will fail to analyze consciousness exhaustively. Nagel argues that "any shift to greater objectivity — that is, less attachment to a specific viewpoint — does not take us nearer to the real nature of [subjective experience]: ...it takes us farther away from it" (1974: 172). Objective descriptions, even if they can translate first person accounts, will take us "farther away" from the what consciousness really is. Any move away from individual experience will abstract over something about that experience, hence leaving it out of the objective description of consciousness.

Flanagan (1985, 1992) responds to this suggestion as follows: Nagel is ambiguous about what he means by "real nature." If he means "real nature" to refer "to the way things seem to some particular person," (1985: 387) then of course a third person description will be "farther away." But there is no mystery why first person accounts are "closer" to the phenomena — people, after all, have the conscious experiences. We are all "uniquely causally well-connected" to our own phenomenology (p. 387); hence, we each have a special relation to how things seem to ourselves. But given the discussion above, this sort of special connection is nonproblematic. As long as the objective viewpoint can still account for the phenomena, then its "distance" from consciousness is irrelevant. If, on the other hand, Nagel means "real nature" to refer to "what is really going on in the cognitive system as a whole," (p. 387) then his claim is simply false. What role conscious mental events are actually playing and how they are physically realized, regardless of how it seems to the first person perspective, are facts that our privileged access cannot unveil. This "real nature" is best understood from a scientific view point.

Once we grant, as we do above, that a naturalist can understand getting an accurate objective description of the subjective point of view as part of the project of understanding human consciousness, then an exhaustive analysis of consciousness should be forthcoming. As Flanagan writes, a theory of this ilk

> will provide a rich autophenomenology, a theory of how the autophenomenology connects up with the actual goings-on, a theory about how conscious mental events — taxonomized into many different classes of awareness — figure in the overall economy of mental life, a theory of how mental life evolved and thereby a theory of which features of mind are the result of direct selection and which features are free-riders, and finally it will provide a neuroscientific realization theory — a theory about how all the different kinds of mental events, conscious and unconscious, are realized in the nervous system. It is hard to see how the analysis could be more exhaustive. (1985: 387)

But again, perhaps this does not take the skeptics' worries seriously. If we assume that "real nature" refers to the way things seem to particular people, then regardless of how well we understand and grant the privileged connection, a move to objectivity must be a move away and will therefore abstract over some aspects of the phenomena. What matters is how things seem to individuals, and if science has to leave that out, for whatever reason, scientific theories cannot capture what we care about in our conscious experiences. So even if we could get all the things Flanagan outlines, we would still be leaving something out.

Nevertheless, it seems to me that the skeptics still shouldn't have to be concerned. Let us consider the nature of the relationship between theories and the world they describe.[20] I read the skeptics as claiming that there are two types of sentences involved in understanding consciousness. First, there are first person sentences that describe our phenomenal experiences. Introspective observations determine the truth values of these sentences (more or less) directly. Second, there are third person theoretical sentences that presumably also describe phenomenal experiences. However, their truth values are more difficult to ascertain since they cannot be directly confirmed by observation.

This picture is by and large correct. We can find a version of the observational-theoretical distinction so prevalent in philosophy of science in our discussion of consciousness. The ways in which we confirm our first person reports of our conscious experiences (our observation sentences) are different from the ways we confirm any third person story about consciousness (the theoretical sentences). And obviously discovering the truth about any third person theoretical account of qualitative experience is going to be somewhat difficult. This split between first person and third person descriptions though does *not* justify the inference from our first person sentences being (more or less) directly observational to the conclusion that they are nonproblematic, hence, special. To make that move, one has to assume that to be nonproblematic is to be directly observational, which just begs the question.

Moreover, this assumption would be false as well.[21] Let us remember how theorizing works. Whenever we explain or predict some phenomenon by using a theory, we assume that the premises concerning observations of the data are relatively straightforward. However, we assume that they are nonproblematic *vis-à-vis the theory we are using*, not that they are nonproblematic *simpliciter*. If our predictions of future observations consistently failed, then we might come to regard our statements about the "hard facts" as suspect along with our theory. Think about the demise of phlogiston theory. Not only did we replace the theory with a theory of oxidation, but we also replaced our observations of substances dephlogisticating with observations of substances taking on oxygen. The data of course remain the same, but the way in which we describe the facts change as our guiding theoretical framework changes. Observation sentences, even observations of the most basic events, are theory laden.

And statements about our own conscious experiences are no different. Quick evidence for this claim comes from the fact that other languages (including ancient Greek, Chinese, and Croatian, and English before the seventeenth century) have no word for "conscious" or "consciousness."[22] Presumably consciousness itself remains unchanged; people from these

adrenaline meter or wisdow wrist will affect our thoughts and emotions linguistic communities have or had perceptual experiences. The point is that they cannot talk about these experiences as we can since they don't regard the mind in the same way we do. Something about *our* epistemic milieu makes us assume the particular first person stance that we do about consciousness. How we individuate conscious experiences via our first person perspective is not transparent, nor is it unproblematic. It can arise only from what we believe to be true about the mind already, from what we have been told about experiences at mother's knee.[23]

We can separate the observational/non-observational distinction from the theoretical/non-theoretical distinction.[24] We don't find a fundamental distinction between first person and third person accounts in terms of theory-ladenness, and we don't (yet) have any interesting defining features for the first person observation sentences. To maintain their challenge, the skeptics must claim that our observation sentences about consciousness — though they be theoretical — describe more about our experiences than any objective account could. Can they do that? I believe that, *contra* Flanagan, they can, but to do so will not help their cause.

Science does not intend to deal with all the intricacies of its subject matter. Instead it uses only a small number of parameters abstracted away from the phenomena in question to explain and predict something (though not everything) about the phenomena. These parameters are influenced by the goals of individual inquiry, the audience for whom the explanation is directed, the history of the study, and so on, and they may differ as each of the constraining factors differ.[25] To take a common and clear example, classical particle mechanics uses point-masses, velocities in frictionless environments, and distances traveled over time to characterize falling bodies. Theoretical physicists only want to explain the general pattern of behavior of moving objects; hence, they can rightly ignore the color of the body, the date of its falling, interference from gravitational attraction, and so on. They predict behavior based only on the position and momenta of extensionless points interacting in a vacuum. Engineers, who have different concerns and address different audiences, would probably want to include gravitational attraction and perhaps the times of the events in their calculations.

Scientists abstract away from the complexities of the actual world and define simpler, artificial domains, isomorphic to the world in only a few aspects. Following Fred Suppe, we can call these imaginary domains *physical systems*, "highly abstract and idealized replicas of the phenomena" that characterize "how the phenomena *would have* behaved *had* the idealized conditions been met" (1989: 65). Scientists calculate the behavior of these physical systems, which they then use to explain interactions in the actual world.

We can see this same picture of how science works in the cognitive and biological sciences as well.[26] The genetic theory of natural selection characterizes evolutionary phenomena in terms of changes in the distributions of genotypes across a population over time as a function of the rate of reproduction, the frequency of crossover, and so on. Behaviorist theories in psychology describe the behavior of idealized organisms as a function of stimulus-response patterns and reinforcement schedules. Other examples include Chomskian theories of competence in linguistics, theories of cell firing in neurophysiology, and computational learning theories in cognitive psychology, all of which describe the behavior of abstract mechanisms under ideal conditions which only approximates the behavior of real phenomena in virtue of a few "fundamental" properties under normal conditions.

Science then does not apply its generalizations directly to data, but rather uses discovered regularities to explain the behavior of physical systems abstracted from the data in such a way that the abstract behavior can be correlated with the actual data.[27] A successful correlation then leads scientists to identify the attributes of the physical system with properties in the real world, thereby explaining them in terms of the hypothesized regularities. Hence, the observation sentences are altered such that they represent what would have been observed if only the few relevant parameters of the phenomena existed under ideal conditions. These altered statements, perhaps in conjunction with some idealized boundary conditions, are used with the theory to make predictions about the physical system. The predictions are then converted into statements about the corresponding data by just reversing the procedure for altering the original observation statements.

We have two moves from the raw observations to predictions of the theory: We translate data into idealized variables and then calculate the theory's postulates from the physical system, boundary conditions, and idealized parameters. The first move is fundamentally counterfactual and always involves pruning away some aspects of the phenomena actually observed. Here is where we would lose something from our first person accounts of phenomenological experience. It is not in translating from a first person account to an objective perspective; rather, it is in using these observational sentences in a scientific theory.

The skeptics are correct when they say that something is left out of scientific accounts of consciousness. Is what is left out important? The skeptics will reply that it is. Any account of consciousness which abstracts away from the actual phenomenal experiences in the manner outlined above will lose the at least some of the properties introspection discriminates in our sensations. Thus, our scientific theories may not be able to discriminate the very means by which we discriminate one kind of perception from another.

This result might prove disastrous for naturalists. If scientific theories cannot identify exactly what we care about in our phenomenal experiences, viz., their feel or quale, then perhaps the limit on theories is too stringent for our purposes. This worry and its implications express themselves most clearly in the problem of the inverted spectrum. It is worth going through this problem in some detail because it illustrates quite neatly what we can reasonably expect from any theory of consciousness. Whether that would be *enough* explanation is a matter for personal taste.

2.2. Inverted Spectra

The problem of the inverted spectrum is a popular tool that philosophers of all stripes have traditionally used in discussing the possibility of developing a theory of consciousness. Recently, however, the thought experiment has come under fire as being trivially solvable in virtue of adopting a materialist framework. We should re-open the case. I believe that the problem of the inverted spectrum is indeed a real problem and worthy of consideration by serious-minded materialists — especially those from cognitive science — because it points out exactly what a theory of awareness or visual processing should account for (given what we know about the brain).

In a nut-shell, the problem of the inverted spectrum is as follows: We can imagine that someone exists whose color spectrum is inverted relative to ours, so that when we perceive redness, she would see blueness, and when we see blueness, she would perceive redness. Further, when she sees what we call "red," she calls it "blue," and vice versa, so that there is no way to tell from outside the head the "quale" of her sensation, so to speak.[28] The difficulty arises from the alleged fact that there is nothing incoherent about supposing this. The logical plausibility of the scenario then supposedly indicates that the connection between how things seem to us and any theory of mind would be radically contingent. Moreover, if how things seem to us is an essential aspect of conscious experience, then any scientific theory of mind would not able to account for (presumably) exactly what it was designed to explain. If inverted spectra are possible, then any account of conscious experience will thereby omit at least some of the properties we can introspectively discriminate in our sensations, properties that we use to distinguish one perception from another. If how things seem to us is fundamental to conscious experience, then science will omit something very important indeed.

Larry Hardin (1988) most recently has launched a detailed argument based on human neurophysiology why such a thought experiment is untenable.[29] I shall first briefly recapitulate Hardin's position before explaining why he doesn't answer those who take the problem seriously. I conclude that the possibility of an inverted spectrum highlights the theoretical limits of any theory of consciousness. However, for exactly that reason, inverted spectra — though they present an honest problem — are not anything cognitive scientists and philosophers of mind should worry about.

Hardin believes that the reason why good philosophers are led astray in taking the problem of inverted spectra seriously is that the discussants never include enough detail about how an inverted spectrum could actually work. He suggests that if we were to articulate enough of what we know about how color processing is carried out (in mammals, at least), then it would become transparent that inverted spectra are not possible.

Here then is our best scientific guess about how color processing occurs in normal (human) vision.[30] Retinas contain at least three different types of cones differentially sensitive to light wavelengths. Often these are called the red, green, and blue cones, but that is somewhat a misnomer because their respective receptive fields are rather large and overlap to a certain extent. It is the *ratio* of relative activation of these three main cone types that determine the hues we eventually perceive. If the ratio of activation levels are the same, we will perceive the same hue, regardless of whether there are different levels of activity in each cone type that leads to the same constant ratio. "Metamer" is the name scientists give to this smallest unit of perceivable color.

Output from the different cones then proceeds to the retinal ganglion. There the three separate activation responses are transformed into two information streams via a complex computation whose details need not detain us here. What is important for our purposes is that this transformation results in one information stream which primarily responds to red and green (the "r-g channel") and one which primarily responds to blue and yellow (the "y-b channel").

The interaction of these two "opponent" channels determines what we see. For example, if the r-g channel is excited relative to its base rate and the y-b channel is not, then we shall see red, a "unique hue," a color determined solely by the activation of one color channel. Likewise, if the r-g channel is inhibited relative to its base rate and the y-b channel is inactive, we see green. *Mutandis mutadis*, the same for yellow and blue.

On the other hand, if both channels are either excited or inhibited relative to their base rates of activation, then we perceive some "binary" hue, such as purple, orange, or brown. Presumably, we can discriminate unique hues from binary ones introspectively as well as neurophysiologically. For example, when we detect the unique hue red, we detect only one color component: red. In contrast, when we detect purple, we also detect that it is comprised of two components: red and blue.

Let us use this machinery to see if we can't tell how an inverted spectrum might work. First, following Hardin (1988: 135-136), let us change our example slightly to discuss the conflation of red and orange. We are to imagine, e.g., Jane, who sees red every time we see orange and vice versa. Is this flight of fancy physically possible in this world, given what we know about the opponent process theory of color vision?

The answer quickly appears to be no. Orange is a binary color and all perceived oranges have yellow and red as constituents. Red, on the other hand, is achromatic. (That is, orange occurs when both the r-g channel and the y-b channel are firing at the appropriate rates. Red occurs when the r-g channel is activated and the y-b channel remains at base level.) Were we to encounter Jane, then it would be easy to determine that her color spectrum is at odds with ours. All we would have to do is ask her whether the hue she uses "red" to refer to has any component parts. If she calls our orange hue "red," then she would presumably answer yes and we would immediately know that something were amiss. Our theory of color vision gives us reason to prefer postulating red perceptions (or a unique hue) over orange ones (or a binary hue) when presenting subjects with something red.

But now suppose that the inversion did not occur across the two types of hue (unique and binary). Instead, returning to the traditional version of the problem, let us suppose that a pair of unique hues are switched. So, for example, we can imagine Henry; he sees green just when we see red and vice versa. Is this inversion possible, given what we know?

Hardin again answers no and he spins a story explaining why. Hardin notes that we perceive different unique hues as having different aspects. For example, we see red as warm and green as cool. He also notes that the r-g channel fires more for red and less for green. Hence, there are physiological differences which might explain the differences in our judgments about unique hues' aspects — "warm" corresponds to a channel's activity being greater than the base rate and "cool" corresponds to a channel's activity being less. Suppose further that this were the case for all possible aspectual judgments. (*Prima facie*, given a materialist position, each phenomenological difference corresponding to a neurophysiological difference appears to be an entirely reasonable supposition — what else could a phenomenological difference correspond to but some difference in the underlying neural base?)

Keeping this result from the supposition of materialism in mind, let us return to Henry and survey the possibilities for inverted spectra. Either Henry makes the same judgments we do with respect to the phenomenal aspects of the hues perceived, or he does not. If he does, then we could easily tell that something is wrong with Henry's color vision, since he would be judging his "red" to be cool and his "green" to be warm. This case would simply be analogous to the red/orange case discussed above.

However, it could turn out that Henry does not make the same aspectual judgments we do; that is, he could claim that what he calls red (actually green) is warm and that what he calls green (actually red) is cool. If this is the case, then again there are two possible scenarios. If Henry is inverted all the way down, so to speak, then either his brain is wired just like ours or it is not. If it is wired just like ours, then conscious perceptions become epiphenominal, for we would have a case of exactly the same physical causes giving rise to different effects. In essence, were this to occur (and if all aspectual judgments corresponded to some neural event), then materialism would have to be false. At least we would have to give up the notion that like causes produce like effects, the basis for all scientific generalizations. Hardin understandably believes that this radical conclusion is a *reductio* of the premises and, hence, that there is no conceivable way (conceivable in the sense that it would be possible given what we generally take to be true about our world) that Henry could be wired like us and yet have an inverted spectrum.

The final possibility remains. The "flavor" of Henry's color perceptions could differ from ours along with his internal wiring.[31] If this were the case, then Hardin suggests that the best we could say is that Henry's phenomenal experiences are *unimaginable* from our point of view, not that they are *inverted*. He asks:

> Can we coherently represent to ourselves just what those experiences would be like?....[Henry] will, we say, see green as...warm. But exactly how could phenomenal green be experienced as...warm and yet be green? If there is a "residue" of green which is separate from its polarity, that residue would correspond to nothing in experience or imagination, yet it is only the ostensible imaginability of the hue inversion which makes its possibility intuitively plausible. (1988: 138)

Hardin concludes that we either will have good reason to believe that others' perceptions of red and green are like ours, in which case their spectra would not be inverted, or their color experiences would be unimaginable, in which case their spectra are not (truly) inverted either.

And so it would go for any possible inversion relation. As long as materialism is true, and as long as our perceptions have aspects to them, then for any possible set of inversions, (theoretically) we should be able to find some physical difference that would give us reason to prefer the mapping we already use between color terms and percepts to any possible inverted mapping.[32]

However, the sort of answer that Hardin gives — that science will tell us about others' qualitative experiences as soon as we have done it properly — doesn't give skepticism its due. If Hardin's story in fact details how color perception works, then he would be right and truly inverted spectra would not be possible. But the difficulty is that we don't know how color perception actually proceeds. The sad truth is that we know so little about how perception occurs in brains that it is extremely premature to claim that a completed scientific account of the mind would include information about individual experiences.

Of course, we do know some things. We know about the receptive fields and the firing frequencies of normal mammalian cones. That is, we understand how to determine metamers for any particular animal. Single cell recording of the activity of various cones indicate the wavelengths to which various cells best respond. Moreover, these sorts of recordings can be done noninvasively so that it is fairly easy to determine the response properties of cones in alert adults. In addition, because we have mapped the distribution of cones types for humans (and other mammals), we can gauge what the input should be for the retinal ganglion. Beyond this point, however, what we know becomes progressively more fuzzy.

The opponent processing theory was designed to cover processing beyond the retinal ganglion. And it certainly has the reputation for being the best psychological theory of color vision to date. Unfortunately though, there is precious little independent evidence supporting this psychological theory. Indeed, when we begin to dig for corroborative data even the slightest, the depth of our ignorance becomes painfully obvious.

For example, it is not at all clear that the color terms we use in describing our everyday experiences pick out natural kinds with respect to our psychology.[33] Notice that our folk color terms form the base of the opponent process theory — hues are parsed in the theory just as we individuate them in ordinary conversation. And if our folk divisions do not correspond to Nature's "joints," then any theory that relies on those distinctions should be suspect.

The skeptics are assuming that the particular qualitative aspect of a quale is the essential aspect because it is what we use to identify it from a first person point of view. After all, this individuation does play an active and fairly successful role in our everyday interactions and the conceptual framework in which it is embedded does have many of the earmarks of a type of empirical theory.[34] It is clear that introspection is by far the most immediate and direct indication of what sensations we are experiencing. It certainly seems as though we have special access to the intrinsic nature of our conscious experiences.

On the face of it though, it is doubtful that our ordinary color divisions would carve our phenomenological spectrum into natural kinds simply because other societies parse their color field in such radically different ways. Some cultures have kind terms for far more colors than our primary red, green, yellow, and blue. To wit: the Jörai, a Vietnamese linguistic group, have twenty-three color kind terms. The Uzbek-speaking Ichkari women from Afganistan refuse to classify colors as being similar at all, claiming things that "this is like calf's dung and this is like a peach; you can't put them together" (Burns and Shepp 1988, as discussed in van Brakel 1992).[35] Other linguistic communities individuate colors into fewer kinds than we do. The Arunta color term "tierga" refers to (what we call) yellow, blue, and green. Mazatec "sasa" denotes (what we call) blue, blue-green, and blue-violet. Further, some social groups use languages that give different names for the same hue if the objects with that color have different uses. The Mexican Comaltepec Indians distinguish colors in terms of animate and inanimate objects. Turkish speakers divide their color world on the basis of natural versus man-made objects. Mandarin Chinese separates colors in virtue of whether the objects are for ritual or daily use.

In light of this ethnographic research, should we suppose that our common-sense individuation of the color spectrum is exactly right? Correlatively, should we conclude other cultures are just sadly mistaken about which hues fall under the different kind terms? I submit that we have no obvious reason to do so. Absent additional evidence, assuming four and only four color kinds is clearly Western prejudice.[36] As members of this society, we've picked out certain aspects of our qualitative experiences as the important aspects for identifying our color sensations, and we use those aspects as "hooks" upon which to hang our folk labels. We centered on those particular aspects because they allow us to converse successfully among ourselves within our linguistic group. Had the taxonomy we chosen been a failure, we certainly would have tried a different tack.

The bottom line is that linguistic practice alone does not tell us much about how things really are, which, as I noted at the beginning, should not be too surprising. The folk theories of different cultures parse the world in different ways, which is exactly what we would expect. Our conscious inner world of color does not exist already carved into kinds any more than the external world does. And whether the Western individuation of sensations constitutes a natural kind individuation is an empirical matter, regardless of how powerful our intuitions. And, empirically speaking, it is too soon to tell what the natural kinds of color phenomena will be exactly.

In any case, if we cannot definitively assert that there are exactly four unique hues, then we have little reason to adopt the opponent processing theory of color vision, for that theory turns on the pair-wise combinations of four primary hues. Nothing apparent prevents us from postulating that we have twenty-three unique hues, with the remainder made from combinations of those, or, following the Ichkari, that there are no n-ary hues at all.

Indeed, even within the Western tradition the assumption of four primary hues is fairly recent and somewhat controversial. Isaac Newton (1952) divided the color spectrum into seven categories: red, orange, yellow, green, blue, indigo, and violet.[37] And some modern theories of color processing are based on these Newtonian divisions. For example, Paritsis and Stewart note that "when we look at the analyzed narrow band of sunlight through a prism as Newton did, we see that seven colors are emphasized....The above phenomena may be considered as an indication that, at the cortical level, colors are classified into seven classes of cells" (1983: 109). Moreover, Thomas Young, the originator of the trichromatic theory of color vision, asserted that there were only three primary colors. And Munsell, who devised the widely used Munsell Color Chips, identified five primary hues: red, purple, blue, green, and yellow.[38]

Of course, we have yet to consider neurophysiological evidence for the r-g and y-b channels, so perhaps we are premature in our assessment that the opponent processing theory is on such shaky ground. If we could unearth some anatomical or physiological data that dovetail with the brain processing hue by combining four basic colors, or, better, data that unequivocally corroborate the opponent processing theory, then the ethnographic comparisons of different linguistic communities' use of color terms would be irrelevant, for we would have independent confirmation for our assumption of four basic hues.

Unfortunately, from the neurobiological perspective, the situation looks bleak as well. The simple fact is that we have no direct physiological evidence for *any* psychological theory of color processing. We know precious little about visual processing once we move to the higher levels of cortex where presumably the actual percepts reside, and what we do know about lower level processing is ambiguous. For example, it turns out that there aren't any cells below the level of the lateral geniculate nucleus sensitive only to wave-length (i.e., sensitive to colors alone). The most specialized cells we do have, the so-called "single opponent" cells, cannot tell the difference between a large colored spot and a small white spot. Hence, it seems that they process color and contrast simultaneously. This means that computations involved in determining chromaticity and brightness take the same neural pathway (Lennie and D'Zmura 1988, Mollon and Sharpe 1983). The remainder of the color-sensitive cells are tied to even more functions, for they are responsive to spatial information as well.

This sort of multi-functional arrangement makes sense in the brain because broadly tuned cells with overlapping receptive fields can process more information and do it more quickly than can a set of finely-tuned cells with only local representations (Rumelhart and McClelland 1986: chapter 3). However, such coarse-coding makes it difficult for those trying to develop information processing theories of the mind/brain, for it becomes unclear how to assign processing jobs to the cells. Do these cells primarily determine hue and only process brightness and shape derivatively? Do they process shape first and foremost with color being an added bonus? Or is their function a combination of all three tasks so that we have incorrectly divided the computational labor in our information processing models? We can't yet conclude that these cells are indeed in the business of determining hue and not primarily engaged in something like processing an object's figure.[39]

In addition, cells responsive to the long and middle wave-lengths do not have a single receptive field. What they are most sensitive to at any particular moment is influenced by their previous firing patterns, how their neighbors are reacting, and what the rest of the brain is doing (Tanaka 1993). Moreover, what these cells respond to maximally over time are not the alleged unique hues. Instead, it appears they are keyed to wave-lengths for our binary colors (Lennie and D'Zmura 1988, Mollon and Sharpe 1983, Ottoson and Zeki 1985).

Finally, because the action potentials, EPSPs, and IPSPs of neurons interact nonlinearly, we have a fundamental problem in extrapolating from the threshold sensitivities of individual cells to larger phenomenal experiences (more on this point in chapter 6). We don't know what algorithms the brain uses and we can't profitably speculate because the degrees of freedom are too large. So, until we can better understand network interactions, we need to be extremely cautious in moving from single cell data to higher level effects. In any event, we cannot now predict qualitative effects from the recorded behavior of a set of neurons taken individually.

The conclusion that we are forced to draw is that we do not have solid neuroanatomical or neurophysiological evidence supporting the opponent processing theory. Of course, the theory is still useful in predicting certain behavioral effects. And it still remains the best psychological theory we have. However, its foundation derives from a Western linguistic prejudice; it can muster little support from underlying neurophysiology. Hence, the only reason we use this theory is its success in accounting for our behavior (including verbal reports).

However, if we have no reason other than explanatory utility to adopt the opponent processing theory, then Hardin's reply to those who take the problem of the inverted spectrum seriously just assumes what he wants to prove, *viz.*, that there is a consistent material marker for all just noticeable differences in phenomenology. But absent support for our hypotheses concerning visual processing, we cannot make claims about what sort of neural events correlate with our phenomenology. If there is no hard evidence for an hypothesis, then obviously we cannot assume that what it claims is true. Hardin is mistaken when he claims that if we just understood the scientific details, then the problem of the inverted spectrum disappears, for we have few scientific details at which to look. He has produced one scenario in which inverted spectrum are not possible, but the bottom line is that we do not yet have a reason to accept his story.

Nevertheless, it may be the case that materialism alone will rule out the possibility of an inverted spectrum.[40] Let us return to Hardin's earlier point that if others are wired in the same way we are, then if inverted spectra are possible, phenomenal experiences are epiphenomenal, but if others are not wired in the same way we are, their phenomenal experiences are unimaginable. If this be correct, then regardless of how the science turns out, truly inverted spectra are not possible, for either inverted spectra are impossible, phenomenal experiences are not part of the physical world, or the qualitative character of others' experiences is beyond our imaginative capacities.

However, the more general argument also entails problematic assumptions. In order for this argument to work, we would have to assume that *all of the phenomenal discriminations we make reflect innate wiring patterns.* Consider the following. Suppose the contrary; suppose that our phenomenological experiences are not tied to our genetic heritage. (This is not necessarily a spooky thought. For example, the quality of our experiences could depend upon how our brains are shaped by the environment. That is, the history of our "nurture," and not our "nature," foretells how things will seem to us.) If the relevant neural connections are not hardwired, then the physical identity of brains would be orthogonal to the functional identity of psychology. Hence, as long as we could show that others are psychologically identical to us, then it is possible that we could imagine what their experiences are like. At least, nothing rules out this possibility yet.

Do we have reason to suppose that phenomenological discriminations don't reflect innate neural connections? We have some reasons for believing our experiences of hue are probably not tied to innate brain structures common to all color perceivers. I should stress that we do not know what is involved in color perception. However, I do believe that the following facts are relevant when thinking about what is likely to be important.

(1) *Individual brains are extremely plastic.* It is well known that when kittens have their eye-lids sutured together at certain critical periods, and so are deprived of visual stimulation, cells in their visual cortices lose their responsiveness to visual cues (Cyander *et al.* 1976, Sherman 1973, 1977). These cells might then respond to inputs from other sensory systems. The volatility of the somatosensory system in monkeys is well-documented in this regard.[41] This same type of effect has been reported with respect to the auditory cortex in some deaf humans. Indeed, deaf "speakers" of sign languages have visual cortices more sensitive to peripheral stimuli than normal English-speaking hearing subjects (Neville and Lawson 1987).

Moreover, if the brain itself is damaged in some way, then (depending on when the lesion occurred) other brain sites may carry out the processes that normally took place in the areas lost (Kolb 1992). We see this effect most vividly in some hemispherectomies. These patients have had an entire hemisphere of their brains oblated and yet they somehow manage to maintain normal functioning (Bishop 1983, 1988, Hacaen 1976, St. James-Roberts 1981). It would be surprising if hue processing could not be similarly affected by these sorts of interventions. If so, then it would be a mistake to tie the qualitative feel of various colors to particular and specific brain structures, for these sorts of data suggest that no brain structure is either sufficient or necessary for any higher order information processing.

(2) *Individual experiences vary widely.* It is not the case, for example, that the perception of color always depends upon visual input. In some hapless folk, one type of sensory stimulus leads to the perception of another (a condition known as "synesthesia"). For instance, one woman has been reported who sees red lightning bolts whenever her beeper buzzes; another who feels vertical columns whenever he tastes chocolate mint (Cytowic 1993).

For a less dramatic — but no less surprising — example, Al Prestrude (personal communication) has documented that the rods in fair-skinned red-heads do not follow the same recovery pattern when stimulated as the rods in subjects with darker complexions and hair do. One result of this difference is that red-heads have more difficulty driving at night with oncoming traffic because they tend to be "blinded" by the headlights for longer than either blondes or brunettes. How our brains react to incoming stimuli differs across subjects so that we cannot assume how something seems to others is easily and straightforwardly derived from knowledge of environment stimuli. In particular, to know exactly how things seem to an individual seems to require knowledge of that individual's particular brain, for it is not yet obvious what counts as a "standard reaction under standard conditions." We have little reason to expect that the perception of an object's color should be any different.   *non sequitur*

(3) *Brains cannot be entirely genetically hardwired.* There simply is not enough genetic material to program all our 10^{11} or so neural connections. Instead, it is more likely that natural selection has chosen a general blue-print for the basic structure of our brain and experience then does the fine-tuning. In support of this conjecture, it is interesting to notice that the density of brain synapses increases at a remarkable rate during the first months of life. For example, baby monkeys have about twice as many synapses as they do when they are fully mature, and this "overproduction" appears in all cortical areas and the limbic system (Rakic *et al.* 1986). Similarly, in humans, synaptic exuberance seems to peak at about two years, after which the number of synapses decreases steadily until adulthood.

Something causes the synapses to disappear over the years. One suggestion is that learning by interacting with the environment retains some connections at the expense of others (Changeux 1984, Changeux *et al.* 1973, Changeux and Danchin 1976, Changeux *et al.* 1984). The general idea is that an organism with an overabundance of synapses possesses the greatest diversity of possible connections among neurons; hence, the best generic blue-print for a complex brain would be one that essentially connected everything to everything. Interaction with the environment then selects or stabilizes a subset of the original neuronal circuits. The rest would just disappear through disuse. "Use it or lose it" may be quite literally true in the brain.

Thus, it is likely that both nature and nurture are responsible for our exact brain configurations. And insofar as our experiences of color depend upon our visual cortices — and these cortices' final neural arrangements depend upon which stimuli the organisms are exposed to — we would expect that each of our individual color processing mechanisms will differ. Considerations of synaptogenesis do not tell us that our processors should differ wildly — indeed, it is possible that we might someday be able to uncover important neuronal constants across all normal adult color processors. However, they don't rule out the converse — it is also possible that there is no microstructure which appears the same in all normal adult color processors.

I conclude that, given what we know about other types of processing in the brain, it would be astonishing if all our visual processing systems turned out to be *exactly* alike. (This possibility, of course, just points out the possibility of multiple instantiability — *viz.*, we may realize exactly the same color "program" on different underlying machines.) This sort of result is neither new in cognitive science nor surprising. However, it is exactly this point that Hardin and Shoemaker overlook.

If we assume that multiple instantiability is a serious possibility — even when the class of subjects is restricted to normal adult humans — the important and interesting question with respect to the problem of the inverted spectrum (and the one Hardin and Shoemaker finesse) is: Can we know whether we perceive roughly the same color spectrum, given that our brains are not structurally isomorphic? This remains unanswered by the mere assumption of materialism if our discriminations do not reflect innate wiring patterns, regardless of whether a just noticeable difference may reflect some change in underlying neural activity for any individual person. Materialism alone cannot rule out the possibility of inverted spectra, for assuming it just tells us that if two people did happen to be structural isomorphs of one another, then they would have the same phenomenal color experiences for the same visual inputs (*ceteras paribus*).

Moreover, if our qualia turn on "soft" wiring, then it seems that any theory which tries to capture qualitative experiences cannot specify what these experiences are like. Any general theory of visual processing will have to abstract over these sorts of individual differences. However, it might be that these individual differences are just what determine the flavor of our phenomenal experiences. Of course, by the assumption of materialism, all qualitative experiences would still have some physical base or other; it is just that any *psychological* theory of visual processing would generalize across what those bases are. And this move is to be expected for any higher level functional theory.[42]

Indeed, depending upon what level of description is relevant for visual processing in neuroscience, a *neurophysiological* theory of color processing may abstract over the base as well. For example, if the computational processes at the level of (functionally described) networks are most important in understanding how the brain "sees" color, then any theory which describes those processes will most likely not include the arrangement of particular neurons. That is, since there are indefinitely many (or at least a very large number of) neuronal configurations which can cause same I/O relations at a higher level of organization, any theory constructed to capture that higher level should not refer to particular lower level instantiations in order to be generally applicable.[43]

If our cognitive theories do develop along these *prima facie* reasonable lines, then any theory of visual processing would only be able to say that we are having some color experience or other, for only that would be describable in higher level functional terms. However, it could not discuss exactly what that experience is like, for that would depend upon individual configurations, which are not part of the higher level theory.

This is not a particularly distressing result from the perspective of science, for such a theory would end up treating perception just like other individual trait in psychology. When psychologists discuss things like I.Q., coping skills, visual acuity, emotional sensitivity, and so on, they explicitly recognize that everyone has them to some degree or other and they scale individuals for these traits with respect to one another according to various tests they have devised. But they also acknowledge at the same time that it is fruitless — even dangerous — to discuss, e.g., what I.Q. *is* apart from their measuring devices. Theorizing about color perception could work just like this. We could devise tests which rank people's responses to colored inputs along a variety of dimensions and we could use these results to predict other behaviors (just as it is already being done in psychology). We might even devise a "theory" to explain these predictions, something like the opponent processing theory. However, insofar as we generalized over crucial individual differences, it would never be legitimate to go beyond these inter-subjective rankings and postulate exactly what those qualitative experiences seem like to the individual subjects.

Let me emphasize exactly what I take my result to be. It is not that there could be individuals psychologically identical to us who lack any qualitative character to their experiences whatsoever (that absent qualia are possible). That is an entirely separate issue and handled in chapter 7. Rather, I am claiming that any theory which does ascribe a qualitative character to someone or something has no obligation to spell out what those experiences are like for any particular individual. It is perfectly legitimate only to claim that the experiences exist, document the effects they produce with respect to various inputs, and use this information to predict future behaviors. Indeed, given the functionalist leanings of psychology today, such a result would not be surprising. We shall have to wait and see exactly how the story unfolds.

Inverted spectra remain a real possibility just because we don't yet know the relevant factors in determining color percepts. At least, it seems that no immediately forthcoming theory of visual processing is going to tell us what others' perceptual experiences are like. This is not to deny materialism — there should still correspond some physical difference or other to every individual quale. However, it is to deny that these differences are *eo ipso* relevant for future theories of awareness.

If inverted spectra are possible, then it is true that accounts of consciousness will omit at least some of the properties we can introspectively discriminate in our sensations.[44] At least this much of the "problem" of the inverted spectrum remains. However, it is not at all clear that these would be the properties we (that is, our brains) actually use in distinguishing one perception from another. It may be that the property which you and I crudely discriminate as "having a sensation of color" is precisely a certain cluster of cells spiking at a certain frequency.[45] Hence, we must reject the more extreme point that the connection of how things seem to us and any theory of mind is radically contingent. For once we disregard our intuitions as tainted by ideosyncratic linguistic practice, then it is no longer clear what is going to be important in explaining vision or awareness.

We can use similar considerations with respect to Hardin's claims about the putatively imaginability of others' color spectra. As long as we do not know what is relevant in accounting for the qualia of our percepts, we cannot make any claims about what we can and cannot imagine. What we could envision successfully will turn on (among other things) what parts of our brains are required for phenomenal aspects and the level of detail needed to specify those parts in an information processing model. We simply don't have enough data yet.

Until a true theory is developed, naturalists need to reason cautiously in order not the beg the questions posed. It is too easy to assume that science will answer everything and that to believe otherwise is to deny something as fundamental as materialism. It may be that the possibility of an inverted spectrum is calling attention to phenomenological distinctions that would make no difference to any scientific explanation of conscious experience. The issues involved in inverted spectra are not as simple as choosing the materialist position.

A scientific explanation of consciousness does require that sensations and perceptions have some common property that plays some causal role but it is indifferent about what that attribute may be as long as the property coincides fairly well with our introspective discriminations. Our qualitative experiences are token-identical with whatever physical states realize them, so it seems that it should be no problem construing *some* attribute of our brain (e.g., neural firing patterns, phase-locked oscillations, the activity of a certain region or cell type) as identical with the intrinsic property of the *type* conscious experience (though see the next chapter). In this case, the skeptic's complaint that a scientific theory of consciousness would not analyze conscious experience exhaustively — though true — would be irrelevant.

To recap: our first person subjective accounts of what it is like to be conscious should be able to be translated more or less faithfully into third person objective language, and even though this translation would preserve all the (important) causal connections among relevant phenomena relative to our explanatory goals, the redescription would abstract over some particular aspects of consciousness. However, though what is left out may be important to our folk conception of consciousness, it may not be important to any particular scientific theory. The difference only underscores the abstract nature of scientific theory and that what is needed for communicative success in personal discourse is not the same as what is needed for predictive success in the abstract physical systems of science.

We have reached an interesting point of rapprochement between the skeptics and the naturalists. Skeptics would agree that analyses of conscious states in terms of their neural realization or causal role can explain certain aspects of our psychological lives. They only deny that "this kind of thing exhausts their analysis" (Nagel 1974: 167). Naturalists agree that a theory which spells out how conscious states are realized in the brain and details the causal role of these states is not exhaustive; this analysis would not include a description of what it is like to be in particular states. Do the skeptics and naturalists actually disagree at all? There are diminished expectations on both sides: Skeptics admit naturalism can find out interesting things, but is not an exhaustive approach. Naturalists admits that naturalism is not exhaustive, but can find out interesting things. Beyond that, we should just wait and see whether what science can tell us is enough to satisfy our curiosity.[46]

Consciousness as a Natural Kind
Chapter Three

I have been acting as though once we presume naturalism, then we can roll up our sleeves and get to work. This is not entirely honest, for there are those who consider themselves both materialists and naturalists but who maintain that there will be no theory of consciousness nonetheless. Proponents of these positions fall into two categories. Either they believe that conscious states do not fall naturally into the taxonomy of psychological functional states, that consciousness crosscuts functionalism (Hannay 1987, Wilkes 1984; see also Block and Fodor 1972). Or they point out that those engaged in these debates have a confused picture of the supposed referents of consciousness, and it is most likely that consciousness is not a natural kind term at all. Our notions about consciousness are fuzzy and probably contradictory, and since no one has devised a suitable replacement for the folk-psychological term, talk about scientific theories of consciousness is premature (Churchland 1983, Dennett 1982, Rey 1983, 1988, Wilkes 1988).

I wish to dismiss their claims. Here I argue that those who dismiss the scientific study of consciousness because they think raw feels play no unique causal role in our mental economy misunderstand how scientific models deal with causal histories. After all, we do posit phenomenological phenomena to explain, e.g., perceptual reports, regardless of the roles they may or may not play in information processing. Uncovering the causal etiology of these perceptual phenomena surely falls within the domain of science (cf., Salmon 1984). If we view theories as empirically adequate models of the world, then no empirical phenomenon is beyond the pale of scientific theorizing. As Richard Rorty (1982) writes, the real problem is not how to study consciousness empirically, but to convince others that, from a methodological point of view, studying it is just like studying anything else.

However, even with this understanding of science, I still have to face the charge that our concept of consciousness is too simple or too vague to help frame the generalizations in a mature science of mind, either as *explanans* or as *explanandum*. One common tactic in developing arguments of this sort is using our intuitions to identify consciousness with some psychological process or other and then demonstrate that identifications of this sort are conceptually confused (*cf.*, Churchland 1983, Wilkes 1988). Consciousness then appears to be simply the wrong sort of term to use in a theory. The virtue of this strategy is that we can discuss consciousness cogently because we eliminate consciousness from our psychological ontology except as a place-holder for some other information process. The problem with strategies of this sort is obvious: consciousness in fact does have some sort of phenomenological feel, and we generally take that feel to be *prima facie* both a necessary and sufficient condition for consciousness.[47] All that the arguments show is that qualia cannot be identified with those psychological processes. I argue that positing conscious experience is needed to account for our behavior. Hence, some theory about consciousness must not only be possible; it will be necessary.

3.1. Explanations and Causal Histories

Arguments that consciousness crosscuts functionalism are fairly interesting since they are accepted and used by people on both sides of the naturalizing fence. Naturalists argue that the domain of conscious states is orthogonal to any psychological categorization; therefore, consciousness must be irrelevant to theories of the mind. For those skeptical about science being able to account for all important aspects of the mind, the fact that conscious states have no place in functional theories of cognitive science only all too vividly illustrates how truly meager the cognitive sciences are. However, neither side is correct since both either implicitly or explicitly rely on unfounded views of explanation in cognitive science. We should focus our energies on developing an explanation of consciousness itself, not on trying to use consciousness as an *explanans* for previously outlined psychological *explananda*.

To see how both sides use this argument, consider the paradigm example of qualia: pain. Naturalists do not deny that the subjective experience of pain exists. However, they would claim that there may be good reasons for believing that the relevant factor(s) for explaining pain behavior (or pains themselves) belong not only to the class of felt pains. Instead, they would belong a larger class including other psychological phenomena, e.g., pains which are not consciously felt, but which influence behavior nonetheless. Because of shared defining features, felt pains and unfelt pains would belong to one explanatory kind in the general taxonomy of mental states in psychological *explananda*. (We are constantly adjusting our posture and position in response to unconscious messages we get about what might become uncomfortable. Some see these sorts of messages on a continuum with consciously experienced pains since they both cause us to adjust our bodies similarly.) It is entirely possible that felt pains will not be a regularity science is concerned with. Some pains being conscious would not have any independent explanatory role in scientific theories (Churchland and Churchland 1981, Wilkes 1984).

Skeptics agree with the eliminativist assessment. However, they draw a different conclusion. Skeptics claim that the eliminative-naturalists are crippling explanations of consciousness because they expect consciousness to fit neatly into their already established patterns of explanation for their already established *explananda* of intelligent behavior. They shouldn't do that. The cognitive sciences have simply parsed the phenomena to be explained incorrectly. For some properties of our conscious states are fundamentally important for any intentional explanation whatsoever. Science overlooks this crucial point; hence, it ignores rather than affirms phenomenal experiences (*cf.*, Searle 1990b, 1992).

However, the eliminativists, as well as the skeptics, lean too hard on the previously established taxonomy of psychological events worth explaining. It is true that (as a general rule) psychological and neurophysiological theories do not discuss consciousness. Nevertheless, we still might want to explain the fact that some pains are conscious in the first place. In this case, consciousness would not be located in the *explanans* of science, but rather as an *explanandum*. Regardless of whether the factors which make some mental states conscious enter into our scientific taxonomy, there is something which entails that some states are conscious and some are not. Tracing the causal factors that lead to this result is a legitimate enterprise. Science need not ignore the phenomena of consciousness; it just may not require them in current psychological explanations of behavior. (In the latter half of this chapter, I argue that they are in fact needed.)

Moreover, outlining the mechanisms of consciousness is the appropriate approach to take because the brain is too complicated to expect helpful quantitative theories that allow for explicit computation of *explananda* from *explanans*. In the more mathematical sciences, we can see examples of explanations that are very close to the "covering law" model of explanation: we can literally derive the *explananda* from the laws describing the behavior of the system and particular initial and boundary conditions. (Think back to the example of determining the location of Venus in chapter 1.) However, in the mind/brain sciences, these techniques wouldn't be helpful. The mechanisms responsible for behavior can be unpacked across many levels of organization in the brain.[48] Here a strategy of "decomposition" and "localization" is much more appropriate (Bechtel and Richardson 1993). In neuropsychological explanations, we develop systematic connections between the data to be explained and various loci of causal interactions in the head. In doing so, we trace a causal etiology of the mechanisms responsible for the whatever it is we want to explain.

To take an example from neurobiology, when accounting for the choeric movements of Huntington's disease, we get a fairly detailed picture of the functioning of the cholinergic neurons and the neurons which synthesize gamma-amino-butyric acid (GABA-ergic neurons) in the striatum, followed by a history of their death in Huntington's patients using data based on CAT scans, PET scants, and magnetic resonance imaging. This profound loss is then connected to a disinhibition of the nigrostriatal dopaminergic system and an over-excitation of the remaining striatal neurons, and a resulting abnormal pallidal output to the thalamus (see Figure 3.1). We finally get an outline of the connection of the thalamus to motor output via the basal ganglia, a disturbance of which is tied to abnormal choeric movements (*cf.*, Kandel and Schwartz 1985: 531-532).

Here we do not see equations that indicate systematic connections between the pharmacology of the brain and involuntary movement; rather, the general mechanism of the disorder (an imbalance in the dopaminergic-cholinergic-GABA-ergic loop) is unpacked in a series of more or less detailed causal stories documenting systematic connections between factors of the mechanism with specific characteristics of the disease. These causal accounts play the same role as the mathematical derivations in physics or chemistry — they both detail a systematic dependency.

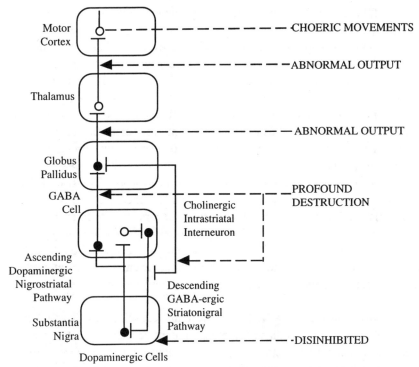

Figure 3.1. Huntington's Disease and the Dopaminergic-Cholinergic-GABA-ergic Loop. *Interaction of neurons that use GABA, acetylcholine, and dopamine in the striatum and substantia nigra, with indications of the effects of Huntington's disease. (Black neurons are inhibitory; white are excitatory.)*

But even if we could successfully develop a detailed multi-level causal etiology of the mechanisms of consciousness such that we find factors in our neurophysiological life positively correlated with the existence of a conscious state, I fear that neither the eliminativists nor the skeptics would be very interested. They both accept that current accounts of human cognition work perfectly well without using consciousness. Even though the skeptics *tollens* where the naturalists *ponens,* they both seem locked into accepting that consciousness itself must have no interesting scientistic causal effects on our behavior (*cf.,* Jackendoff 1987, Searle 1980, 1990, Velmans 1992). Eliminativists think that the events explaining our behavior crosscut the domain of conscious states and the skeptics maintain that this mechanistic account of behavior, though adequate for science, will ignore subjective phenomena.

Still, both the naturalists and the skeptics overlook that consciousness could simply be outside the domain cognitive psychologists are *currently* trying to capture. That psychologists can and, in many cases, do distinguish the information processes relevant to their studies from phenomenal awareness (thus *ipso facto* irrelevant) does not mean that the models they create of these processes entail that consciousness is not a topic for scientific scrutiny (the eliminativists' position) or that they are now somehow fundamentally inadequate (the skeptics' position). The *explananda* and the *explanans* of science change as our understanding of the world evolves. The warmth and phlogiston of yesterday became the heat and kinetic energy of today. So too may attention and meaningful behavior of today become the consciousness and memory stores of tomorrow.[49] Whether a model is incomplete depends on which phenomena it is supposed to be explaining. Since good explanatory models do not try to account for every observational event, that current models omit conscious phenomena is irrelevant to psychology and cognitive science as a whole.

Moreover, since eliminativists do believe that consciousness is a physical state in the brain, albeit a brain state that may not influence the development of subsequent functional brain states or processes, conscious states may be more relevant to understanding cognition than mere noise. Although not part of the causal chain currently under investigation, some states, like consciousness, may index certain processes, e.g., focal attention or certain memory processes, which *are* causally relevant in the circumscribed domain. A causal etiology of this index would then broaden our understanding of how brain events correlate with mental events.

3.2. Qualia as *Explananda*

According to the eliminativists, those who insist on there being some explanatory role for consciousness when psychological explanations work perfectly well without it appear to possess "a certain fetishism...an obsession which, at least since Freud, we have no reason to honor" (Levine 1987). They believe that there simply is no need to regard the "problem" of consciousness as a problem at all for psychological explanation can be complete without it.

But we have seen that even if consciousness does not fit into the current psychological taxonomy, developing a causal etiology of conscious phenomena could be a legitimate scientific enterprise either as its own end, or in a future revised taxonomy. It may also turn out that conscious states index other phenomena which are used in our psychological explanations, and so developing a causal history of consciousness would be a useful extension to our psychological understanding of mind.

However, this position does assume that the category of conscious states is well-formed and coherent. We still must consider a final sort of general skeptical argument directed against developing a scientific account of consciousness which holds that "conscious" and "consciousness" are too ill-defined to serve as fruitful *explananda*. Notions about consciousness are too imprecise and too riddled with unsubstantiated intuition to have it act as a natural kind in science. Nevertheless, as I shall argue in defense of the naturalists' project, we do find at least one common element among all our conscious experiences and this should be enough to start a proper empirical investigation into the mysteries of consciousness.[50]

In general, science studies *natural kinds*, groups of objects whose members are governed by the same set of laws and whose properties are not relativized to any particular personal interest. So, for example, "atom" is a natural kind, but "germ" is not; "gold" is, but "gem" is not. It is not always immediately clear whether some terms form a natural kind, even though they are used in science as such. For example, "memory" in psychology encompasses many diverse phenomena and scientists make several different fundamental distinctions within the category. Currently, we have short-term memory, long-term memory, working memory, as well as procedural, declarative, semantic, episodic, iconic, non-cognitive, somatic memories.... So many different types that it seems possible, even likely, that "memory" will come to be replaced by a set of systematically more useful descriptions.[51] These descriptions then should pick out natural kinds, while the term "memory" would become obsolete in psychology (though it would probably still be useful in other scientific domains, such as computer science).

Science quite often co-opts everyday folk terms into its more rigorous conceptual framework to be used as natural kind terms. Consider, for example, "force," or "mass." These terms have been adapted from everyday language to fit our more precise scientific conceptual framework.[52] But because our folk way of conceptualizing the world is notoriously slippery and vague, the terms have to be repackaged a bit in being translated from one conceptual scheme to another. It is uncontroversial that if "consciousness" were to be used scientifically, it would most likely have to be refined to some degree. What is under dispute, however, is how much we would have to alter "consciousness" to fit in a scientific framework, for somewhere along the continuum of change, the scientific term would cease to be the same term as our everyday one. If it has to be refined enough, then the nay-sayers would be correct in their assessment that (the folk term) "consciousness" does not denote anything suitable for scientific inquiry.

I should pause here to point out that what we are looking for here are not the necessary and sufficient conditions for consciousness. Since any scientific definition must be empirically motivated, scientific terms will come to have a more precise meaning as they become more embedded in the framework of particular empirical theories.[53] And these meanings may differ as the theories differ. The question before us is how significant the meaning change of our common sense notions would have to be with empirical discoveries about awareness in general.

There is well-known evidence that our common sense beliefs will have to be revised rather substantially, raising the clear possibility that "consciousness" is not a natural kind. For instance, our common assumption that introspection of our conscious states gives us reliable and transparent information about ourselves, our motives and experiences is largely false.[54] Schacter and Singer (1962) famously demonstrated that how we understand our emotional states turns on easily available environmental cues, regardless of whether those cues in fact contributed to our emotional state.[55] For a particularly salient instance of this phenomenon, consider research done by Cantor, Zillman, and Bryant (1975). They showed photographs of nude women to male subjects, who then ranked their own subjective sense of attraction. Some of subjects had previously been riding an exercise bicycle to the point of autonomic arousal (flushed face, increased heart rate, panting, etc.); other had remained stationary. Those who had been exercising ranked the nudes as more exciting than those who were not already aroused. That is, subjects attributed a sense of emotional arousal to the most immediate environmental cue, and not to what actually caused their autonomic reactions.

Cognitive dissonance studies also indicate that external factors we discount influence our allegedly purely "subjective" attitudes. If subjects are given the promise of a monetary reward for adopting a certain attitude toward something they normally find repugnant, they are more likely than not to now find that object or situation less distasteful. Interestingly, when queried about why they changed their attitudes, subjects invariably do not cite the promise of a reward as a factor (Bem 1972).[56] Nisbett and Wilson (1977) concur. They have shown, for example, that our attitude towards in individual heavily *an* influences our perception of that individual's accent, mannerisms, physical appearance. However, we are completely unaware of that influence: we believe that we can rank personal attributes independently of our overall reactions. Finally, we know that the size of a person's pupils figures crucially into how we perceive that person (Hess 1975).[57] The larger the pupils, the more friendly or sexually attractive that person appears (Finkelstein and Walker 1976, Green *et al.* 1979, Hicks *et al.* 1978, 1979, Kirkland and Smith 1978, McAffee *et al.* 1982, Tarrahian *et al.* 1979, Tomlinson *et al.* 1978).

Contra the transparency thesis, it is well known that echo-location is the mechanism certain blind people use in maneuvering around objects, even though these people have no idea how they avoid running into things.[58] Moreover, the documentation of blindsight shows that some perceptual judgments do not require conscious activation (Barinaga 1992, Cowey and Stoerig 1991, 1992, Critchley 1979, Fendrich *et al.* 1992, Ptito *et al.* 1991, Weiskrantz 1988, 1992, Weiskrantz *et al.* 1974).[59] Some subjects with lesions in the primary visual cortex, which results in blindness in the left visual field, can still nonetheless make accurate perceptual discriminations in their scotoma when told to guess about the location, orientation, size, and shape of objects.

Finally, our enormous propensity for confabulation leaves few doubts that our conscious states actually tell us little about what of the external world we are experiencing and why we are behaving the way we do. Patients with frontal lobe lesions often deny whatever deficit they exhibit (Benson and Stuss 1990, Joseph 1986, Malloy *et al.* 1993). Patients with Anton's syndrome do not recognize that they cannot see. They behave as though they can see perfectly normally, and they deny outright they suffer any visual impairment. When asked why they bump into things, or why they answer questions about their physical environment incorrectly, they often just invent patently false reasons (McDaniel and McDaniel 1991).[60] In split-brain patients, when the severed hemisphere nondominant for language initiates some physical activity, the hemisphere which does control speech will invent a story to explain what its body is doing. Generally, it does not express puzzlement at the behavior uncontrolled from that hemisphere's viewpoint, nor does it admit that the other hemisphere must be forcing the action (Gazzaniga 1985, Gazzaniga and LeDoux 1978, Gazzaniga *et al.* 1979, 1987).[61] Other common instances of deficit or clinical confabulation include patients with amnesia, aphasia, Alzheimer's disease, Korsakoff's syndrome, multiple personalities, vitamin B-12 deficiencies, and those suffering from sexual abuse (Badalyan *et al.* 1991, Baddeley and Wilson 1988, Berglund *et al.* 1979, Dalla-Barba *et al.* 1990, Gaimotti 1975, Kluft 1984, Kopelman 1987a, b, Mangone *et al.* 1991, Parkin 1984, Sandson *et al.* 1986, Saunders 1991, Stuss *et al.* 1978, Weinstein 1971).

And confabulation is not limited to abnormal brains. It is also a well known difficulty in gathering eye-witness reports.[62] What we remember depends greatly on the context in which we are remembering. And quite often what we remember never actually occurred (Neisser 1982). This sort of confabulation is quite normal; no lesions, deficiencies, abuses, or diseases are involved.

However, that some of our common sense beliefs about awareness need to be revised does not mean that consciousness is not a natural kind. Natural kind terms group sets of individuals, properties, processes, or states of affairs such that laws or principles governing that kind include all the members of that kind. Following Kathleen Wilkes, we can think of natural kinds as lying on a continuum from a strict natural kind in which "virtually all the laws or principles governing the kind...[apply to] virtually all the members of the kind," to "cluster" natural kinds in which "some laws may hold true of all instances falling under that kind" and others "will apply only to the constituent sub-classes," to groups which have little more coherence than a "mere 'set'," in which there are no overarching principles at all, though the laws which govern the subclasses might be structurally analogous (1988: 33-34). That what we generally accept as the overarching principles of consciousness are in fact wrong would only indicate that consciousness is not a strict, or "unitary," natural kind at best. Given the diversity of conscious phenomena, that conclusion should surprise no one. If we stop looking for the unifying principles which govern all and only conscious phenomena, we can still meaningfully ask whether consciousness is a cluster phenomenon suitable to ground scientific investigation or whether it is just a set term serviceable only in our looser everyday conversations.

How can we decide whether "consciousness" marks a natural kind? As Wilkes notes, part of the answer must lie in the usefulness of the laws which govern part or all of the phenomena. As I have suggested above, this is based on pragmatic considerations. But after we decide that a set of proposed laws for a delimited domain are promising enough to warrant scientific investigation, we still must decide whether the laws refer to a true natural kind, or to merely a set. One criterion suggested for a natural kind is that "the laws [which]...relate the various subclasses...should not have their content exhausted by a conjunction of the subordinate laws describing each subclass" (Wilkes 1988: 37). Nancy Cartwright, for example, believes that the "superlaws" in physics are not profitable for just this reason: "what the [superlaws]...dictate should happen, happens *because* of the combined action of laws from separate domains, like the law of gravity and Coulomb's law" (1983: 71).

Would the laws concerning conscious phenomena be analogous to the superlaws in physics? To answer this question negatively, we need to discover systematic relationships among the collection of conscious phenomena useful for science. When Wilkes examines the various types of conscious phenomena, she believes that an interesting criteria for being a conscious state will forever elude us. She considers how varied our own experiences are that we use as referents for "conscious."[63] She notes the following four diverse usages of "conscious:" (1) *"conscious" as a state of being.* We say we are conscious when we are alert instead of comatose. Generally speaking, this is a black and white distinction: we are either awake, or we are not; (2) *"conscious" as a counting adjective used for types of sensations.* We say that we are "conscious of" various locatable bodily states which lie on a continuum of intensity: bare tickles, pins and needles, excruciating pains, and so on; (3) *"conscious" as a nonlocalizable mass term,* to which very different adjectives apply than the "consciousness" of pains. We also say we are "conscious of" different sensory perceptions — visual, auditory, taste, olfactory, somatosensory, and kinesthetic. As Wilkes points out, our pains and the like can be "stabbing" or "throbbing" or "better than before." On the other hand, if our visual experience of a blue cup is "stabbing," or "throbbing," or "better than before" then it is for very different reasons than those we use to ascribe attributes to our pains (1988: 36); Finally, (4) *"conscious" as a delineating attribute.* We use "conscious" in conjunction with the propositional attitudes — we have some conscious desires and some unconscious ones.

Wilkes believes that once we understand how different all these categories of conscious things are, we have no choice but to conclude that dropping the term "conscious" from science would leave nothing interesting out from our investigation of the four sorts of phenomena. (Of course, given Wilkes's arguments, nothing should stop anyone from taking any one of the four criteria as the defining feature of conscious phenomena. For example, the distinction between being responsive to stimuli in the environment versus being nonresponsive is very important to clinical neurology and medicine. Hence, it might be useful for them to use the term "conscious" to refer to patients in the first category and "unconscious" to refer to those in the second. Such a move would entail severely narrowing our common sense notion of the term; nevertheless doing so might turn out be extremely fruitful.)

Of course, whether Wilkes is right is an empirical question and one we have no choice but to leave aside for the time being. Nevertheless, it does seem that, as different as the four categories are, they do all have one thing in common: for each category, it is *like something* to have the relevant phenomena. It is like something to be awake, like something to have our foot fall asleep, like something to hear a bird sing, and like something to want an ice-cream sundae. Perhaps somehow this qualitative "something" points toward a unifying principle. That is, perhaps this points to a defining property that supports and bounds most people's conception of consciousness.[64]

Still, we must keep in mind that our folk psychological expressions are generally tied to "appearances" and not to true "essences." To take Patricia Churchland's example:

> [our folk term] 'fire' was used to classify not only burning wood, but also the activity on the sun and various stars (actually fusion), lightning (actually electrically induced incandescence), the Northern lights (actually spectral emission), and fire-flies (actually phosphorescence). As we now understand matters, only some of these things involve oxidation, and some processes which do involve oxidation, namely rusting, tarnishing, and metabolism, are not on the 'Fire' list....It is only when we understand the deeper nature of the phenomenon that we begin to see how the old classification was skewed. (1988: 285)

How are we to make sense then of our intuition that consciousness in fact does have some sort of qualitative feel, and, in our everyday interactions, we generally take that "quale" to be a *prima facie* necessary and sufficient condition for consciousness?[65]

In a nut-shell, this book tries to answer that question. Let us take the difference in the reportability of the "feel" or quale to be a preliminary statement of our intuitive difference between conscious and unconscious states which we can then tap as the defining characteristics of a physical system.[66]

That is, we can use this property to start setting parameters which we can use in specifying some abstract physical system. At the same time, we should collect relevant data insofar as possible. We can use this information to refine, expand, and otherwise alter our hypothesized physical system. Once supported by data, the system will identify consciousness with some (abstractly defined) processes or events or states of affairs, thereby explaining it.

So, are there any data that suggest that our introspective reports capture some regularity important in science? If so, then we can use them to help "operationalize" our intuitive ideas concerning what is really important. I think there are. Recent work on the different memory systems of the brain clearly shows that perceptions subjects claim to have experienced consciously affect behavior differently than perceptions they apparently had, but were not aware of. It turns out that there is a significant difference in the way representations are processed when subjects consciously retain a priming stimulus versus when subjects receive a prime subliminally (Marcel 1980, 1983a, 1983b).[67] For example, the effects words with multiple meanings have on the processing of a subsequent word which is semantically related to one of the "priming" words' meanings have been recorded under two conditions. First, primes are presented slowly enough that subjects are consciously aware of them. Second, priming words are flashed so quickly that the subjects do not perceive them consciously. These are referred to as "masked" stimuli (Marcel 1983b).[68] It turns out that when unmasked, or when presented slowly, the word "PALM" facilitates processing "WRIST" only when it is preceded by the word "HAND"; when it is preceded by "TREE" it delays processing of "WRIST." However, when the word "PALM" is masked, it facilitates processing "WRIST" regardless of what precedes it. That is, whether we are consciously aware that we have seen something differentially affects later behavior; in this case, it affects the time it takes for us to indicate that we recognize subsequent words.[69] Something about a state *being conscious* (as evidenced by verbal report) alters our range of behavioral responses. And insofar as our verbal reports and our reaction times are independent of one another, we can separate our judgments about our qualitative experiences from whatever it is that alters our motor behavior.

Contrary to what the eliminative naturalists claim, we do in fact need to posit something besides our ability to issue reports and our perceptions in order to account for our behavior.[70] Indeed, we need to posit some theoretical entity introspectively accessible to us, tied to our intuitive notion of qualia, and indexed by our reports about what it is like to have a particular experience, for this is needed for a complete psychological theory. It makes sense for the moment to let our folk expression "qualia" stand as the name for this psychological place-holder, since the two are (at least for now) intimately related. Though much of our folk-understanding of consciousness is false, one aspect does ground phenomena needed to explain our behavior. This aspect I take as our first-pass conception of consciousness. The rest of the book is devoted to supporting, refining, expanding, better defining, and ultimately "reducing" this notion such that we can ultimately understand consciousness in purely naturalistic and non-mysterious terms.

3.3. Promissory Notes

I recognize that I will not have convinced any skeptics that a naturalist theory of consciousness is forthcoming with my quick example of implicit priming. All I have tried to do here is clear some conceptual space for consciousness in current psychology theorizing. I claim that positing (something like) conscious experience is needed to account for our behavior, regardless of currently popular views in the cognitive sciences. Though this theoretical posit cannot rely on the *particular* qualitative attributes of individual experience, it is intimately tied to qualitative experience as a whole. Scientific data show that verbal reports about our conscious experience index something fairly well, though what this thing is, how it is structured, what it does, and where it is located has yet to be uncovered.

Furthermore, as we search for these answers, we must be careful to guard against our dualistic intuitions telling us that mental states are phenomeno-logical billiard balls, without any interesting or relevant physical structure. Indeed, there may be no legitimate way to abstract a consciousness from the brain (or relevantly similar brain-like structure) containing it. If we disregard these dangerous inclinations that preclude taking our gray matter seriously, it becomes easier to explain consciousness. "Consciousness" could refer to something like a set of dynamical neuronal firing patterns that directly correlate with our qualia. And having a certain quale would be the brain exhibiting some particular dynamical structure or other.

Of course, simply stipulating that we should ignore our intuitions concerning consciousness is no answer to the skeptic. Those who find the problem of the explanatory gap a compelling argument against developing theories of consciousness will have found little reason to change their opinions thus far. However, I do think that I have provided enough evidence to suspend heavy reliance on intuition pumps regarding the feasibility of explaining consciousness. That done, my job now is to put up or shut up, as it were. I take the remainder of the book to be an argument by example against the Nagelians (and McGinns)[71] of the world. Locating consciousness in the brain is but one step to overcoming their cognitive dissonance. This project forms the bulk of chapters 4, 5, and 6. Using these results to answer more specific concerns regarding exactly when in processing stream we are conscious, of what (relative to other active processing streams) we are aware, and who should exhibit these phenomena forms a second step. This I do in chapters 7, 8 and 9. Only after I have developed a framework for discussing consciousness naturalistically and scientifically will I return to the problem of the explanatory gap. In chapter 6, I try to provide a more complete answer to the serious "mysterian."[72] At least, I spell out one naturalist's response.

Now, let us roll up our sleeves and get to work: I start with a modest question: what are the major psychological and neurophysiological differences between conscious states and unconscious ones?

A Multiple Memory System Framework
Chapter Four

The previous chapters argued that not only is a scientific theory of consciousness an intelligible goal, but we need one in order to account for some behavioral evidence from psychology involving the (partial?) activation of memories. We can find a difference between conscious and unconscious processes. Hence, a likely place to begin building an explanation of conscious phenomena would be via exploring those differences.

Here I adumbrate an interdisciplinary framework for understanding consciousness within current information processing paradigms. The framework turns on the premise that there are at least two distinct and independent systems of memory,[73] only one of which is relevant for consciousness. As I discuss in chapter 5, I construe "memory" broadly. In brief, our "memory" systems process incoming stimuli as well as store previous experiences because there is actually little distinction between the storage of previous perceptions and processing current ones. In particular, mental states use the information stored in their "weights" to "interpret" incoming data such that they fit into meaningful units or schemas. By accounting for the interaction of our "conscious" and "unconscious" memory systems in processing incoming stimuli, we will thereby give a causal history of conscious perception.

I use this framework to construct an hypothesis about how to understand consciousness with respect to our mnemonic processes. I then examine what it tells us about the conscious experiences of infants, amnesics, and other animals. Finally, I suggest the sorts of neuronal firing patterns that correspond to conscious experience. Though admittedly speculative, these ideas will at least illustrate the type of theory we should develop given the evidence at hand.

The remaining chapters then extend my particular hypothesis and the general theoretical framework. Chapter 7 examines the problem of absent qualia and argues that theories of the sort I develop entail that absent qualia are not possible. Chapter 8 compares my approach with the higher level "executive" theories from psychology in order to clarify the ways in which consciousness is actually a structure in the higher-level information processing paradigm. Chapter 9 replies to Daniel Dennett and Marcel Kinsbourne's worry that we will never be able to narrow the temporal window enough to pinpoint when conscious processing begins. Using experiments in evoked response potentials as a bridge between cognitive psychology and neurophysiology in memory research allows us to refine our story along the temporal dimension, as well as to make more explicit connections with underlying neuroanatomy. But as a beginning, this chapter outlines the relevant data for building a large scale multi-level framework in which to situate consciousness. It pulls evidence from neurophysiology, developmental psychology, clinical neurology, and cognitive psychology and focuses primarily on priming studies and what they can tell us about normal processing in human memory.

4.1. Converging Evidence for Two Independent Memory Systems

Psychologists in the mid-1970's hypothesized that there were two distinct processing mechanisms for long-term memory (Anderson and Bower 1973, Collins and Loftus 1975, Keele 1973, LaBerge 1973a, b, 1975, LaBerge and Samuels 1974, Posner and Snyder 1975a, b, Schneidner and Shiffrin 1977, Shiffrin 1975, Shiffrin and Geisler 1973, Shiffrin and Schneidner 1977, Turvey 1974). First, there was an automatic form of pattern matching that occurred when appropriate inputs simply activated a learned sequence of elements in long term store (LTS). This sort of memory response was strategy-free, massively parallel, and largely unconscious. It did not require any attentional mechanisms, apparently had few capacity limitations, and was beyond subject control. Second, controlled processing referred to a temporary activation of a sequence of elements in LTS that was created easily enough, but unlike automatic access, demanded attention and subject control. As a result, it had a more limited capacity and was dependent upon conscious processing strategies.[74]

However, there is now substantial converging evidence from the various cognitive sciences that instead of different types of access to the same memory system, there are (at least) two separate memory systems in the brain, only one of which supports conscious perception. We already know from chapter 3 that stimuli which are not consciously perceived, but which are registered nonetheless (in an "automatic" memory task), can influence behavior, and they can influence behavior differently from stimuli which are consciously seen (in a "controlled" memory task).[75] And these differences between automatic and controlled memory processes do not seem merely to reflect differences in the types of retrieval mechanisms we have when accessing a single underlying system. At least two distinct neural systems are involved in automatic versus controlled memory processes. Data from infant studies show that these systems mature at different rates, and tests involving adult amnesics indicate that one system can be impaired while the other still functions normally.[76] Understanding how these different systems function and interact would put us well on our way to developing a functional causal history of the conscious processes.

4.1.1. Neurobiological Evidence for Two Memory Systems

In charting the neural sites for "automatic" memories in other (simpler) organisms, neurobiologists have had the most success when concentrating on habituation, classical conditioning, or imprinting. The neural mechanisms necessary and sufficient for exhibiting these types of learning are slowly becoming understood and how to generalize these findings to more complex creatures like ourselves is also becoming clearer. In general, studies have found that learning an automatic behavioral response only modifies already existing circuitry specialized to perform the behavior (Davis *et al.* 1982, Groves and Thompson 1970, Tischler and Davis 1983). No additional circuitry is needed to initiate or to maintain the learned responses.

To take a particular example, consider the nictitating membrane/eyeblink response in rabbits. A 350 msec tone (the conditioned stimuli) is paired with a 100 msec corneal airpuff (the unconditioned stimuli). Rabbits extend their nictitating membrane and blink as the conditioned response to the tone + airpuff. After several hundred trials, the rabbits will exhibit this response as the tone sounds, but before the airpuff occurs. The minimal circuitry that appears necessary for performing the conditioned response includes the cerebellar deep nuclei, afferent connections to the cerebellum via mossy and climbing fibers, and efferent connections through the superior cerebellar peduncle (Gellman and

Miles 1985). (See Figure 4.1.) It is not yet clear exactly where the synaptic changes occur along this circuit, or even how many places for synaptic change there are, but the evidence does indicate that classical conditioning for the eyeblink response requires only this specific and limited circuitry.[77]

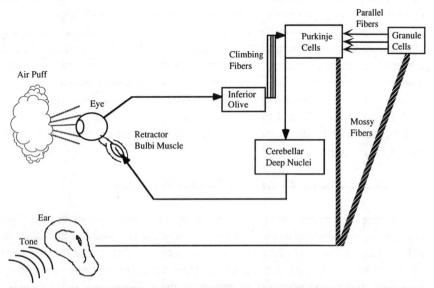

Figure 4.1. Proposed Minimum Circuitry for Conditioning of Rabbit Nictitating Membrane Response. The Purkinje cells receive information about the eye airpuff from the climbing fibers, which start in the inferior olive. They also receive information about the tone from the mossy fibers, the cerebellar granule cells, and the parallel fibers. The Purkinje cells then signal the retractor muscles to contract via the cerebellar deep nuclei. If the signals from the climbing and parallel fibers occur simultaneously, then relevant synaptic connections are strengthened and the behavioral response is learned (based on Gellman and Miles 1985).

Even though generalizing from any particular neurophysiological explanation to all instances of learned automatic memory is dubious, we can draw the following broad conclusions nonetheless. First, the sites for automatic memory are (generally speaking) identical to the sites which underlie the stimulus input to behavioral output circuit. Accordingly, automatic memories are diffused throughout large portions of the brain and there is no single area dedicated to recalling these memories. Second, because the actual neural circuit responsible for the behavior changes when some new response is learned, this new behavior will occur whenever that circuit is initiated (disregarding any behavioral override mechanisms from above). This sort of relatively permanent change in underlying circuitry explains how these sorts of simple memories can be recalled rapidly, automatically, and in parallel. It also explains why there are apparently no capacity limitations on this "system" and why it is beyond subject control.

The apparent minimal requirements for (at least certain types of) automatic memory contrast with the story behind the "controlled memory" related to qualitative experience, for apparently laying down the memories in a controlled memory system requires the hippocampus and adjacent areas of cortex. Larry Squire and Stuart Zola-Morgan have developed an animal model for this memory system based on studying a variety of bilateral lesions in the medial temporal lobe in monkeys.[78]

The most extensive bilateral lesion in the medial temporal lobe system that Squire and Zola-Morgan study, the H+A+ lesion, includes the hippocampal formation (the dentate gyrus, the hippocampus itself, the subicular complex, and the entorhinal cortices), the amygdala, and the surrounding perirhinal and parahippocampal cortices. Monkeys with this lesion are severely impaired on memory tasks that require direct access to memories of previous episodes, although they can still learn skills at normal levels. For example, the lesioned monkeys cannot perform a delayed nonmatching-to-sample task.[79] However, these same monkeys can be trained in classical conditioning paradigms. In particular, they show normal performance in the incremental learning of skills and habits, including object and pattern discriminations (Mahut and Moss 1984, Malamut *et al.* 1984, Zola-Morgan and Squire 1984).

Later, Squire and Zola-Morgan discovered that damage to the amygdala did not affect controlled memory performance; instead, this memory was impaired when the cortical areas surrounding the amygdala were damaged. Indeed, memory is disrupted when only the perirhinal and parahippocampal cortices are lesioned, but the hippocampus and amygdala spared. These investigations allowed them to map the major neural components of the controlled access memory system in monkeys (and presumably in humans as well). It consists in the hippocampal formation, including entorhinal cortex, and the adjacent perirhinal and parahippocampal cortical areas. (See Figure 4.2 for a schematic view of the medial temporal lobe memory system.)

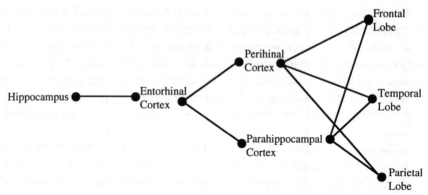

Figure 4.2. Medial Temporal Lobe Memory System. The hippocampus receives the majority of its input from the entorhinal cortex. The entorhinal cortex in turn receives most of its input from the perirhinal and parahippocampal cortices. The frontal, temporal, and parietal lobes input to the perirhinal and parahippocampal cortices. All of these connections are reciprocal (based on Squire and Zola-Morgan 1991).

We apparently use this medial temporal system to form long-term memories stored in an explicitly accessible form.[80]   These memories would then inform and guide the interpretations of our conscious perceptions.   Immediate memory and the perceptions themselves probably lie in the distributed activity in cortex or neocortex, but if we are to learn these experiences such that we can later recall them explicitly, the hippocampus and related structures must be active during perception (and perhaps later learning as well[81]). However, the medial temporal system's involvement in forming consciously accessible, long-term memories appears only temporary — memories which initially depended on an intact system were later unaffected by H+A+ lesions, indicating that these memories become reorganized, perhaps as the result of slow synaptic change in the neocortical areas.

Squire and Zola-Morgan suggest that the medial temporal system may act to conjoin disconnected events or stimuli features which are processed and represented in distributed form throughout neocortex. They hypothesize that we can recover a previous perception or thought because the hippocampus and related areas maintain a "sketch" of how the distributed set of representations fit together into a single coherent event. In essence then, the hippocampus would "index" or summarize the memories to be formed. This system would thus be important for rapidly processing episodic information in conscious perception. Other types of learning, such as the skills, habits, and conditioning mentioned above, would lie outside the scope of this system (or at least do not require it), and, generally speaking, are acquired at a slower pace and are not stored in such rich detail.[82]

Here then we find one possible difference between the neurophysiological components supporting the processes related to conscious and nonconscious phenomena. Conscious phenomena are connected to the medial-temporal lobe memory system that underwrites explicit and meaningful recall, whereas unconscious processing can be found in the diverse areas throughout the brain. Perhaps if we could understand what fundamentally differs between those two systems, then we would be well on our way to defining the difference between conscious and nonconscious processing.

In any event, there is neurobiological evidence for (higher order) mammals having at least two memory systems, one that reflects only changes in the neural circuits underlying the learned behavior and one that depends upon a medial temporal lobe hippocampal system to support its memories. The first memory system roughly corresponds to psychology's "automatic memory" system, while the second is analogous to its "controlled memory" system. We should now explore the psychological properties of these two systems to differentiate better the types of processes associated with conscious phenomena from the processes disconnected from conscious access.

4.1.2 Infants, Amnesics, and the Dual Memory System Hypothesis

The hint from neurophysiological research that there might be two different memory systems in some mammals which operate independently of one another is echoed in psychology's infant developmental literature. We can tentatively align the memory system that infant habituation-novelty preference tasks and some conditioning paradigms tap into with the automatic memory system mentioned above, and the memory system that underlies object search tasks and other such paradigms with the controlled access memory system. Moreover, even though the automatic memory system seems to be present at birth, the richer explicit system apparently does not emerge until eight or nine months after birth.[83] These data focus more specifically on the differences in the causal powers of the two systems and they allow us to begin to chart the development and expression of consciousness in human cognition.

Psychologists use an infant's preference for attending to novel objects to index the amount of information the infant has stored in memory about some aspect of the world. If an infant looks at a repeatedly presented face less and less as time goes on, but gazes far longer at a new face, then, scientists argue, the response pattern of "habituation" and "recovery" indicates that the infant has formed some sort of memory for the first face. But, as many have noted, such behavior does not necessarily indicate very sophisticated mnemonic processing on the part of the infant. We could think of the infant's performance simply in terms of "facilitated processing" of familiar stimuli, rather than as controlled access to explicit knowledge about the previous exposure to the face. One hypothesis is that a young infant's differential attention to novel and familiar stimuli merely reflects changes in the cognitive procedures involved in perception (Schacter and Moscovitch 1984: 184-185). That is, we can think of an infant's performance as indicating the activation of an automatic memory system analogous to the systems supporting habituation or classical conditioning in simpler organisms.

Apparently, the differential attention in infants is unaffected by the length of time between the original habituating exposures and later novelty tests.[84] Fagan (1971, 1973) found that infants did not forget familiar stimuli with 30 second, 24 hour, and 48 hour delays between the study and test periods.[85] Interestingly, these habituation effects in six to nine month old infants do not occur in cross-modal shifts between study and test, nor do they in intermodal study or test situations (Gottfried *et al.* 1977, 1979, Mackay-Soroka *et al.* 1982, Rolfe and Day 1981, Rose *et al.* 1978, 1979), even though in intramodal conditions, younger infants show reliable preferences for the new items over changes in orientation (Cornell 1975, Fagan 1979), representational format (Dirks and Gibson (1977), and motion (Moscovitch 1984: chapter 3). (Year old infants are largely unaffected by cross-modal, intermodal, or intramodal testing.) Since, as Schacter and Moscovitch (1984) note, we also see long-term habituation in lower animals, including the leech, earthworm, and rat (Castellucci and Kandell 1976, Gardner 1968, Leaton 1974), the habituation-novelty effects we see in infants are probably mediated by a fairly primitive, evolutionarily early, memory system — a memory system aligned with nonconscious processing.[86]

We can also train infants in simple operant conditioning paradigms, similar to those successfully used in rats with hippocampal lesions.[87] Moreover, there is evidence that general cues, and not the attributes of particular items, maintain these responses.[88] That is, three to five month old infants seem only to learn associations between stimuli and response and do not explicitly remember the contexts in which the learning episode occurred. Consider Papousek (1969) for one such example. He trained infants to turn their heads to the right when they heard a tone to receive a squirt of milk. After they had acquired the response, the infants would continue to turn their heads, even though they were no longer hungry. Indeed, the infants would continue to turn their heads, even though they refused to drink. Finally, when quinine was substituted for milk in the experiment, infants continued to turn their heads and accept the squirted liquid, despite its bitter taste.

These perseverative behaviors do resemble the behaviors of hippocampal rats, who will continue to run mazes, ignoring any reward because they are no longer hungry or thirsty.[89] The rats' perseverance stems from a memory system that does not require the hippocampus and surrounding areas to mediate the conditioned responses, since it appears only when the medial temporal lobe system is missing. Likewise, perseverance in young infants may indicate a non-functioning controlled memory system, and they too may only have access to the more primitive automatic memory.

On more "explicit" memory tasks, which require the long-term retention of particular events (such as the previously mentioned delayed matching-to-sample), infants less than a year old performed poorly, similar to monkeys with H+A+ lesions (Brody 1981). In human infants, AB error is the most common type of forgetting studied in explicit memory tasks. Piaget (1954) noted that infants can find an object repeatedly hidden at some location A, but after finding the object at A several times successfully, they will continue to search there when the object is now placed at location B, even though the move to B was done with the infant watching. Infants engage in similar behavior when they search for their mothers who leave the room through door A for the first few trials and door B in later trials (Corter et al. 1980, Zucker 1982).

Why would a young infant be unable to overcome perseverative tendencies, and how is this failure connected to fully mature memory systems? Schacter and Moscovitch advance the hypothesis that a young infant's AB error indicates rapid forgetting. They point out that the frequency of the error depends upon the delay between hiding the object at B and when the infant is allowed to search for it.[90] At first blush, this hypothesis may appear far-fetched since it requires infants to forget much in a relatively short period of time. However, this sort of rapid forgetting is exactly the same sort of mnemonic difficulties that plague hippocampal amnesics. Perhaps infants have the same sort of mnemonic abilities as amnesic patients and hippocampal rats, with their performances reflecting an incomplete controlled-access explicit memory system. Infants then would be like adult amnesics and hippocampal rats in that none would have access to an explicit memory system — the system would be damaged in amnesics and the lesioned rats and still immature in infants.[91]

In support of the suggestion that both infants and amnesics lack an explicit memory system but do have access to an automatic one, Schacter and Moscovitch report that amnesics perform exactly like infants in an AB̶ type of search task. Indeed, many amnesics continue to search for an object at its previously hidden location even though the new "hiding" place is in plain sight. Schacter and Moscovitch argue that proactive interference from search trials at location A cause the apparent perseverance in amnesics. (This interpretation fits with other studies which show that amnesics are very susceptible to the effects of such interference (Kinsbourne and Winocur 1980, Warrington and Weiskrantz 1974, Winocur and Weiskrantz 1976).)

Other evidence that amnesics only function with the more primitive "automatic" memory system intact includes the fact that they can learn skills and exhibit classical conditioning effects (Brooks and Baddeley 1976, Graf et al. 1984, Moscovitch 1982, Parkin 1982, Schacter and Graf 1986b, Shimamura 1986, Squire and Cohen 1984, Weiskrantz 1984, Wood et al. 1982). Weiskrantz and Warrington (1979) point out that even though the conditioned responses of two severely amnesic patients were near normal, they could not recognize the conditioning apparatus with which they had interacted upon numerous occasions. Indeed, HM, a well-known amnesic who has had his temporal lobes removed in both hemispheres, can learn to perform a variety of motor skills, all the while insisting that he could not remember events connected to previous trials, including trials that had taken place only minutes before (Corkin 1965, 1968, Milner et al. 1968).

Interestingly enough though, spared learning in amnesics is not confined to motor skills; many of the retained abilities are either perceptual or cognitive (Squire and McKee 1992). For example, amnesics can learn to apply the Fibonacci rule over several trials, even though they all claim "unequivocally that they had never seen or done this task before" (Wood et al. 1982: 174).[92] They can also learn to solve the Tower of Hanoi problem, to read mirror script, and to complete sequential patterns (Cohen 1984, Cohen and Squire 1980, Nissan and Bullemer 1987). Brooks and Baddeley (1976) found that amnesics can put a jig-saw puzzle together faster if they have completed the same puzzle before. In fact, their learning curve was much the same as that of normals. Finally, amnesics read sentences much faster a second time through, compared to reading them for the first time (Moscovitch 1982).

In addition, amnesics use the prior presentation of words when completing sentence fragments (e.g., adding an "LE" to "TAB__" when they were previously shown "TABLE" in a list of words). Indeed, they do so as much as normal controls do,[93] though the amnesics cannot even recognize the words in later recognition tasks, and the normals have no trouble explicitly recalling the words (Graf et al. 1984, Jacoby and Witherspoon 1982, Warrington and Weiskranz 1970, 1974). Further, amnesics show identity priming effects in lexical decision tasks — they are faster to decide whether a string of letters is a word or not when the string is proceeded by itself (Moscovitch 1982).[94] (Though the evidence is still controversial, these priming effects appear to persist at least a week after exposure (McAndrews et al. 1987).[95]) Data along these lines suggest that amnesics retain some information from learning episodes that cannot be recalled consciously. Hence, the preserved mnemonic skills in amnesics must be due to a memory system that is neurophysiologically and psychologically distinct from the medial temporal system (damaged in amnesics) that Squire and Zola-Morgan hypothesize underwriting explicit recollection.

If we assume that these experimental paradigms tap into analogous memory systems in monkeys, rats, infants, and amnesics, then we know much more about the processing capabilities of automatic and explicit memory systems. For example, the automatic system appears to be little more than facilitated processing of familiar stimuli. It is modality-specific, though not specific to orientation, motion, or representational format; it cannot recall specific episodes, rather only the general cues needed to generate conditioned behavioral response. And it encompasses both perceptual and cognitive information, as well as more traditional motor skills. Explicit memory, on the other hand, is more sophisticated. Not inextricably connected to any particular modality, it can recall facts associated with specific events in a subject's life.[96] If I am correct in believing that consciousness is somehow aligned with explicit memory, then it too should be multi-modal and tied to particular facts within particular experiences. This conjecture is investigated below.[97]

4.1.3. Characterizing the Two Memory Systems

At present, even though different fields agree on their descriptions of the experimental results, they disagree over what those results mean in terms of general principles from which to posit underlying causal mechanisms. Borrowing from artificial intelligence terminology,[98] scientists have generally characterized the difference between the two systems as the difference between "procedural" memory and "declarative" memory.[99] Procedural memory, or, as it is often called, "implicit" memory, requires changing later processing functions in virtue of information passing through the system. This "knowledge" is expressed implicitly through differential procedural operations. Declarative memory, on the other hand, refers to the specific outputs of some processing function. This information is explicitly representable in conscious recall. In young infants, H+A+ lesioned monkeys, and some amnesics, the procedural memory system is believed to be intact, and the declarative memory system impaired.

This characterization of the distinction is similar to the one Mort Mishkin makes between a "habit" system, which depends on the strengthening connections between stimulus and response, and a "true" memory system, which entails explicit representations of experiences (Mishkin *et al.* 1984). Yet other suggestions of how we should characterize the differences among the various memory tests abound. They include distinctions between "cognitive" and "semantic" memory, "semantic" and "episodic" memory, "horizontal" and "vertical" associations, and "skilled" memory and "conscious" recollection (Kinsbourne and Wood 1975, 1982, Moscovitch 1982, Schacter and Tulving 1982, Warrington and Weiskrantz 1982, Wickelgren 1979).

That these distinctions cross-cut one another in their details is uncontroversial; however, each still remains faithful to the same broad picture of the phenomena. They all make the following points: the first memory system deals with information automatically accessed given certain inputs. It expresses its knowledge indirectly through differentially affecting behavioral responses to the same task, instead of through some overtly given verbal answer or meaningful gesture. The second memory system concerns knowledge about specific circumstances surrounding events. Though it too may differentially affect behavioral responses, memory in that system can be recalled in (more or less) propositional form (in humans at least).

However, none of these simple dichotomies really does full justice to all the data which have been amassed concerning multiple memory systems, for we get conflicting results using different memory tasks. For example, identity priming in lexical decision tasks lasts a long time in amnesics, while masked priming in normals (which gives rise to the same immediate behavioral results as identity priming in amnesics) only lasts for a few seconds, if that. (No one is sure yet what the significance of the difference is. I hope to make clearer in the following discussion how complicated the relations among our memory systems actually are.) When we go on to include data from different experimental paradigms, as I do below, the picture gets even more unclear. But though the ties become more tenuous, there are some fairly broad points that each of the accounts have in common — enough, I believe, to make the set including the different models a viable interdisciplinary framework.

4.2. Priming

One reason that the data discussed above fit so well together — even though they are derived from different animals — is that they are amassed using common methodological frameworks. Neurophysiology, developmental psychology, and clinical neurology all use versions of the same basic tasks in testing their respective hypotheses concerning mnemonic processes. These common frameworks allow for easy conversations among the different investigative groups and for making fairly straightforward connections among the theoretical paradigms.

Nevertheless, any models derived from the data can at best only function as analogs of one another. We must be careful that this sort of tie is not the Achilles' heel of multiple memory theories. It is too easy to assume that because each of the models comes from a different discipline, each thereby acts as strongly confirming evidence for the others. However, the investigations on the different animals could be showing similar results simply because similar experimental tasks were used. Because analogous tasks weaken the mutual independence of the theoretical models, and thus their worth as confirmed of one another, in order to strongly confirm the models developed in different fields, we need to use different experimental paradigms organized around different principles and assumptions.[100]

A set of data that would be useful for any proposed model of multiple memory systems would be the priming data mentioned at the end of chapter 3, since it was these data that highlighted the differences between conscious and unconscious processing the first place. But how priming data are supposed to fit into some dichotomy similar to the ones discussed above is not clear. Though some argue that priming effects are just another instance of procedural memory,[101] we do find instances of "double dissociation" between priming and skill learning (Schwartz and Hashtroudi 1991). (That is, we find some patients who exhibit normal priming though have impaired skill learning and others who can learning skills but not exhibit priming.) For example, Alzheimer patients show impaired priming and normal motor skill learning, while Huntington's disease patients show normal priming effects using recognition and recall tests, but (controlling for motor deficits) have great trouble learning new skills (Butters *et al.* 1990, Ferraro *et al.* 1993, Grafman *et al.* 1990, Heindel *et al.* 1988, Perfect *et al.* 1992).[102] (Even repetition priming itself is not a unitary phenomena. We also find a double dissociation between two types of priming among stroke victims. Patients with temporal-parietal lesions show priming effects for stimuli repeated a short time later, but no priming effects if the repeated item occurs more than 5 stimuli presentations after the original presentation. Patients with dorsolateral prefrontal lesions show the opposite effects (Kersteen-Tucker and Knight 1989). These type of results suggest that one sort of priming may be affiliated with short term memory (which is connected with our frontal lobes — see chapter 8 for discussion), while the other is tied to long term store, the general topic of this chapter.)

In response to these sorts of concerns, Schacter (1990) argues that priming depends on both the activation of already established explicit memories in the declarative system and on some sort of new "perceptual" representations that can influence performance independently of conscious recall.[103] However, in some cases it seems that priming also reflects the influence of new declarative representations on behavior, even though these representations somehow fail to gain access to conscious awareness.[104]

To explain priming is going to require a more complicated picture than a simple procedural-declarative distinction, since the phenomena seem to operate when the two (or more) memory systems interact. Once we expand our pool of relevant data to include results from experimental paradigms other than versions of delayed nonmatching-to-sample, we can see inadequacies in the simple automatic-versus-controlled or procedural-versus-declarative characterizations of our memory systems. On the other hand, though, if we could develop some account of how priming works and which systems it uses in the brain, we would then have a start in understanding the differences between conscious and unconscious processing in humans, as well as how such processing interacts. Moreover, since we can get differential priming effects in normal adult humans, priming studies also present us with a way of investigating the various memory systems and their processes in normal human brains that would help control for any confounding effects brought on by species, age, or collateral lesion damage. In the following sections, I discuss priming in normal adults in more detail and then present a framework for understanding human memory systems and consciousness based on those data. I illustrate how different experimental paradigms lead to different accounts of automatic and controlled memory, and without attempting to resolve all the conflicts, I sketch an account of our memory systems that includes the majority of the evidence and that can serve as a framework for analyzing consciousness functionally.

4.2.1. Word Completion and Perceptual Identification Tasks[105]

Tulving, Schacter, and Stark (1982) gave a word completion task to normals, similar to the one mentioned above for amnesics. Subjects studied long lists of low-frequency words and were then given a yes/no recognition test and a fragment completion test one hour, one day, or one week later. (In half the test conditions, the recognition test preceded the completion test; in the other half, the completion test came first.) They discovered that, as with amnesics, previous exposure to a word facilitates a subject's ability to complete a fragment of it. The magnitude of this priming effect did not diminish over time; in contrast, recognition performance declined severely over a week interval.

Similar results have been reported in perceptual identification tasks. Here, subjects attempt to identify a word presented during a brief (approximately 35 msec) exposure after having studied a word list that includes items to be repeated in the identification task. Facilitated identification occurs even after a 24-hour delay between a single-study exposure and the identification task, but, as before, recognition memory declines significantly over the same period.[106] In addition, graphemic information is retained over long intervals in perceptual recognition. Indeed, remembering without awareness can be tied to a particular episode, a particular modality, and a particular font (though not to a particular environment).

Altering the test conditions of this basic paradigm tells us much about the various and complementary properties of the different processing systems underlying perceptual identification and explicit recall. For example, manipulations of the level of processing (brought about, e.g., by the instructions to examine a list of words for instances of the letter "r" versus instructions to examine the list for concrete nouns) have no effect on the perceptual identification results, but they do substantially affect success in later recognition. Perceptual priming does not transfer well across modalities, whereas recognition memory appears largely unaffected by changes in the modality of presentation from study to test sessions. Perceptual priming is insensitive to the amount of attention devoted to the task, whereas recognition is greatly affected by level of attention (Jacoby and Dallas 1981).[107]

This evidence suggests that there is a fundamental difference between the memory system(s) used in the more implicit priming tasks and the one(s) tapped in the explicit recall tasks. The first memory system apparently does not require explicit memory of the study episode. Nevertheless, some sort of elaborative processing of the stimuli does occur since subjects must have at least some minimal representation of the stimuli before any sort of behavioral priming effect appears (Graf and Schacter 1987). In addition, this pre-existing representation must be modality-specific since changes in modality do affect implicit priming.[108] In contrast, the second memory system allows one to recall particular learning events and is sensitive to the length of time between study and test and to whether the subjects are asked to process the words in the list semantically, as well as to the number and spacing of repetitions among words. Moreover, this memory system is probably not tied so closely to modality since explicit priming effects are not sensitive to modality changes.

Because we generally do not see implicit priming with non-words, some believe that the priming effects elicited through the so-called implicit memory systems really reflect just a specialized early lexical decision system (Forster 1981, Forster and Davis 1984, Forster et al. 1987). However, Feustal, Shiffrin, and Salasoo (1983) offer data suggesting that we can get repetition priming effects for non-words if the non-words are repeated sufficiently. We can see this effect even when the repetitions occur so rapidly that the subjects do not consciously see the letter strings (though the effects are smaller for non-words than words). In fact, the difference in latencies for word versus non-word identification are additive to the difference due to the repeated presentations.

Feustal, Shiffrin, and Salasoo conclude that implicit priming effects must be due to some type of episodic memory images not consciously accessible, and they suggest that the superior priming for words over non-words is due to some "unitized codification" of known words which facilitates an automatic, rapid identification. That is, after five repetition occurrences, nonwords are processed in "chunks" just like real words are, since words and nonwords are primed equally well after that much exposure (Salasoo *et al.* 1985).[109] Indeed, after a year's delay, subject performance is essentially equivalent for the old nonwords, the old words, and the new words. Learned nonwords are remembered in a unitized form similar to real words.

Because these sorts of repetition effects decrease with delays of as little as a day, Salasoo, Shiffrin, and Feustal believe that the lexical decision task with repetition priming depends on facilitated mnemonic processes for the repeated words with relatively short lag. Here though we also find a good lesson in the difficulties of interpreting memory data. On the one hand, word completion and perceptual identification priming do not seem to fit a simple spreading activation, rapid decay model for either implicit or explicit memory because this priming is differentially sensitive to various contextual factors, and lasts on the order of weeks (Jacoby and Dallas 1981) — it cannot simply be a lowering of the threshold of a previously formed semantic "logogen" in explicit memory. On the other hand, repetition priming seems to be exactly a lowering of activation thresholds in some memory system, since it lasts only for a few seconds. Do these sorts of priming rely on different memory systems, tap into different processing procedures, or some combination of both?

No one has a good answer (though I suggest a possible resolution to the dilemma below). We are witnessing a clear instance of the type of experimental task partially determining the picture of the phenomenon to be explained. Virtually the same experimental subjects engaged in two different types of psychological tasks (both of whose goals were to differentiate implicit from explicit memory) and — even though the background assumptions driving the paradigms seem to be essentially identical — they consistently gave diametrically opposed results. These sorts of results not only confuse any picture one might have of implicit and explicit memory in normal humans, they make the links among the different animal models in pursuit of a unified conception of memory more tenuous as well, since they rely on a common experimental paradigm to tie themselves together.

As I stated above, we have to be very careful not to let different animal models mutually support one another in virtue of their sharing similar experimental tasks. If experimental paradigms determine the effects such that the effects are an artificial result of the task, then all we would have would be an artificial and illusory connection among the different animal models. We would not be focusing upon the real underlying causal mechanism (indeed, we could not be sure that there even is one) and hence could not hope to create a single theory of memory. What we need is converging evidence from different sources so that we do not have to rely too heavily on any one experimental paradigm.

Nevertheless, these results do give us some information about our memory systems that we did not have before. For example, it is clear from these experiments that there probably is an episodic basis for the perceptual identification and repetition effects, which is very different from what we believe to be true about any procedural or skills memory system. This postulation is bolstered by Jacoby and Dallas's (1981) observation that prior exposure to low frequency words increases perceptual recognition priming. Why would one additional exposure have such an effect? Perhaps, as they suggest, some early implicit perceptual system is in fact storing a few contextual factors. Thus this memory system would be a processing system faintly reminiscent of a semantic memory built out of episodic traces.

Schacter suggests that we understand these sorts of implicit priming phenomena as depending on a "perceptual representational system" that is distinct from our more explicit memory and from a procedural or skills memory. Though some sort of elaborative processing must occur for the creation of a "perceptual" memory, these perceptual systems retain only the "structural" information of stimuli, and not its semantic character (since, among other things, new associations among words can lead to interference in performance in the second system, whereas the first system exhibits no such AB, AC interference effects for pairs of normatively unrelated words (Graf and Schacter 1987, Schacter 1992).)[110] These perceptual systems must also operate apart from procedural memory because they are more than simply independent, facilitated, input-output circuits. They feed into explicit memory and facilitate processing there (or in short term store) by increasing or decreasing the activation threshold for "structurally" similar representations. They are non-semantic, though cognitive, and they operate automatically and independent of subject control.

Even though including different sorts of experimental paradigms does muddy our conception of mnemonic processing, it also demonstrates that we probably have three types of memory systems, not just two. The neurophysiological study of classical conditioning in rabbits, the developmental psychology tests of infant habituation, and clinical neurology's skill learning tasks for amnesics probably investigate one type of memory; word completion paradigms, and other cognitive priming tasks, tap a different sort of memory; and finally the experiments on the medial temporal lobe system in monkeys, the lesioned hippocampi in rats, and object search in older infants and amnesics are designed to study a third sort of memory (the one hypothesized to be aligned with conscious phenomena). This third sort of memory we have yet to characterize fully with respect to the other two, and it is the most important system because its outputs perhaps just are our conscious percepts. In particular, we should understand the relationship between the two episodic memory systems. It should now be obvious that an account of these systems is crucial for any "causal history" explanation of consciousness.

4.2.2. Properties of Explicit Memory

Let us now focus on separating the differential processing attributes of the perceptual processing system and the explicit, controlled access, system by outlining the specific causal properties of explicit memory associated with consciousness. Looking at different experimental paradigms that are connected to differential mnemonic processing should prove useful for uncovering the various capacities of our memory systems and how they interact. If nothing else, these experiments should once again refine and extend our conception of our (three) memory systems by increasing the list of processing attributes for the explicit, controlled access memory system (in contrast to the structural/perceptual memory system).

In our consciously accessible (explicit) memory, we find only a particular segmentation and interpretation active at a time for each stimulus. A quick example of this phenomenon appears in Figure 4.3. We can see the Necker cubes as both opening upward to the left or both downward to the right, but never as opening in both directions at the same time. A second point the Necker cubes suggest is that in matching incoming stimuli with some semantic hypothesis, our conscious explicit system tries to account for as much of the data as possible with each semantic "guess." Even though the two cubes are two separate perceptual objects, we nonetheless perceive them as a single unit.

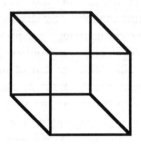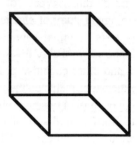

Figure 4.3. Necker Cubes.

Anthony Marcel (1980, 1983a, b) generalizes this observation and argues that what determines whether two logically separable events are in fact judged as a single unit is whether our semantic "schema" treats them as lying within the same parsed segment of its unitized description. We do find evidence for this sort of unitization or chunking in both the auditory and the visual domains. Bregman and Rudnicky (1975) demonstrate that it is easier to distinguish tones when subjects believe the tones belong to separate perceptual events In their experiment, subjects heard a cyclic signal stream consisting of the tones Y X A B X Y. The frequency of X was lower than that of A or B, and the frequency of Y was lower still. Normally, identifying the order of A and B is made more difficult when they are surrounded by X tones. However, moving the frequency of Y closer to that of X allows the X tones to be subjectively "captured" into a "schema" which parses X and Y as one unit, and consequently, the A and B tones become easier to distinguish.

In the visual domain, Dember and Purcell (1967) and Kristofferson et al. (1975) have shown that when subjects are presented with a target and a mask within a short time frame, they treat the target and mask as one unit. That is, subjects are aware of only one perceptual event. But if the researchers add an extra stimulus and manipulate the presentation rate such that the subjects parse the new stimuli and the mask as one unit of information, then the target remains left as an independently recoverable unit.[111] Obviously, there are limits to what counts as a boundary for some perceptual event — objects located too far from one another physically or temporally cannot be unitized. But still, these experiments indicate that we interpret incoming stimuli and we can only (consciously) perceive things in virtue of our interpretation.

Experiments like these help underscore the differences between our two episodically based memory systems and give us a start in delineating the differences between conscious and unconscious mental events, as well as a few clues about how the two systems interact. For example, it appears that the output of our perceptual memory system need only include the structure of the incoming stimuli, but can perhaps encompass more than one "interpretation" for each stimulus.[112] In contrast, the content or output of our explicit memory system seems to be the most economically fruitful semantic hypothesis. (At least, we are conscious of only a single interpretation at a time.)

(Cognitive psychologists' "meaning analysis" refers to a similar process. Like other functionally characterized processes, meaning analysis entails that we assign meanings to things in virtue of the input to the system and the relation of what is activated to other cognitive "nodes." We know where we are and what our environment is like by assimilating analyzed sensory inputs into pre-existing "schemas," whose assimilation in turn can modify the schema.[113] "Meaning is equated with [the] structure [of cognitive schemas]. Thus, a set of events on which we cannot impose any relations is meaningless. Meaning is not some sum of meanings of individual elements, but, instead, 'the structure itself is meaningful'" (Mandler 1984: 51). Cognitive psychologists argue that we comprehend events in terms of the relations that exist among the stored units in the schemas which the events have activated, and so only sensory signals which stand in special relation to other internal representations count as a true representational input.)

The final section below summarizes the general principles concerning the operation of our three memory system gleaned from all the data presented thus far. These general principles are elaborated in chapter 9, where I introduce ERP research as further corroborating evidence and show how this research serves as a conceptual bridge between psychology and neurophysiology. Before I discuss conceptual bridges though, I first sketch one way in which consciousness may fit into the picture we can draw (chapter 5), speculate on the neural correlates for conscious interpretations (chapter 6), step back to see if this framework gives us a reply to the philosophical problem of absent qualia (chapter 7), and then compare this hypothesis with the more popular "executive" theories of consciousness from cognitive psychology (chapter 8).

4.3. Tripartite Memory

Pulling all these data together, I suggest that our three memory systems could be organized as follows.[114] One system contains habits and skills, and other such "memories," and is probably located among the corticostriatal connections of the brain.[115] This system actually appears to be little more than a collection of task-specific behavioral responses. That is, the system does not store representations of particular events, but rather only learned responses to specific cues.[116] However, it is not quite fair to call this memory system a "procedural" memory, for not all of the memories are embedded action responses (Forster and Grovier 1978); many of the learned "procedures" in humans are in fact semantic (Jacobson 1973, Kristofferson *et al.* 1975, Tipper 1985, Tipper and Driver 1988).

Similar to, but not identical with, this system is a perceptual memory system resembling the one Schacter hypothesizes to underwrite implicit priming tasks. There is evidence that this system is not semantic (though it is episodic). That is, it appears that this system is sensitive to only a restricted and rather crude set of an input's many "microfeatures."[117] Given that the members of this set roughly correspond to a stimulus's shape or form microfeatures, I shall refer to the memory system as a structural (ST) system.[118] As implied, the ST system is modality specific and sensitive to font and graphemes, but not to the environment surrounding the stimuli. Further, it is not sensitive to the type of processing the stimuli receive (e.g., semantic versus phonetic), nor to the amount of attention focused on the task.

The general mechanism for acquiring memories in the ST system is probably similar to the mechanism that underlies consciously accessible memories. That is, memories in these systems are most likely formed through individually remembered episodes being laid on top of one another.[119] However, the memories in the ST system are more primitive (perhaps a disadvantage from not working with the hippocampal "tagging" system) and what is remembered from each episode is not context specific.

Each mnemonic trace, once laid down, operates as a self-contained unit for pattern matching and so, because we see no AB, AC interference, does not depend on neighboring memories for input or support. Though this system does not contain semantic information itself, since we do see some semantic priming in the lexical decision paradigms, we can infer that the system influences the activation of the hypothesized "declarative" memory system that underwrites intentional behavior. My hypothesis is that the ST system has multiple outputs which input to, or at least somehow affect, conscious declarative memory, and in virtue of priming certain schemas in declarative memory, it indirectly influences behavior.[120]

Whether priming output behaves in accordance with the spreading activation, rapid decay, model largely depends upon the type of task given a subject.[121] Recall that priming effects in lexical decision tasks show a rapid decay over fairly short time intervals, while perceptual identification and stem completion show no such decrease, even after long delays. Moreover, we see clear semantic priming with lexical identification in the declarative system, but we see little with perceptual identification. I suspect these apparent inconsistencies in the data reflect differences in where the priming effect actually occurs along the chain of processing from this relatively primitive system to our more sophisticated hippocampal memory system.[122] (See Figure 4.4 for illustration.) The "implicit" effects from, e.g., word recognition and perceptual identification occur fairly early in the processing chain, perhaps as enhanced inputs to the declarative system. The more "explicit" effects from things like lexical decisions, recall, and recognition reflect processing in the declarative system itself.

The explicit memory system is the one that forms the basis for short-term memory and consciousness itself. Although the larger hippocampal region and its connections to neo-cortex lay down the memories in this system,[123] the memories themselves are probably located only in the cortex (although the medial temporal region may have to maintain the cortical regions for several years before the memory is completely established there[124]). More specifically, this memory system is thought to be located in the diverse regions of the cortex that are responsible for analyzing and processing incoming sensory data. For example, area TE in inferotemporal cortex may be the storehouse for visual memories (Horel 1992), Mishkin 1982).[125]

Lynn Nadel (1987) suggests that this system might have evolved to supplement the first system by storing the spatial contexts of incoming sensory information.[126] Now, however, this system captures not just immediate physical surroundings, but all sorts of contextual information, for example, the temporal arrangement of events. Indeed, the defining characteristics of this memory system are not just the vast amount of information stored in content addressable form, but also the complex associations that tie together or bind different mnemonic objects into complicated unified wholes. In short, this system stores particular episodes and "schemata." Because this system is so closely allied with remembering the relevant details and connections among specific events, I shall refer to this explicit, controlled access, system as semantic (SE) memory.

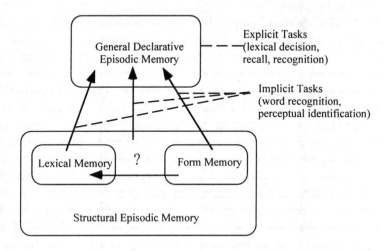

Figure 4.4. Memory Systems and Priming Tasks. *The ST system probably contains at least three component parts: episodic memories that carry no specific information about context; a lexical memory, specialized to help us communicate rapidly; and a memory for forms or structures. The lexical and form memories are created by overlain episodic memory traces. This perceptual memory system inputs to the SE declarative memory system, which supports consciousness. Lines of input are shown with arrows. It is possible that explicit tasks tap directly what is activated in semantic memory, while implicit tasks reflect the input from perceptual memory to declarative. Different places in the stream of processing have different computational properties, so explicit and implicit tasks elicit different processing effects.*

In contrast to the ST system, memories in the SE system have a tendency to diminish rather rapidly over time, possibly through some consolidation procedure. This system is sensitive to the level and type of processing a task demands, as well as to the amount of attention devoted to a task, and it can transfer information from one modality to another without loss of that information. It is definitely an interpretive, semantic system, with only a single hypothesis about the meaning of the incoming stimuli apparently active at a time. It also shows AB, AC interference, indicating not only that semantic ties among groups of data exist but also that they are not easily broken once formed. (See

Table 4.1 for specific processing differences between the two systems.) In contrast to our older and more primitive ST memory system, this system's units are not stable for a long period of time, nor do they function independently of one another. Rather, various semantic "interpretations" exist only transiently,[127] and exactly what the interpretation looks like depends to a large degree on the surrounding activity of the cortex at the time of sensory input.

Table 4.1. Processing Attributes of SE and ST Memory

Semantic Memory	Structural Memory
Amnesics can't form	Amnesics show effects
Attentional effects	No attentional effects
Directed forgetting	No directed forgetting
Effects decay over time	Little decay over time
Graphemes important	Graphemes important
Levels of processing effects	No levels of processing effects
Need fewer cues for recall than for priming	No data available
Only one interpretation active at a time	Multiple structural "interpretations" possible
Shows AB, AC interference	No AB, AC interference
Requires elaborative processing for storage	Requires minimal processing for storage
Little affective priming	Affective priming
Slower, controlled identification	Automatic, rapid identification
Few exposure duration effects	Exposure duration effects
Storage of environmental contexts	No storage of environmental contexts

Before moving to exactly where I think consciousness fits into this framework, I would like to pause for a moment and explain how this framework relates to the philosophical problems discussed in the first three chapters. Our ultimate goal is to develop an abstract but relatively unified conception of consciousness such that we can regularly predict its appearance in a physical system (presumably by tracing its causal etiology). This abstract conception would turn on, among other things, first person reports of what it is like to experience something or other (under some suitably rigorous conditions), though the conception would be articulated in a third person language that preserves all the relevant causal powers of what is described in this first person perspective. This conception may not, and probably won't, capture the experiential difference among the different qualia within a single modality. However, it should include what separates conscious thoughts from unconscious ones (in terms of causal efficacy, of course).

Developing such an abstract conception would probably give cold comfort to the nay-sayers. For those in the grip of the problem of the explanatory gap, it must seem that I am merely answering some "easy" question (to use David Chalmers's phrase), such as, "What are our mnemonic processes?" and pretending that that answer serves as a reply to the truly "hard" question, "What is consciousness?" Here I can only beg the reader's indulgence. In order to answer the hard question, one has to begin by working on some small piece of it. I have chosen to answer as my small piece, "What separates conscious thoughts from unconscious ones?"

I take it that the multiple memory system framework I sketched here serves as a version of a physical system directed toward elucidating that question. Our next task is to explore the occurrence of consciousness (abstractly conceived) within the multiple memory framework. It is my contention that this framework contains (more or less) the parameters necessary to explain consciousness by locating it in its proper psychological and neurophysiological causal nexus, for memory and perception are inextricably bound together. (At least, perception and our two episodic memory systems are intimately related.) Hence, on to my next small piece: Where and how do conscious perceptions fit into what I have said about ST and SE memory?

Where does knowledge of objects, as contrasted with percepts, appear?

Conscious Perception and Semantic Memory
Chapter Five

The last chapter urged that explaining how the ST system influences the SE, how the SE determines which interpretation is active for some set of stimuli, and then what exactly an "interpretation" amounts to in purely naturalistic terms should be part of any causal etiology of conscious processing. Though such a story would not tell us *why* we are conscious, it would give us a better idea of *when* we are conscious with respect to other cognitive activities. The specific processes and interactions of the ST and SE systems are part of the processes leading to conscious phenomena, so identifying the components of those systems relevant to consciousness would specify the relevant parameters in our physical system for awareness. This chapter represents a step in that direction. Here, I gesture toward when and of what we are conscious within the multiple memory framework.[128]

The last chapter intimated that conscious perceptions were connected to activity in the SE system. Hence, we need to learn more about that system. Ideally, as we learn more about the systems that influence SE memory, we will be able to argue that whatever is (primarily) activated in the SE system itself is conscious, and that exactly what becomes active depends upon the incoming stimulus, input from ST memory, and what was previously activated in the SE system. So then, consciousness would become just a particular unified interpretation of some phenomenon.

This chapter expands upon that hypothesis first by better articulating what is meant by an interpretation in SE memory and where consciousness fits in and then by seeing what this hypothesis tells us about the apparently degraded conscious experiences of infants, amnesics, and other animals. The next chapter speculates how one might understand qualitative states purely neurophysiologically as a more direct answer to the problem of the explanatory gap in perception.

5.1. Perception and Memory

The traditional view of visual processing asserts that when we recognize an input *as* something, we match our perception of a new stimulus with items stored in episodic memory. Following Humphreys and Riddoch (1987), Martha Farah compares the process to "finding a book in a library" (1990: 96). Given the pervasiveness of computer models of the mind, perhaps a more apt example would be searching for a file on a personal computer. When we want to find a particular document on our computer, we type the name of the file into a search program. We can think of our typed names as representing in some abstract fashion the actual name that the computer "knows" in a machine language. Presumably the search program then goes through our hard-disks comparing the names of the items stored there with what we have typed into the program. And once we find the document we are looking for, we can then access all the information stored in it. We can think of what we type into the search program that the program uses to locate the missing file as analogous to our perceptions, and the names on stored files as analogous to long-term memory representations in the SE system. When a match between a perception and a long-term memory representation occurs, we then retrieve the memory and we access all the information associated with the perception.[129]

Though this model reflects familiar computer analogies in cognitive psychology, there are some reasons for believing that the traditional account of visual perception is wrong. In particular, it appears that there is a more symbiotic relationship between perception and memory; that is, our perceptions affect our memories and what we have previously experienced affects what we see. Fast evidence for this fact comes from linguistic processing. One we have learned a language, then it is impossible to hear someone speaking that language as merely making sounds. We always hear the languages we know *as languages*. Contrast this phenomena with hearing languages we do not know. In these cases, we can enjoy the rhythms of Spanish or the guttural inflections of German or the singsong of Chinese without hearing the sounds as a language. (This point became especially salient to me when I realized that I had no idea how English sounds to those who do not speak English. I had always assumed that it would sound more or less like German. Imagine my surprise when an Italian woman informed me that English sounds like snakes hissing.)

So, what I know about languages shape how I perceive them. Indeed, what I know can shape my perceptions radically. Our auditory systems "fill in" absent phonemes so that the resulting strings of sounds are meaningful (Linsker and Abramson 1970). We literally hear speech sounds that have either been obscured or replaced by noise (Warren 1967, Warren and Warren 1970). The visual system works in an analogous fashion. For example, in Figure 5.1, we see the second letter in the first word as an H but the second letter in the second word as an A, even though these "letters" are shaped in exactly the same way.

T/\E C/\T

Figure 5.1. Ambiguous Letters. We see the phrase unambiguously, even though the H and the A are ambiguously presented (originally from Selfridge 1955).

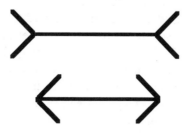

Figure 5.2. Müller-Lyre Illusion. We see the upper line as longer than the lower line, even though they are actually the same length.

These effects are not limited to language either. Persons living in Western cultures exhibit a robust reaction to the Müller-Lyre illusion (see Figure 5.2). We experience the upper line as distinctly longer than the lower, even though they are actually the same length. However, members of cultures in which lines and angles do not play a large role do not experience the illusory effect. For example, the Zulus live in round huts, plow their land in curves, and use few sharply angled artifacts. And they appear to be affected by few of these sorts of illusions (Gregory 1966). Once again, what we already have learned about the world shapes how we perceive it.

These sorts of examples suggest that the computer search model of matching imputs to stored representations is not correct. Moreover, the familiar computer analogies in cognitive psychology do not comport with clinical evidence concerning how visual processing breaks down. This is especially true for visual agnosia, a condition in which patients are unable to recognize the class to which an object belongs.[130] Patients who exhibit this deficit have difficulty recognizing a variety of visually presented objects. They cannot name them, nor can they nonverbally demonstrate that they know what the object is by grouping the objects into semantic categories. However, they are able to recognize the objects in other modalities by touching them or by listening to their characteristic sounds or by hearing verbal descriptions. These patients can also copy drawings of objects and they can match pairs of drawings as the same or different — even using objects they do not recognize.[131]

According to traditional accounts of the syndrome, these agnosias indicate the loss of some stored visual memories. That account entails that the agnosic patients should have normal visual *input* processing since perceptions are distinct from the stored memories hypothesized to be damaged. However the data concerning agnosia suggest that visual processing is in fact impaired in some important ways. Patients with agnosia are very slow to copy and match drawings. They are also much more sensitive than normals to visually degraded stimuli. Finally, they often claim that their vision impaired, and on sophisticated tests of visual perception (feature integration, closure tasks, and distinguishing possible from impossible figures), they do not score in the normal or near normal range.[132]

Data along these lines suggest that visual perception is not normal in these patients, and consequently, it seems unlikely that the agnosic deficit is due solely to impaired stored visual memories. If it were possible to find agnosic patients without any visual deficits, then they could count as evidence for the existence of two types of abstract visual representation (perception and memory). But since these cases do not seem to exist, that fact casts doubt on the viability of the computer model of memory retrieval.

We should conceive of perception and mnemonic processing very differently. We need an abstract conception that is more plausible neurologically and consistent with the phenomena of language processing, learned perceptual illusions, and memory deficits mentioned above.[133] A more accurate conception of perceptual processing emerges from "connectionist" or parallel distributed processing models. Parallel distributed processing (PDP) refers to a type of computer modeling that uses networks of interconnected units to process information in parallel. Each node is structurally identical to all the others, and each takes concurrent incoming signals and uses them to compute the value of its output. Once the computation is complete, these nodes either "excite" or "inhibit" their neighboring nodes by sending a positive or negative signal up the connecting pathways. The paths that connect the nodes have different "weights" whose values specify the strength of the connections between each pair of nodes. The system is parallel in that many nodes carry out their computations and output their signals at the same time. The weights interact with the output signals traveling along the connection via some propagation rule, which determines the exactly value of the signal that inputs to the next nodes in the network. Input to nodes is a function of the connection's weight strength and the value of the signal traveling along the connection, and the subsequent output is a function of the input and some transformation rule within the node. The idea underlying these models is that complex information processing can emerge from the interactions of large numbers of these simple processing nodes.[134]

This sort of processing is also called "processing by constraint satisfaction" because we can think of each unit trying to satisfy the constraints imposed upon it by neighboring input connections and relative weights. When the network as a whole eventually settles into a relatively stable state we can say that represents the best "hypothesis" concerning the input. So, for example, in a word recognition network, the network will settle into a state that is most consistent with the activation pattern and information from previous "perceptual" experiences as stored in the connection weights.[135]

Farah argues that satisfying several constraints at once appears to be how actual object recognition works as well. While shape seems to determine our low-level images of objects, it is well known that shadows, viewing angle, occlusion, and so on, often distort what we are able to see. The trick in vision is to extract the real shape of the object from all distorting factors. To do so, we need to find an interpretation of the input that conforms to the features of some known object shape as well as the prevailing set of conditions for perception.[136]

What is important for our purposes is that in these sorts of "connectionist" models is that there is no distinction between the "perception" of a stimulus input and memory. The connection strengths, the summing functions, and the incoming data determine which pattern the network will settle into, and this activated pattern then corresponds to the hypothesized identity of the object. Nothing is "matched against" some other pattern; what it "perceives" depends upon the "memories" it holds in its connection strengths.

Hence, once we have "trained up" our own networks, we cannot help hearing the sounds of our language as our language, or disambiguating letters in context, or seeing the various Gestalt illusions. Changing the weights connecting our nodes in learning determines how we perceive, and not just understand, our world, for perception and memory operate within the same distributed net. Likewise, damage to the memories would also impair perception. (Farah hypothesizes that in agnosia either the nodes themselves or the connections among nodes are probably impaired.)[137]

If we adopt a PDP view of mnemonic processing, then it is easy to see why there is no easy distinction between recall and interpreting current input stimuli in SE memory. Both activate the same network and then affect it in similar ways.[138] To say that conscious percepts reside in activated SE memories then is just to say that we have a conscious percept whenever we use the SE system to recall previous experiences or to interpret incoming data; that is, we have a conscious percept whenever the SE system is activated. More specifically, a conscious percept is an interpretation of incoming stimuli in the SE system in light of the previous (interpreted) experiences we have had (just because those interpreted experiences are what determines the connection strengths and activation levels of the nodes).

This symbiotic view of perception and memory is corroborated by recent work in positron emission tomography (PET) and magnetic resonance imagining (MRI). Using these brain imagining techniques, which are sensitive to the active areas of a brain in more or less real time, scientists have verified that when we think about or imagine some object, the same areas of the brain are activated as when we are actually seeing that object. Remembering the red car you just saw yesterday utilizes in the same networks in the brain (to a remarkably fine degree) that were used to see the red car in the first place. As Michael Posner (1993) concludes, "These [sorts of] findings support the general idea that processes initiated internally from instructions can activate the same sensory areas where these computations are performed on actual sensory events." Once again, we see that perception and memory are physically and inextricably linked.

5.2 The Case of SB

Additional evidence for this perspective comes from an entirely different quarter, in the fairly rare cases of early childhood blindness followed by regaining sight in adulthood. I shall focus on patient SB who regained his sight at age fifty-two with corneal transplants (Gregory and Wallace 1963). He is the most famous blind patient who later regained his sight and probably the most thoroughly studied. However, the earliest comprehensive scientific discussion of this situation dates back to von Senden in 1932.[139] His book *Space and Sight* recounts all the known examples of blind individuals who have later recovered their sight and their reactions to discovering a visual world.[140] Interestingly enough, the first recorded case of this phenomenon occurred in 1020. Philosophically, the question of what happens when people regain their sight after being impaired for most of their lives became important after Molyneux posed the question to Locke in 1690.[141]

What is interesting about SB and other similar patients is that they can visually recognize the objects immediately after surgery that they could previously recognize by touch, but they are essentially blind to previously unfamiliar objects. For example, SB could recognize and name all the capital letters, which he learned by touch as a boy in school, but he could not recognize any lower case letters (of any size) to which he had not been exposed as a child. (See Figure 5.3 for more examples.) One obvious conclusion to draw here is that in order for signals from the eyes to be interpreted as a visual percept and hence be meaningful, we must connect them with objects or events in the world that have been previously experienced and encoded in semantic memory.

Richard Gregory compares the essential blindness of SB with Wittgenstein's "aspect blindness." Wittgenstein (1953) asks of an imaginary aspect-blind person confronted with a Necker cube: "Ought he to be able to see the schematic cube as a cube? For him it would not jump from one aspect to another. The 'aspect-blind' will have an altogether different relationship to pictures from ours." As Wittgenstein could have surmised, SB did not experience the Necker cube reversals we do. Instead, he saw meaningless patterns of lines. (In general, he hardly saw pictures as depicting objects at all.)[142]

Figure 5.3. The Vision of SB. (a) The first drawing is SB's attempt to sketch a double-decker bus, made 48 days after his operation. All the features shown were probably previously known to him by touch. The front, which he could not have known by touch, is missing. (b) The second drawing was made six months later. Now SB adds writing, and the "touch image" of spokes on the wheels has been corrected, but he still cannot craw the engine cover. (c) A year later, there is yet more detail, but the very front of the engine is still missing (from Gregory and Wallace 1963, reprinted with kind permission by Dr. Richard Gregory).

Wittgenstein saw aspect-blindness as central to understanding how we move from arbitrary input "symbols" to the meaningful language. Gregory indicates that we should expand Wittgenstein's perspective such that in SB's case — and in any instance of conscious perception — we could include other sensory systems besides sight and hearing whose "symbols" we interpret and such that meaningful nonlinguistic interpretations are possible. I concur and think that we should consider any sensory signal as a potential input "symbol" to be read and understood.

If Gregory, Wittgenstein, and I are right, then in order to perceive some stimulus consciously and meaningfully, we have to *interpret* the input signal in terms of what we already know. Psychological creatures use their own mnemonic histories to "ground" their percepts contentfully, as it were, and this interpretive grounding allows for the percept to be experienced consciously. (This again recalls psychology's "meaning analysis.") *Why* this type of interpretation should give us consciousness is not clear, but that it in fact *does* seems correct.

Perhaps another way to illustrate what I (and what Gregory and Wittgenstein) have in mind is to consider blindsight again (Barinaga 1992, Cowey and Stoerig 1991, 1992, Critchley 1979, Fendrich *et al.* 1992, Humphreys *et al.* 1992, Ptito *et al.* 1991, Weiskrantz 1988, 1992, Weiskrantz *et al.* 1974). Recall that patients with lesioned striate cortex may claim to be unable to see; however, when asked to guess about the location or orientation or other gross features of objects in their scotoma, they are surprisingly accurate in their responses. Obviously some visual processing is occurring outside the retina-lateral geniculate nucleus-cortex route,[143] but whatever it is (perhaps via the superior colliculus), it is nonconscious. My hypothesis predicts that any such processing would be "aspect blind" because it could not rely on SE memory; hence, it would have to be non-interpretive, purely syntactic, and unsophisticated relative to our conscious perceptions. And this is exactly what we find. Blindsight patients can only discriminate coarse non-semantic features in their blindsight areas, such as distinguishing X's from O's, circles from triangles, and vertical lines from horizontal. They cannot read letters or words as such, interpret figures as representing other things, or infer the presence or absence of objects on the basis of partial information in their blindsight regions. They can make simple identifications, the kind one would expect if relying solely on ST memory, but cannot do so meaningfully, as we do when we are conscious.

5.3. The Consciousness of Others

If consciousness is to be identified with an interpretive activation in SE memory, then we should be able to pinpoint where consciousness resides in the brain, for we know quite a lot about the neurobiology of our memory systems. This section looks at what the hypothesis claims about the location of conscious awareness in our nervous system and then examines how we should think about the consciousness of others. (This project will be repeated in a more general form in chapter 7 when I examine the problem of absent qualia.)

5.3.1. The Location of Consciousness

The last chapter suggested that SE memory required a myriad of components. The hippocampal system and its connections to neocortex are responsible for laying down the memories. That is, they are responsible for altering the connection strength among the nodes in light of previous and current experiences. However, once such changes are complete — once the network is "trained up" — the contributions of the hippocampal-neocortical circuit diminish or halt altogether. The memories of the SE system themselves are not located in a hippocampal system. Instead, they are found in the diverse areas of cortex that process incoming sensory data. The medial-temporal lobe region helps to establish the connections within cortex that allow for sophisticated interpretations (i.e., mnemonic associations) of incoming stimuli, but it is the cortex itself that houses the memories, consequent interpretations, and conscious awareness.

Notice then that the real difference between ST and SE memory, once SE memories are firmly established, is in the *type* of information stored, not in its general location. Both ST and SE memories appear to be distributed throughout our sensory cortices. However, the ST system cannot capture rich contexts or semantic associations, for each individual mnemonic trace is self-contained, isolated, and relatively sparse. In contrast, SE memories are extremely interconnected and as a result of being more distributed have the computational capacity to represent the immediate details surrounding incoming stimuli. (Perhaps being stored in essentially the same location allows for the ST system to influence activation in the SE.) As I stated above, why activations in SE memory are conscious and the activations in ST memory are not is unclear, especially given their contiguous locations. Perhaps just the

What about pandemonium?.

difference in mnemonic type (self-contained, structural, and sparse versus interconnected, semantic, and complex) is enough. I do not know.

To repeat: Two important features differentiate activated memories in the SE system (and the corresponding interpretation of present events) from activated memories in the ST system (and the corresponding response to current input): the rich associative interconnectedness among relevant mnemonic states in the SE system and the fact that the associative ties of the SE system are semantic, not structural or syntactic. Which of these features (if either) is necessary or sufficient for consciousness is not clear. All we can say now is that in order to have a conscious perception, we have to be able to interpret incoming data using the rich autobiographical information stored in the SE system.

It appears that what makes for this difference between the two systems just is the addition of the sophisticated hippocampal filing system. However, this would not entail that the hippocampus itself in necessary for consciousness. Rather, having the hippocampal system participate in laying down SE memories allows for those stored memories to be conscious. The system, in conjunction with the cortical areas in which the memories are actually stored, is sufficient for our perceptual awareness. If the hippocampus participated in laying down the memories, then we can later use those memories in consciously interpreting incoming stimuli.

At this juncture, I can make no claims about what I think is necessary for consciousness beyond activation of SE memory. Nevertheless, the weaker conditions I outlined do raise questions about whether infants and amnesics are conscious since their mnemonic systems obviously differ from ours. The next two sections examine what the hypothesis of consciousness being identified with activated SE memories would tell us about conscious experiences of those lacking proper SE systems. (This issue is raised again in chapter 8.)

5.3.2. Infant and Amnesic Consciousness

Young infants, as you may recall from chapter 4, do not appear to have a true semantic memory. Instead their memories appear to be structurally-based S-R loops. In particular, infants perseverate inappropriately in their behaviors and cannot perform simple memory tasks like delayed matching-to-sample.

What underlying mechanisms could account for the difference in performance between normal adults and young infants? I submit that it is not a difference in the hippocampal system or in the sensory cortices, as one might expect, but rather in prefrontal cortex.[144] Nevertheless, because infants cannot store incoming information in richly interconnected semantic networks — the only defining characteristic of conscious mnemonic processing that we have able to uncover — we should conclude that they are not conscious.[145]

There is now evidence, primarily from local lesions studies in the macaque and rhesus monkeys, that the capacity to perform delayed-response tasks depends on the bilateral integrity of the dorso-lateral prefrontal cortex[146] as well as the hippocampus and related medial temporal areas (Goldman-Rakic 1987, Malamut et al. 1984, Zola-Morgan and Squire 1984). The most intriguing finding is that a number of principal sulcus neurons fire in a pattern time-locked to the delay period of a delayed-response task (Fuster 1973).[147] These neurons become active when the target stimulus is first presented, and then show increasing activity during the delay, and finally, cease firing at the end of the delay (Fuster and Alexander 1971, Kojima and Goldman-Rakic 1982, 1984). Furthermore, these neurons only increase their firing rate during the delay when the stimulus must be remembered in order to complete a task. These results provide excellent evidence that the frontal lobe plays a role in processing absent information.

Interestingly enough, these neurophysiological results *cannot* be replicated in infant monkeys with underdeveloped prefrontal lobes. The frontal lobe is a rather late maturing system — it is not until one and a half to three years after birth that prefrontal cortex approaches adult form in humans. Whatever the principal sulcus neurons are doing early in life has nothing to do with remembering important stimuli.[148]

I conclude that young infants' brains are simply arranged differently than ours and that they differ functionally as well. In further support of this point, recall the discussion in chapter 2. Synaptic density drastically increases during post-natal development. Baby monkeys have about twice as many synapses as they do when they are fully mature, and this "overproduction" appears in all cortical areas, including the frontal lobe, the motor, somatosensory, auditory, and visual cortices, and the limbic system (Rakic et al. 1986). In humans, synaptic exuberance appears to peak at two years postnatally, after which it decreases steadily for about the next 15-20 years.

Why do we see this change in brain organization and structure during the first years of our lives? My suggestion is that laying down memory traces themselves selectively reinforces some connections at the expense of others.

The general idea is that an organism with an overabundance of synapses possesses the greatest diversity of possible connections among neurons. Interaction with the environment selects, or "stabilizes," a subset of the original neuronal circuits. The rest then disappear through disuse.[149] So, until enough of the brain is stabilized such that proper SE memories can be maintained, infants must rely upon cruder forms of memory. Hence, their perseverative behaviors and S-R loops.

Does this discussion suggest that infants are not conscious? Synaptic over-production does appear in the hippocampus and surrounding areas, just as in other parts of the brain, so perhaps we should just claim that we don't know what duties *that sort of* hippocampus is performing, just as we don't know the duties an infant's pre-frontal cortex performs. In this case, it would be premature to say that infants are not conscious, for we simply don't know enough yet. However, it is clear that whatever jobs are being done by the various lobes of the brain, infants cannot form proper SE memories and those do appear to be necessary for conscious awareness in humans. Granted, the mature hippocampus is only one possible route to those memories, so the fact that the hippocampus might not be performing that service is no reason to deny sentience to a being (see discussion on amnesics below). Nevertheless, we have no evidence that infants have the proper sorts of memories at all, regardless of how they are formed. Given the discussion in the previous section and how we have defined consciousness in our attempt to explain it, we should be skeptical of any claims that young infants are aware.[150]

Amnesics are a little easier to understand — even though their behavior resembles that of young infants — just because they do have severely damaged hippocampal areas. Amnesics cannot form new SE memories — so much is clear. However, quite often they can access the memories previously "filed" by their hippocampal system before it was damaged or oblated. In these cases, the amnesics are conscious. They interpret incoming stimuli in light of what they can recall from their (admittedly incomplete) SE system.

An interesting case to consider along these lines is Clive Waring, a British-born patient who lost his hippocampus and portions of his left frontal lobe through viral infection (Restak 1988). He is remarkable in that he professes to have no awareness of *any* events prior to his present circumstances. He always believes that he is just conscious for the very first time. Indeed, he fills pages of diaries with those words to record that momentous, though always repeating, occasion: "I have just awakened for the very first time....I am now conscious for the very first time...." And then he goes back and crosses out previous entries as not having been correct, for he does not believe that he was conscious yesterday, or a few minutes ago, when he wrote that he was.[151]

What are we to make of him in light of our previous discussion? Do we want to say that he is not conscious because he apparently cannot access his previously formed SE memories, even though he is constantly professing that he is always just become aware? I think that he is conscious. However, I also believe that he can access some parts of SE memory. For example, he always recognizes his wife as his wife (although he has apparently forgotten their child). He explicitly recalls who she is whenever she walks into the room. He can also recognize other things as those things: playing cards, diaries, pens, pianos, some friends, and so on. This sort of behavior would seem to suggest the activation of SE memory. What he cannot seem to remember though is himself. Perhaps that is why he always seem to be just waking up to himself — he has no retrievable context in which to place who he is. It seems that he cannot interpret himself *as* anything. Nevertheless, though I would not want to claim that his "inner life" is a rich as mine, it certainly does seem to be of the same type.

And the same considerations go for any amnesic. They cannot form all the connections that I can because they have lost the ability to create new SE memories. However, the SE memories that they can access are used in the same way I use mine — in part, to interpret incoming stimuli as something. Therefore, amnesics are conscious.[152]

5.3.3. Animal Consciousness

As an additional bonus, we can use these sorts of considerations to determine when and whether other creatures are conscious. Since much of this framework of chapter 4 relies on animal models fairly heavily, it is important to understand when we should assign qualitative experience to other animals. Knowing when and whether other animals have qualitative experiences should provide an additional line of support to any interdisciplinary theory of consciousness as well as extend the framework itself by refining our understanding of the operations of the SE system. We can use the general principles we have already developed to organize data relating to the mental capacities and processes in other animals, which in turn will clarify the properties peculiar to an SE system.

Certainly examples that show that animals must remember particular events about their environment abound. For instance, after training, a rat in a radial maze (a maze which has eight runways around a central starting point, arranged like spokes emanating from the hub of a bicycle wheel) with food placed at the end of each runway will re-enter each runway an average of less than once per trial until all the food has been consumed (Olton 1978, 1979, Olton and Samualson 1976). Because they use different patterns of exploration for each trail run, the rats must remember which runways they have already visited and these memories must be particular to the trial they are running. We can conclude that rats can create and use a map of food locations for particular occasions.

Pigeons also seem capable of something similar. They can be trained to peck a particular sequence of colored lights in order to receive food (Straub *et al*. 1979, Terrace 1984). They are able peck this sequence regardless of the order in which the lights were arranged on the response keys. This fact indicates that the pigeons must be able to remember temporal sequences that are not tied to specific stimuli in the environment. Would these examples count as instances of an SE memory system similar enough to ours to support conscious thought? To answer this question, let us contrast rat and pigeon behavior with the types of memories primates are able to form and use.

As mentioned in chapter 4, chimpanzees are easily able to perform matching-to-sample identity discriminations. Shown an object, like an apple, as a sample, they are able to learn to select the apple from a set consisting of an apple and a banana. In addition, they also apparently understand the relationships between abstract figures — a large red triangle and a large blue triangle are matched with a small red circle and a small blue circle. Most interesting though is that they are able to remember, match, and discriminate on the basis of an analogy. Shown half an apple as the sample, they can select a half-filled jug of water as the match instead of a whole apple. Indeed, these analogical discriminations can extend to relationships between pairs of objects. When first shown a can opener and a can as a pair, chimpanzees can later select a key as the appropriate analog for a padlock (Gillan *et al*. 1981, Woodruff and Premack 1981).

Pigeons, on the other hand, can barely perform matching to sample for objects physical identity (D'Amato *et al*. 1985, Mackintosh 1987, Mackintosh *et al.* 1985). What capacities do chimpanzees have that pigeons do not? Chimpanzees can use analogical reasoning for specific episodes, which requires that they can remember particular aspects of particular objects and later compare those aspects to similar attributes of different objects. This type of memory and reasoning means that they can understand objects or events *qua* an instance of some generalization and that they can recall specific instances of those objects or events and manipulate them to solve problems. Pigeons in contrast seem only to remember specific sequences of objects or events, without being able to categorize attributes of those objects or events.

This difference recalls Gregory and Wittgenstein. They suggested that conscious experience requires interpreting incoming stimuli such that we see events in terms of some aspect or other. These aspects form the semantic markers we use to analyze and remember data. Gregory goes on to suggest that this "aspect-sightedness" separates conscious thought from other sorts of cognitive processing and that we can only develop the cognitive capacities necessary for such conscious interpretation by physically interacting with the world. But regardless of whether we accept his stronger position, it is at least clear that chimpanzees are aspect-sighted, while pigeons are aspect-blind. Chimpanzees analyze their world in terms of shared or dissimilar attributes, while pigeons can only react to a sequence of events, and not its meaning.

Since pigeons are not able to abstract properties away from the events that contain them, I suggest that their "semantic" memory system is not like ours. Part of what makes our SE system semantic is that we remember particular episodes in our lives as similar or different and analyze them as they relate to one another. As we saw in the priming paradigms, semantic priming — which relates to the interpretation our memory system gives to some incoming stimulus — is peculiar to SE memory. ST memory can only analyze the form of represented objects and then use that analysis to influence which interpretation the SE system gives. So, we should say that at best pigeons have only a severely degraded form of SE memory and that probably all they really have are ST systems.

We, on the other hand, not only remember particular sequences of events important to our well-being, but we always understand those sequences in a certain light. As we saw with Marcel's subliminal priming data and with the example of the Necker cube, for each event, we have only one — but always one — interpretation. Primates seem to have a similar sort of ability. They not only retain particular episodes in their lives, but they can understand those episodes as being related along some dimension. They too apparently use meaning analysis in the same (or similar) way cognitive psychologists hypothesize that we do.

Of course, this difference in ability does not answer the question of whether chimpanzees are conscious and pigeons are not, but it does give us reason to argue that chimpanzee are functionally similar to us in a way which suggests they might have phenomenal experiences similar to ours, and that pigeons are not functionally analogous, so how to understand their experiences is an open question. Though we may are not able to answer definitively whether rats and pigeons are conscious, insofar as we wish to maintain that the SE system is central to our experiencing qualia, then we should also accept that primates experience qualia too.[153]

Though much more work needs to be done in filling in the details, it should be clear at least in which direction I am heading. Conscious perceptions and thoughts just are activations in SE memory. This is how to understand consciousness with respect to the physical system outlined in the last chapter. I recognize though that the skeptics should not be any more convinced by this story than any other one, especially because an activation in SE memory in no way *seems like* what we experience consciously. At least, the intuitive link between the two is tenuous at best. In the next chapter I address this complaint, while also trying to cash out what I mean by an "interpretation" in less metaphorical terms.

How Do We Get There From Here?
Chapter Six

I would now like to turn my attention to the "harder" problems in understanding conscious experience. A common complaint of any theory of consciousness is that it is never clear why it should be *that* that is conscious. One "hard" problem in explaining consciousness is articulating why the answer given is a reasonable answer to the question, What is consciousness?, and not a reasonable answer to some other question, such as, How do our memory systems work? In this chapter, I circle around this problem. As will be clear in the discussion, I don't have much patience with some versions of this difficulty (*viz.*, the version that drives Flanagan's New Mysterians). However, I do think that other, less cantankerous, versions are worthy of careful consideration. Nevertheless, I shall keep my goals modest. Even if I don't succeed in mollifying the mysterian skeptic here, I at least shall cash out some of the metaphors I have been using in the previous chapters in neurophysiological terms. This will at least add to the empirical testability of my thesis, while the philosophical skeptics may still attack on more familiar conceptual grounds.

Perhaps the clearest description of this problem is given by Kathleen Akins and Steven Winger (forthcoming) in their discussion of "Marr's Paradox."[154] Though it is now widely agreed that Marr's theory of vision is false, his theory still provides a nice in to the problems involved in conscious perceptions because the theory is so clearly articulated. And Akins and Winger believe that what they say of Marr's theory will apply *mutatis mutandis* to any other computational theory of perception.

6.1. Marr's Paradox

Consider how Marr's (1982) theory roughly goes. David Marr was interested in visual processing as shape recognition. To that end, he postulated a hierarchy of four processing levels that progressively extract and compute more and more abstract object shape information from our activated two-dimensional retinal array. The first level corresponds to the retinal array itself. A grid of light intensities forms the primitive representational information from which we construct our perceptions of objects. The second level is a "primal sketch" which calculates the spatial organization of the various points of light intensity. Representation at this level consists in things like zero-crossings, discontinuities, boundaries, groups, and so on. Next is the "2.5 D sketch" which has moved from the zero-crossings and boundaries to edges, orientation, and depth. Akins and Winger compare the representations at this level to "line [drawings] with dotted lines (discontinuities in object surface) and arrows (surface orientation)" (forthcoming: 4). Finally, there is the completed "3 D sketch" which uses the information from the previous level to calculate the actual shapes and spatial orientation of objects. The completed three-dimensional "objects" are represented then in terms of "volumetric primitives" attached to "stick figures" (4).

What is important to notice about this hierarchical theory is that *none of the representations at any of the levels correspond to what we consciously experience in the visual domain.* Our visual experiences are rich, continuous, unitary, and semantically loaded. They do not *seem like* the output of any of the stages of visual processing.[155] Moreover, this claim would seem to hold true for *any* hierarchical theory of vision. (Both Akins and Winger suggest that retinal images might resemble our perceptions, but that seems wrong to me. My retinas respond to a two-dimensional array of various wavelengths impinging on them; I experience three-dimensional objects projected out into space.)

Here then is the paradox: On the one hand, we think that our conscious perceptions are tied to some stage of whatever processing stream we have. On the other hand, we think that our conscious experiences have to resemble the computational (or brain) states that instantiate them. However, nothing in our alleged stream resembles our experienced perceptions. Hence, a conflict.

And this conflict is but one version of a common theme in perceptual psychology and philosophy of mind. Other versions include the previously mentioned explanatory gap in philosophy, the "problem of perception" in neurophysiology, and the "binding problem" in psychology, all three discussed in this chapter. The basic question is: how do we get there from here? How can we explain conscious perceptual experiences, given what we know about the brain, its structure, and its computations? Our intuitions, such as they are, fail us completely. Our perceptions are unified and complex. However, we know that brains divide their processing tasks into small, manageable pieces, and then segregate those tasks across the gray matter (more on this below).

Daniel Dennett (1991) intimates that both of the conflicting assumptions that lead to Marr's Paradox are false.[156] Hence, no conflict. He argues that our "Cartesian theater" intuition — that there must be a single place in psychological processing which is conscious — is fundamentally misguided. There is no such thing. Instead, the content of many different processing streams might become conscious, depending upon where we probe. We don't process information and then parade the results in some place; rather, we only represent things once, and, depending upon what we do with the information then, it might be conscious (or not) at that time. In essence, he replaces our metaphorical theater with a metaphorical probe.

However, this move does not solve the problem. Moreover, Dennett's proposed "solution" does not work for exactly the same reasons the traditional pictures don't work, for his Multiple Drafts Model is but a tarted up version of the same old story. That is, Dennett buys into the guiding principles of the computer model of the mind/brain — a mistake, as I suggest in chapter 5. If we want to solve Marr's Paradox, we are going to have to be a bit more radical.

Consider: either Dennett's "probe" is some sort of moveable Cartesian Theater with the powers to produce our experiences in all their unified richness, or it is much weaker. If it is the former, then we have not rid ourselves of Cartesianism at all — we have just made it a traveling side show instead of New York Broadway. If it is the latter, then consciousness would depend heavily on the (content of the) processing stream probed. In this case, we are back to Marr's Paradox again, for in no processing step do we find anything that resembles what we see or hear.

How do we solve this difficulty? Of course, something is conscious in our brain. However, that nothing in the processing stream *resembles* our experiences is not problematic. No one, so far as I know, seriously believes that the representations in our brains *exactly* resemble our phenomenal experiences. That is, no one believes that corresponding to our experience of a blue triangle is something in our brains that is blue-ish in hue and triangular in shape. But once we deny this very naïve view, we are left without a clue about what to *count* as a resemblance. Even the general sort of isomorphisms we should even be looking for it is unclear.

This, of course, is the mystery that drives the purported problem of the explanatory gap, as well as shows fallacy in the mysterians' reasoning. The mysterians claim that since we can't even imagine how we would recognize a solution to the problem, one must not exist. Better to claim: so much the worse for our intuitions. There are lots of things we can't image — 5-dimensions, superstrings, the beginning of the universe, infinity, the size of a quark — but personal inadequacies should not stop science. We should not be moved by what we can or cannot imagine *a priori*.

But even if we dismiss the philosophical problem of the explanatory gap as a failure of imagination, there are other, perhaps less gripping, difficulties of a similar stripe. Our visual experiences seem detailed, consolidated, and "non-gappy"; however, the visual system in the brain is fundamentally distributed. Dennett pushes on our intuitions and suggests that we don't perceive what we think we do.[157] Our visual experiences are a lot more serial and fragmented than we think. He might be right, but this alone is not going to solve our problems. We *do* experience richly bound perceptions (we know this because, as I discuss below, we can make demonstrable mistakes in binding features together); so how do we do this if there is no theater?

Dennett errs in his analysis when he claims that we do not re-represent things to ourselves, for we do that continuously. The first things that should strike anyone studying the brain are the massive feedback loops. There are as many things traveling back downstream as there are up. I argue below that it is simply a mistake to talk about or assume a processing "stream" with "higher" and "lower" levels. It is more accurate to envision dynamical loops exhibiting resonating frequencies and the visual system operating as a single complex unit.

Moreover, if we think along these lines, we can also see Dennett's second mistake. He suggests that any contentful representation could become conscious if appropriately probed. However, I live in a world that is object-filled and me-centered. Those are the only sorts of visual representations I have. All my color experiences have shapes, and vice versa. And if there aren't shapes out there, then my brain does its best to convince me that there are. I can't be aware of any other sort of visual representation. But if there aren't separate streams that process information in a step-wise fashion, if there are only unitary dynamical loops disturbed by sensory input, then it should not be surprising that there is only one sort of experienced perception.

If the perspective I advance in this chapter is correct, and if what corresponds to our visual perceptions are higher order patterns of bifurcation in an attractor phase space (these are defined and discussed below), then the problem of visual perception and the binding problem disappear. If the traditional computational perspective is wrong, and sensory processing is not piece-meal, step-wise, and segregated, then there is no need for some theater or other to tie things together. In this case, Dennett would ultimately be right about the need to dismiss our intuitions in this matter; he just fails to do so himself.

Here then is how I shall proceed. I first outline a brief history of this problem of unified perception, since it enjoys a rich tradition in both philosophy and psychology. I use that history to motivate the currently accepted solutions to the binding problem in psychology. Finally, I discuss the problem as it appears in neuroscience, arguing that the most popular solution (synchronized 40 Hz neural firing oscillations) does not work. I conclude by sketching my own solution to the problem, which, not coincidentally, helps cash out the metaphorical "SE interpretations" of the last few chapters, as well as gives my answer to those who want to know what our perceptual experiences resemble in the brain.

6.2. A Brief and Potted History

The problem of how our minds tie together outputs from different assemblies has been entertained, in one guise or another, at least since the eighteenth century. Hume (1753, 1777), most famously, suggests that, in virtue of the law of association, sensory impressions cause unified conscious perceptions as a result of occurring in spatial-temporal bundles. The "force of custom" carries the imagination to conceive objects as unified sets of impressions when given disparate sensory experiences. Further, when we sense a new token of some impression-type, the law of association also calls forth the corresponding concept from memory.

Association is crucial here. Objects, especially as considered over time, display many features, each of which could cause some sensory experience.

However, when these experiences occur together, they are bound as a unit in virtue of their association with one another. Nevertheless, Hume himself noticed that association alone is not sufficient to explain our fairly stable ideas of objects (especially when these ideas are projected into the future, for which we could have no corresponding impressions) since our sensory experiences are diverse and fleeting. Somehow we must process our impressions so that they are stable enough to create ideas of objects as well as retrieve memories of other objects. To make up for associationism's obvious inadequacies, Hume assumes that the faculty of "imagination" can smooth over the connections among ideas even though few connections actually exist among impressions.

As Patricia Kitcher notes, Kant too recognized that using simple association as the only mechanism for combining disparate impressions such that we perceive a single unified object leads to a binding problem: "If... cognitive states reproduced one another...just as they happen to come together, this would not lead to any determinate connection of them, but only to accidental heaps" (A121, as translated in Kitcher 1990: 70). While agreeing that interaction in the world causes our conscious perceptions of the world, Kant argues that perceptions become unified only when the mind actively synthesizes them.[158]

A set of mental states must be tied together into one overarching percept in order to represent an object successfully. We can't derive this unity from the objects in the physical world themselves, since we only have access to continually and wildly fluctuating sensory inputs. Therefore, *we* must somehow bind the information contained in our various transient cognitive states together. "Synthesis" then is "what gathers the elements of representation together and unites them in a definite content" (Kant: A77/B103). In a process similar to mathematical computation, synthesis adds different cognitive states together into a single representation. Given some set of sensory inputs, we should always get out some stable output, though the output need not be the same for each instance of the same set. (Consider, e.g., the Necker cubes or the ambiguous letters from chapter 4.)

Though Kant provides no story about the underlying nature of representations or the rules of synthesis, Kitcher argues that his account is compatible with current information processing theories of mind, which hold that the best way to understand cognition is to understand how mental "symbols" are manipulated in virtue of some governing functions. In fact, we can trace this "syntactic" notion of mind historically through major branches of psychology.

Structuralists tried to uncover the fundamental bits of conscious experience (Brentano 1874, Ebbinghaus 1902, Kulpe 1893, Muller 1827, Stumpf 1883, Titchener 1896, 1898a, b, Wundt 1874, 1896); the Gestalt psychologists attempted to categorize the rules our minds use for combining different inputs (Koffka 1922, 1935, Kohler 1920, 1929, 1947, Wertheimer 1912, 1967); Freudians investigate the ways our minds link together beliefs and desires (Freud 1895, 1900, 1910, 1933, 1938); and finally, modern representational theories of the mind insist upon some language of thought with syntactic rules to account for how the mind can faithfully represent the outside world.[159]

However, even though Kant is correct in pointing out Associationism's shortcomings, his account of synthesis as a way to overcome the Humean flux of impressions is not without difficulties. We must be careful to distinguish the need to stabilize the constantly changing incoming sensory data long enough to "read" an impression off of them, the need to unite the stable impressions into coherent groups so that we can separate, e.g., objects from their surrounds, and the need for some rule (or set of rules) by which we can relate our impression-sets to similar stored memories. Kant blurs these three distinctions. Overlooking the initial need to segment incoming sensory data into stable impressions, he writes that the law of association is too weak to create coherent groups of impressions and yet talks as though he were discussing tying our impression-sets to remembered ideas.

Nevertheless, Kant's arguments against Hume parallel recent discussions in psychology as scientists are realizing that spatiotemporal contiguity or any simple rule of association is not going to be enough to yield determinate and unified visual percepts since individual features are processed separately. We can understand modern cognitive psychologists who study the binding problem as reacting to sort of Gibsonian hypothesis of easy and veridical perception.[160] These psychologists regularly point out that the sensory information we receive is too crude for simple combination or associative algorithms to give rise to our sophisticated mental perceptual representations. They conclude that we must actively bind the various features of objects together, so that what we see are synthesized constructions of our world.

This binding problem of modern psychology, as did the "binding problem" of the eighteenth century, arises in the construction of visual percepts. Generally speaking, psychologists believe that in order for us to interpret incoming stimuli semantically (that is, in order for us to perceive some object as that object), our brains first extract constant features from an incoming array of light patterns, then construct temporary (pre-) representations from the patterns, before they can begin to associate the object representation with its meaning.[161] However, as I have already stated, the brain processes visual data in segregated specialized cortical areas.[162] For example, (roughly speaking) the inter-blob region computes the orientation of lines and edges, the intralaminar pathway responds to color, and the magnocellular stream calculates movement (Ramachandran 1990, Ramachandran and Anstis 1988, Zeki 1992). Nevertheless, the features computed separately must somehow become united after processing in these initial distinct areas, since our conscious experiences reflect the various features and sub-contents as joined together in a single interpretative unit or as a single percept.

However, given what we know about the segregated nature of the brain and the relative absence of multi-modal association areas in the cortex,[163] how conscious percepts become unified into single perceptual units is not clear. If we lack true association areas, then the more popular (and intuitive) neurophysiological solutions to psychological binding, such as "grandmother" neurons and convergence zones, cannot be correct. But, if we could figure out how and where the brain joins together segregated outputs, we should be able to localize the neuronal processes correlated with perceptual experiences in detail (thus generating a serious reply to the mysterians).

In what follows, I discuss ongoing research in visual perception in which the scientists involved are deliberately and conscientiously making explanatory connections between perceptual awareness and neural oscillatory firing patterns. I critically examine some data apparently relevant for understanding the neurophysiological underpinnings of perception. In particular, I examine the possibility that 40 Hz oscillatory firing patterns in cortex are important lower level neuronal events related to perceptual experiences.[164] I conclude that these connections are premature and that the binding problem may in fact be an artifact of a misguided "Kantian" perspective on visual processing. A neo-Humeanism of simple processing rules (in the form of nonlinear dynamics) may solve (rather, dissolve) the problem.

6.3. Psychology's Binding Problem

One way in which we gain empirical access to our brains' binding procedure through the study of illusory conjunctions. We can force our brains to make mistakes when it combines the shape and color features to create a representation if we present the stimuli rapidly and if our attention is divided. For instance, if subjects are briefly shown a stimulus consisting of red X, a green T, and a blue O that is flanked on both sides by numbers and are asked to notice and repeat the numbers, they might see (and later report) a blue X, a green T, and a red O (Treisman and Schmidt 1982). Indeed, some are so convinced of their perception that they do not believe that the actual stimuli were otherwise. The obvious hypothesis is that their brains, taxed by the difficult task, incorrectly bind the separately processed colors and shapes together.

Ann Treisman (1986) takes evidence along these lines to suggest that we have neural signals which convey the presence of distinctive features; we have "feature maps" for length, color, cardinality, orientation, curvature (but not verticality or straightness, since tilt is apparently represented relationally by some standard not positively signalled), some topological properties, like connectedness and height/width ratios, as well as movement and differences in stereoscopic depth. Later stages of processing must integrate the information from the early feature extraction phase into temporary object-specific (pre-) representations. We then focus our attention onto the objects to combine these features into consciously perceived representations. Treisman hypothesizes that focused attention operates by means of a "master map" of locations that registers the presence and discontinuities of color. It selects all the features present at the attended location, binds them into a temporary object schema, and then compares that schema with stored descriptions.[165] Illusory conjunctions can arise before we access our semantic knowledge of familiar objects, and we require both the conjoined features and the activated associated semantic memories before we can get awareness of a perception (Treisman and Galade 1980).

So, the illusory conjunctions at least stem from poor location information in some aspects of mental processing.[166] Not everyone though shares Treisman's conclusion that lack of attention is also necessary. For example, William Prinzmetal believes that poor spatial resolution is responsible for the illusory conjunctions. (He also believes that poor spatial resolution can explain the neon colors effect, a visual illusion in which achromatic figures take on the color of an overlaid grid of colored lines.) Similar to the Gestaltists, he holds that external organizational principles, such as contiguous areas, common surfaces, subjectively defined groups, and syllable-like units in words, work to constrain what little spatial information we have (Prinzmetal and Keysar 1989). We have a set of processing functions that determines color, texture, etc., and that information is "integrated" over previously defined objects or surfaces (Prinzmetal and Keysar 1989: 165). Against Triesman's master map theory of feature integration, Prinzmetal argues that while diverting attention may indeed decrease spatial resolution (and so indirectly increase illusory conjunctions by further limiting location information), it also affects feature identification and perceptual organization (Prinzmetal *et al.* 1986). In support of his position, he points out that illusory conjunctions are more likely to occur when features are part of the same perceptual "unit" and that we are more uncertain of where things are within a group than across groups (Prinzmetal 1981).

He suggests that the algorithms we use in visual processing are designed to filter noise and fill in absent stimuli using the most economical coding possible. One distinct possibility is that the algorithms compute borders accurately, but compute colors much more coarsely.[167] So, in comparison to our calculations of luminance, our processing of hue has lower resolution. (Prinzmetal's suggestion is that V1 and V2 might perform these computations by using low spatial resolution for small changes in luminance and a higher resolution for large changes.[168] Such an algorithm would in fact filter noise and could fill in any missing information using a very economical coding.) Furthermore, relatively poor color resolution in any algorithm would be compounded by visually sensitive neurons integrating information over receptive fields, which omit spatial information. However, the ubiquitous reciprocal connections in our visual system (Van Essen 1985, Van Essen *et al.* 1992) would allow feed-back among the various stages of processing so that our subjective perceptions about object organization could influence our color judgments, and we would then bootstrap our way up the hierarchy to a full-blown interpretation. He posits that we already have object representation "templates" which we use to constrain feature processing and to help determine which processed bits should be united together into one percept. (See Figure 6.1.)

The point here is not to adjudicate between the two proposals for solving the binding problem. Rather, I wish to suggest that binding understood as a process of hooking together disparate psychological units is fundamentally misleading. That is, a Kantian story in which the brain actively engages in some processing to tie various features together might not be required. Instead, a more Humean perspective in which the "tying together" falls out of some other sort of (simple) processing might be more accurate. "Binding" might be a property inherent in the structure of our brain's firing patterns — in particular, "higher level" order superimposed on individual cells' activity.

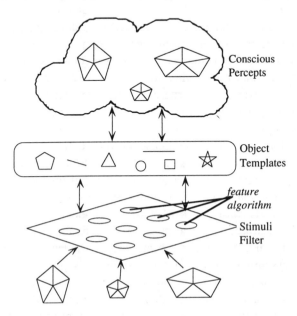

Figure 6.1. Prinzmetal's Object Template Constrained Feature Processing. Prinzmetal suggests that we have object representation "templates" which are used to constrain feature processing and to help determine which features should be united together to form an object hypothesis. Reciprocal connections in our visual system allow the feedback among the stages of processing so that our final perceptions also influence feature judgments.

6.4. The Problem of Perception in Neuroscience

The binding problem also surfaces in neuroscience as scientists realize there is no central cortical "informational exchange," given the dearth of "association" areas. Psychology's original question of how disparate perceptual features can yield single interpretations for objects becomes for neurophysiologists: How do brains link together the various outputs from different processing modules such that some system activates unified percepts? And as we come to know more about the brain and how it is organized, it becomes clear that there is going to be no simple solution to neuroscience's version of the binding problem.

The biggest obstacle to solving the problem stems from accepting parallel distributed processing as the fundamental computational mechanism of the brain. Since we understand ourselves as growing, developing organisms, we must hypothesize that the different mental "symbols" we use to represent objects or aspects of objects in the real world have to be able to co-exist within the same physical hardware. Most importantly, new symbols cannot require new pieces of hardware, for otherwise our brain would have to grow each time we think an original thought or have an original perceptual experience. However, if the brain is in fact fundamentally and massively parallel, we are left with what von der Malsburg (1987) calls the "superposition catastrophe."[169] That is, if we take mental "symbols" to be different subsets of coactive neurons within the same brain structure, as they are in the classical framework of neurobiology, then if more than one symbol becomes active at a time (as they surely must, given what we know about feature extraction and later binding), they become superimposed by coactivation and any information carried the original differentiated subsets is lost. The lack of internal structure of neuronal assemblies in the classical framework prevents computational combinations, which, in turn, rules out most interesting mental calculations.[170]

Jerry Fodor and Zenon Pylyshyn (1988) argue that this coactivation conundrum entails that the parallel distributed architecture of the brain is merely a lower-level implementation of a higher-level discrete symbol manipulating device. Segregate each cell assembly unit to physically distinct areas of the brain, e.g., the different parts of the topologically organized somatosensory system in the postcentral gyrus of the parietal cortex. The firing patterns of the different cell assemblies can "speak" to one another through select connections among areas. The symbols can then interact across the areas as unstructured units since all the lower level detail within cell assemblies is lost at the higher level of connected groups of segregated areas. In this way, the parallel architecture masquerades as a von Neumann-style computing device.

However, as von der Malsburg argues, this solution can only work in severely restricted environments with a specific set of patterns, since slicing a system up into so many subsystems destroys most of a machine's flexibility. Requiring a different subsystem for each interpretation would not permit the machine to respond to new and different stimuli very efficiently. Moreover, given the sophistication of the human mind, it also places too heavy a burden on either phylogenetic development or ontogenetic organization because each distinct subsystem would have to be either already programmed in or would have to develop quickly in response to each distinct but representable stimulus. Such a solution probably would allow only incomplete and abbreviated interpretations of the rapidly changing external world. Finally, since the solution assumes a different dedicated physical subsystem for each concept, it entails that symbol patterns for new input or newly learned concepts require new and different areas of the brain, and this violates what we know about how brains develop. The basic problem is that most physical connections within the head (that we know about) just develop too slowly to allow for the rapid conceptual learning we continually exhibit if changes in the physical connections were the only mechanism for representing new ideas.

6.4.1. The Addition of Time

But if using the physical connections studied thus far among neurons to tie different subsets of firing patterns together cannot work, obviously the brain must find additional degrees of freedom elsewhere. Time is a likely candidate, for mental and biological functions operate on two different time scales. There is the psychological time scale, characterizing mental processes and ordered on tenths of a second; there is also the faster time scale ordered on only thousands of a second. The mean unit activity of neurons evolves on the longer psychological time scale, but the activity of a single cell fluctuates around the mean on the faster time scale.[171] It is possible that correlating the activity fluctuations of a set of coactivated neurons could thereby bind that firing pattern into a single unit. Several such units could coexist if their activity is desynchronized relative to one another, thus solving the superposition catastrophe.[172]

Here then could be the procedure our parallel and distributed perceptual systems use to synthesize disparate feature contents into a single unified interpretation. Given the complexity of what we represent in the environment and the flexibility and computational demands on our representational machinery, it seems the simple answer to the binding problem — that all binding requires is a serial architecture — must fail. Something occurring in a lower level of neural organization must be importantly relevant. That is, single cell activity (which would underlie and support higher level averaged activity) may be the appropriate place to look for the causal mechanisms in order to account for the "higher level" perceptual phenomena.[173]

However, it is difficult to translate questions dealing with how populations of neurons interact to questions concerning how a single cell behaves. Since each area of the brain is composed of a staggeringly enormous number of neurons, recording the firing pattern of a single cell may not capture any relevant higher level patterns or processes. Indeed, since there are tens of thousands of cells in each visual column, any one cell from which a scientist records could have a function orthogonal to the task at hand. And until neuroscientists could make the leap from studying single cells to studying populations of cells, many interesting questions concerning visual perceptual experience in the nervous system were simply unapproachable.

But within the last ten years or so, two sorts of techniques have emerged as ways to start studying the behavior of larger numbers of neurons: multiple simultaneous recordings from single cells, and multiple-channel electroencephelograph recordings from relatively small populations of cells. As a means by which to connect neurophysiological structures with larger neurophysiological or psychological functional units, these procedures allow scientists to examine the intrinsic dynamic operations of circumscribed cortical areas and to start assessing their relevance for visual perception. In particular, when coupled with computer technology (which permits simultaneous visual stimulation of different areas in the visual field keyed to the cells whose spike trains are being recorded), they gave scientists a way to start determining the principles of visual processing within single cortical areas. The function of the distributed systems connecting the various visual subsystems can then be studied using mathematical correlation methods to assess the cooperative firing across groups of neurons in different areas.[174]

6.4.2. One Possible Neurobiological "Solution"

Though it is still largely unknown how the visual system links features of a visual scene together, neuroscientists are beginning to give a few answers to some of the smaller questions and are starting to speculate on what principles might underwrite psychology's larger story. For example, Reinhard Eckhorn and his research group at Philipps University in Germany took simultaneous multiple recordings of single unit activity, multiple unit activity, and local slow wave field potentials from areas 17 and 18 in lightly anesthetized cats with independently drivable microelectrodes.   They evaluated their data for receptive field properties, orientation and direction tuning, and short-epoch cross-correlations between various combinations of the different types of recordings and discovered that the neurons of an assembly partly synchronize their outputs through a transition to a phase-locked oscillatory state. Assemblies relatively far from one another which have similar receptive field properties — including assemblies in different areas of the brain — synchronize their activities as well if they are stimulated at the same time. Operating at a frequency between 40 and 80 Hz (the gamma range), these oscillations occur in all three types of recordings. (See Figure 6.2.) Eckhorn speculates that this sort of oscillatory pattern may serve as a general mechanism for binding of stimuli features in the primary visual cortex by linking excitatorially connected neurons with similar receptive fields. In this way, the dynamic assemblies would "define" an object in virtue of resemblance among features (Eckhorn *et al.* 1988a, b, c, Eckhorn *et al.* 1989).[175]

There are three possible sources for the oscillations in area 17 (Jagadeesh *et al.* 1992): intrinsic membrane properties in presynaptic cells (e.g., the interneurons or the pyramidal cells), oscillations in thalamic input, or intracortical feedback pathways (Freeman 1975, Ghose and Freeman 1990, Llinas *et al.* 1991, Rhodes 1992, Silva *et al.* 1991, Steriade *et al.* 1991). However, it appears that intrinsic membrane properties have little effect (Jagadeesh *et al.* 1992, Gray 1992), so some rhythmic synaptic input probably leads to the oscillatory behavior. Using single and multi-unit recordings, Charles Gray and Wolf Singer have shown that the dorsal lateral geniculate nucleus of the thalamus in anesthetized cats shows no general synchronized oscillation pattern in the gamma range, suggesting that the synchronous oscillations are probably cortical phenomena alone Gray and Singer (1989), Gray *et al.* (1992).[176] These results strongly suggest that the brain uses these temporal patterns for some peculiarly cortical activity.

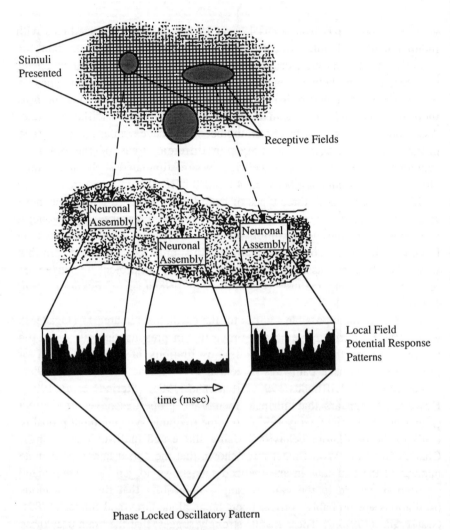

Figure 6.2. A Sketch of Eckhorn's Synchronized Neuronal Assemblies. Spatially separated neural assemblies with similar receptive fields synchronize outputs through a transition to a phase locked oscillatory state for simple stimuli (the grid pattern shown here). Scientists can record the phase locked transitions using local field potentials, as well as by simultaneous multiple recordings from single unit activity and multiple unit activity. Neural assemblies that do not have similar receptive fields, even though they are spatially contiguous, do not synchronize their outputs.

Moreover, Gray and Singer have shown that phase-locked synchronization across spatially separate columns for cells with similar orientation preferences are influenced by global properties of the stimulus. (Indeed, such synchronization has been found between neurons in area 17 of left and right cerebral hemispheres (Engel *et al.* 1991).) When two short light bars move in opposite directions over two similar receptive fields, the responses of the cells show no phase-locking. When they move in the same direction, the cells are only marginally synchronized. When the cells are shown a single long bar of light, their responses are strongly phase-locked.[177] (See Figure 6.3.) These effects indicate that phase-locked oscillations depend on various large scale aspects of the stimuli, such as form or motion, which local responses cannot reflect when taken individually. Therefore, the synchronization may also serve to represent the higher order features in a pattern. For example, it may help in figure-ground segregation (Gray *et al.* 1989).[178]

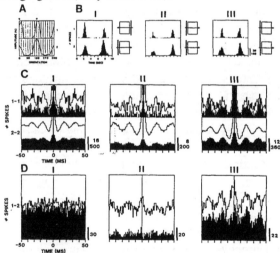

Figure 6.3. Phase-Locked Oscillations Depend on Global Properties of the Stimuli. (A) Orientation tuning curves of neuronal responses recorded from two electrodes (1,2) show a preference for vertical light bars. (B) Post-stimulus time histograms of the neuronal responses for the following stimulus conditions: (I) two light bars moved in opposite directions, (II) two light bars moved in the same direction, and (III) one long light bar moved across both receptive fields. (C, D) Auto-correlograms (C, 1-1, 2-2) and cross-correlograms (D, 1-2) computed for the neuronal responses at both sites (1 and 2 in A and B) for stimulus conditions I, II, III in B. For each pair of correlograms except the two displayed in C (I, 1-1) and D (I) the second direction of stimulus movement is displayed with unfilled bars (reprinted with permission from Nature (Gray et al., 1989) Copyright 1989, Macmillan Magazines Limited).

Although the phase-locked oscillations may yet turn out be an artifact of some other, more fundamental, process,[179] it also may be that "[stimulus-evoked] resonances are a general phenomena, forming the basis of a correlation code which is used within and between different sensory systems and perhaps even throughout the entire brain" (Eckhorn *et al.* 1988: 129).[180] And as modelers in artificial intelligence pick up on the mechanism of phase-locked oscillations and explore the principles underlying this sort of binding solution,[181] it does appear that this hypothesis provides the ideal sort of answer to psychology's binding problem.

In fact, it is congenial to both Triesman's hypothesis of a master map of locations in which attention is used to tie features together and Prinzmetal's notion that organizational assumptions in perception plus feedback from higher level processes accounts for perceptual binding. For example, Kammen, Koch, and Holmes (1991) have demonstrated that some nonlocal feedback must play a fundamental role in the initial synchronization and the dynamic stability of the oscillation. And this higher level comparator could exist either as Treisman's central feature-locator attentional mechanism or as Prinzmetal's lower level, distributed recurrent feedback loops.[182] Moreover, in investigating the architecture required to segment and bind more than one object at a time, Horn, Sagi, and Usher (1991) have stumbled across something like the illusory conjunction effect in their computer simulations of oscillatory binding. It is no wonder then that phase-locked oscillations are being taken seriously as a new and exciting solution to superposition catastrophe and the binding problem. (This too is a "Kantian" solution: the brain actively binds together separately processed features.)

6.4.3. Problems with Neuroscience's "Solution"

However, the neurophysiologists who suggest that synchronized oscillations are the key to solving the binding problem are guilty of confusions about stages in processing.[183] The sort of underlying model of mental function which neuroscientists assume divides visual perception into three different stages: segmentation, binding, and association, each of which the brain actively pursues using some computational means or other.[184] (See Figure 6.4.) Early stages in the visual system must be dedicated to parsing the incoming two-dimensional pattern of retinal stimulation into cohesive features. They must somehow figure out how to indicate that this neuron over here with this particular receptive field is signaling a bit of the same feature as that neuron over there with that particular receptive field. Differential response properties of cells, as well as the axonal and dendritic connections among individual neurons, could carry out some of these required "computations." However, since our perception of single features must remain constant across such disruptive events as blinks, saccades, head movements, changes in lighting, etc., the architecture of the neural net probably will not be able to handle the task alone. The brain must also actively segment incoming data. And only after the brain determines which features are present can it begin to bind them into unified objects (though top-down expectations most likely do play some role in determining which features the brain decides are there). Some of this binding may be architecturally constrained as well. For example, the connections between topological maps in different areas can preserve the approximate spatial relationships of objects in the external world. However, since our world is in a constant flux and we are constantly being exposed to novel visual stimuli, purely "structural" architectural solutions again will fall short. Finally, only after this initial processing can the brain assign meanings to the bundles of features through associating the temporary object hypotheses with previously encountered stimuli and their related associations.

What Eckhorn and his group and Gray and his colleagues have indexed is *segmentation*, not binding. They presented their cats with very simple stimuli, a bar or a grid pattern, and then tested the response of cells with similar receptive fields *for single features* (*cf.*, Figure 6.4). If two cells are sensitive to similar orientations, for example, then their experiments predict that the cells will fire in phase-locked synchrony if the visual system is shown a bar in that orientation. This is no trivial result, but it does not show what would happen if two cells, one color responsive and one orientation responsive, were both activated by an appropriately colored and oriented bar. In fact, in cells they tested, Gray and Singer (1987, 1989) found that if neurons in different hypercolumns were sensitive to different features, but still responded to the same particular input, then these cell were *not* phase-locked.[185]

Moreover, the difficulty with generalization to a population which plagued single cells recordings affects the multiple unit recordings as well. Scientists currently can record from such a small number of neurons at a time that we have little assurance the behavior we are witnessing reflects the general trend, even within a particular column. (In this particular case, the difficulty is compounded by the fact that not all the neurons probed became phase-locked, even though they had the proper receptive fields (Gray *et al.* 1989).)[186] I think that the seriousness of this objection cannot be over-emphasized. The greatest number of simultaneous single unit recordings in a single brain area of a moving organism is only about 150. While this represents a tremendous technological achievement, it only captures about ten percent of the cells in any column. Without additional sorts of controls, generalizing from this small of a statistical sample is dangerous. We simply have no way of knowing that the cells being recorded from represent how the majority of the cells in that area are behaving.

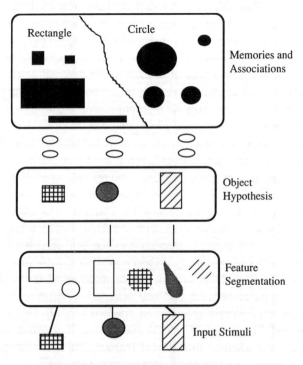

Figure 6.4. Segmentation, Binding, and Association. Early stages of visual processing parse the incoming two-dimensional stimuli patterns into simple cohesive features (feature segmentation). The next stage binds these features into perceptual objects, in conjunction with some top-down expectations of which features and objects are actually there (object hypothesis). Finally, these "guesses" about which objects are present are associated with memories of previous experiences with similar objects (memory and association).

So, without additional converging evidence that the brain uses phase-locked oscillations to tie together disparate features into a single object, it is premature to conclude that these oscillations form a binding mechanism. Given current state-of-the-art technology, we are simply unable to devise single cell (or local field potential) experiments that would be able to test the oscillation hypothesis definitively. I must conclude that those who see phase-locked oscillations in individual neurons as the additional temporal process which overcomes superposition woes celebrate prematurely. Though oscillations may be the correct answer, we do not have anything near conclusive evidence linking phase-locked oscillations with the psychological phenomena of binding, and perhaps more importantly, multiple unit recording technology itself falls short of being able to support our higher level functional analyses. Methodological limitations appear to halt any sort of actual explanatory connection between individual neural firing patterns and psychological effects right here. Neuroscience cannot (now) provide the link that psychology requires between bound perceptual unity and individual neurons simply because neuroscience lacks the tools to do so.

6.5. A Different Approach

Until neurophysiologists are better equipped to probe orders of magnitude more individual cells simultaneously, about the only other avenue currently available for uncovering a neurophysiological index for the binding mechanism is to look at data farther removed from the behavior of the individual cell, with the hope of providing a different sort of connection between sensory input, neuronal behavior, and motor output, on the one hand, and psychological phenomena, on the other. However, any move farther away from the individual cells necessitates abstracting over some neurophysiological details. In this instance, the individual cell would no longer be able to be the explanatory currency of neurophysiological accounts of psychological phenomena. Instead, we would look for relevant invariant structures at, for example, the higher level of EEG waves.

Interestingly enough, with a perspective more removed from the behavior of the individual cells, we find a different sort of order on top of the temporal order described above. Perhaps we could tie bound conscious perceptions to the particular activated *assemblies* of neurons in the SE system by borrowing from Jean-Paul Changeux's theory of "selective stabilization" (Changeux 1984, Changeux and Danchin 1976, Changeux *et al.* 1973, Changeux *et al.* 1984) and Walter Freeman's use of chaotic principles (Freeman 1975, 1979a-c, 1983, 1987, 1994a-c, 1995a, b, Freeman and Baird 1987, Freeman and Schneider 1982, Freeman and Skarda 1985a, b, Freeman and van Dijk 1987, Freeman *et al.* 1988).[187]

In this section, I rely on concepts which may be unfamiliar to non-mathematical readers. Therefore, it might be helpful to pause here briefly to give a very brief introduction to chaos theory. Put very simply, any real dynamical (changing) system, which may be described or modeled by using non-linear equations, is capable of displaying chaotic behavior, which can be thought of as follows. Small changes in the initial input conditions of a chaotic system can produce dramatic changes in the form or behavior of the system. These systems are exquisitely sensitive to small perturbations. In a dynamical system, any settling down into a relatively long-term, stable form or behavior is called an "attractor." That is, the attractor is the state a dynamical system settles down to over time. In the case of a truly chaotic system, the behavior never repeats exactly, though it may often come close. A change in the qualitative form of an attractor is called a "bifurcation." In this context, a bifurcation describes a transition from one relatively stable state to another.[188] The environment, or set of dimensions in which any dynamical system operates is called the phase space.

The foregoing offers a possible solution to the binding problem in terms of the dynamics of chaotic systems which I here suggest includes cortical neuronal assemblies. That is, sensory input disturbs our cortex's natural spontaneous behavior such that it forces various assemblies of neurons to fire in stable attractor based patterns.[189] What the patterns look like would depend upon the sorts of connections among individual neurons that had been forged in virtue of previous activity and corresponding memories. These "attractors" would then serve as our neurophysiologically realized "interpretation" of the incoming stimuli.

Walter Freeman measures the EEG activity on the surface of the olfactory bulb of adult rabbits during the presentation of odors paired with water in a classical conditioning paradigm (Freeman 1978, Freeman and Schneider 1982, Freeman and Viana Di Prisco 1986, Viana Di Prisco 1985). What he and his group find is that the EEG shows a brief transition from a state of low level irregular activity to a high amplitude coherent oscillation with a distinctive spatial pattern of root mean squared amplitude.[190] These transitions are correlated with specific odor recognition responses and change with learning. The dynamical transition occurs at the peak of a 3-8 Hz "respiratory slow wave" caused by the surge of inspiration-driven receptor input. The high amplitude coherent burst has a dominant spectral peak in the 40-80 Hz range, and it emerges from the low level phase-locked background activity which "rides" the respiration waves. (See Figure 6.5.) During the burst, the EEG from the whole surface of the bulb oscillates at a common frequency, but, more importantly, it exhibits a specific spatial amplitude pattern which remains (approximately) constant when the animal is not learning to recognize any new stimuli (Bressler 1984, Freeman 1975, 1978) (See Figure 6.6).[191]

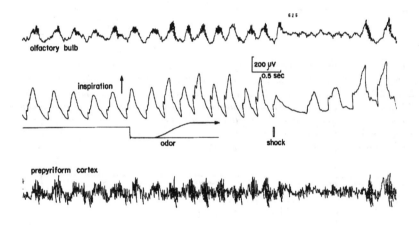

Figure 6.5. Coherent Burst "Rides" Inspiration Slow Wave. Upper trace — unfiltered EEG for a single channel in olfactory bulb shows respiratory slow wave (4 Hz) with "burst" (50 Hz) at the peak. Middle traces — pneumograph output showing actual lung movement and trace below showing timing of conditioned stimulus odor release and shock for aversive conditioning. Lower trace — unfiltered EEG of prepyriform cortex. (Copyright 1982, The Society for Psychophysiological Research. Reprinted with permission of the publisher and the authors from Freeman and Schneider 1982).

This sort of 40 Hz activity with respect to olfaction was first reported in Adrian (1942). Later Lavin *et al.* (1959) and Hernandez-Peion (1960) extended the oscillation results to include other sensory stimuli besides olfactory inputs. What is important to notice for our purposes is the relationship between perception, learning, and memory: new odor associations affect the shape of the oscillatory patterns tied to previously learned odors. As rabbits learn more about their "world," they "categorize" the same smells differently, and these different "categorizations" affect how they "perceive" future odors. (See Figure 6.7.)

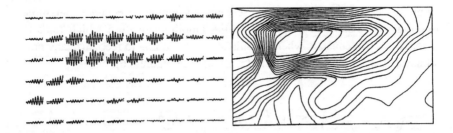

Figure 6.6. Spatial Amplitude Pattern for Learned Odors. Common carrier wave emerged from 60 EEGs recorded simultaneously from the olfactory cortex of a rabbit as it recognized a scent (left). The wave is nearly the same in each recording, except that the amplitude varies. The shape of the carrier wave does not indicate the identity of the scent. That information is contained in the spatial pattern of amplitude across the cortex, which can be displayed as a contour plot (right), much like the plots of elevations in topographic maps (from Freeman 1991, reprinted with kind permission by Dr. Walter Freeman).

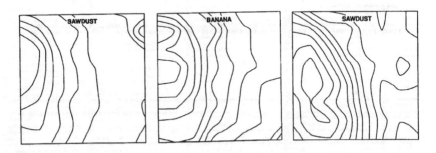

Figure 6.7. The Influence of Experience on Perception. Contour plot at the left emerged consistently from bulbar EEGs of a rabbit what had been conditioned to associate the scent of sawdust with a particular reinforcement. After the animal learned to recognize the smell of banana (middle), however, reexposure to sawdust led to the emergence of a new sawdust plot (right). The change shows that bulbar activity is dominated more by experience than by stimuli; otherwise, sawdust would always give rise to the same plot (from Freeman 1991, reprinted with kind permission by Dr. Walter Freeman).

At first blush, this sort of spatial order might be surprising, since EEG waves reflect a macroscopic voltage averaged over the seemingly independent microscopic activity of hundreds of densely interconnected neurons. On the other hand, appearances aside, our neurons do not function independently of one another. Moreover, spatial order in EEG waves occurs in many places in our central nervous system. In the rabbit, systematic interactions between the bulb and cortex are most likely responsible for the coherent oscillations. One hypothesis is that this larger scale order is similar to the sort of order which emerges in the scroll waves of concentration in the Zhabotinske reaction, in the formation of Bénard cells of convection in fluid dynamics, or in populations in ecology (these forms of order are also explained by attractor patterns in non-linear dynamical systems) (Segal 1965, Winfree and Strogatz 1983, Yorke and Li 1975). In any event, we can see the spatial amplitude pattern as a higher level structure that emerges from lower level neuronal behavior which we can use to document an animal's response to environmental stimuli.

6.5.1. Bifurcating Dynamical Systems

Although the EEG can only reflect the aggregate behavior of individual neural activity, it is possible that the patterns it reveals concerning the relative density of the underlying activity are in fact the relevant information-bearing states in the system, and that therefore the details of the individual neuronal events are not important in that regard. That is, the decomposition and localization of psychological information processing events would bottom out at a level above the individual cell. Indeed, Bill Baird points out that because the firing rates for individual mitral cells in the bulb are about one pulse for every fifth cycle of a 50 Hz EEG burst, there would be no way to track input by studying the mean pulse rate of single cells (Freeman 1979a, Baird 1986a). Moreover, when responding to deterministic input, the spiking activity of bulbar neurons are Poisson distributed in time, similar to the pattern of radio-active decay (Holden 1976). This apparently irreducible stochasticity of individual neurons (probably introduced in the activation of synaptic transmission of post-synaptic channels or in processing in the microtubules (Hameroff 1994, Harth and Wong 1973)) means that only ensembles of cells perform reliable computations which the macroscopic averages then reflect. In sum, it may be that the macroscopic spatial and temporal patterns form true macrostates,[192] and the dimensionality of space for the higher level patterns is the space of "information" processing.

Though superficially similar to Fodor and Pylyshyn's position that the underlying distributed architecture merely implements unrelated algorithms, this picture of what that higher level "algorithm" looks like is very different. We would consider different brain areas as discrete systems in which an influx of energy (the sensory input) causes the current state to destabilize and bifurcate into a new ordered state that itself becomes momentarily stable. Computer models of such systems exhibit this sort of behavior. Inputs that the system has learned trigger one pattern more than the others, allowing that pattern to win a "growth competition." Freeman and Baird both extrapolate from their research on the olfactory system and argue that this mechanism of competing instabilities forming stable patterns is used for creating temporary object interpretations,[193] as well as for forming dynamic associative memories.[194] The system recognizes an input as belonging to a particular input category when the spatial pattern of sensory synaptic input pushes the resting state of the system into a different and stable oscillatory pattern.[195]

Freeman and Baird argue that we should think of the informational oscillatory patterns as either inhomogeneous limit cycles or weakly chaotic attractors. One advantage of using this sort of analysis is that we can describe these sorts of bifurcation paths within a multi-dimensional state space using rather simple nonlinear equations. One would expect a huge dimensionality with extremely complex trajectories to characterize the informational state space for complex polymodal creatures like us; however, periodic or chaotic attractors typically only occupy a fraction of the dimensions. Simple order (low degrees of freedom) out of seemingly random and noisy disorder (very high degrees of freedom) is the hallmark of this sort of nonlinear dynamical analysis.

Walter Freeman and Christine Skarda envision the entire cortex to contain such systems interconnected by cortico-cortical fibers (Freeman and Skarda 1985a, 1985b, 1990, 1991, Skarda and Freeman 1990). And there is some evidence that this perspective is warranted. Areas in which stimulus-evoked oscillations occur include the rabbit olfactory cortex, the cat, hedgehog, and rat olfactory systems (Adrian 1942, Bressler and Freeman 1980, Gault and Leaton 1963), auditory cortex and the hippocampal areas in the cat and rabbit (Basar 1972, 1983, Basar et al. 1987, Basar and Ozesmi 1972, Basar and Ungan 1973, Freeman and Barrie 1994), the hippocampus of guinea pigs (Charpak et al.

1992), and the monkey, cat, and rabbit visual cortices (Basar *et al.* 1987, Bressler 1994, Freeman and Barrie 1994, Freeman and van Dijk 1987, Kruger and Mayer 1990). Furthermore, similar resonances were found in EEG-recordings in humans above the association, limbic, and motor areas, as an evoked response in the auditory pathway, cerebellar cortex, and neocortex (Basar 1972, 1980, Basar *et al.* 1976, Basar-Eroglu and Basar 1985, Krieger and Dillbeck 1987, Turbes 1992), and in primary motor and the sensory cortices using magnetic field tomography (Llado *et al.* 1992, Ribrary *et al.* 1991).

If this view be correct, then the sequence of patterns that the oscillatory networks pass through over time, or the bifurcations from one attractor to another, constitute the "computation" of the system (Dynes and Delautte 1992, Eggemont 1991). These oscillations entrain the "micro-activity" of individual neurons in various areas of cortex into a well defined macrostate, while, at the same time, gating irrelevant "noise." The movements from macrostate to macrostate operate on the longer psychological time scale; and a shorter time scale used for, e.g., voluntary saccades or changes in motor behavior, perhaps reflects an internal clocking interval at which sensory data are sampled and the networks are nudged toward a stable pattern. (Bill Baird makes this suggestion.[196]) The resultant "perceptual states" of the networks act as input into the motor regions, which then enact some sequence of motor outputs. Motor states also presumably feed back into the perceptual states and cause transitions there as well.[197]

The picture of mental "computation" which emerges from bifurcation dynamics and resonant frequencies is very different from a classical von Neumann computing description in which the syntactic structure of mental "sentences" is the currency of cognition. First, this type of system dynamical approach is inherently multi-level (whereas the traditional computer metaphors for the mind operate on only a single level of analysis). The underlying microstructure actually determines which pattern will emerge, but the higher level series of bifurcations through which the network goes are the interpretive states. Second, the oscillatory patterns as described change their shape as the system learns more about its environment. There is no constant "syntax" over which functional algorithms can operate. Third, the patterns of oscillation that emerge as we learn to recognize and categorize stimuli are the basic units of cognition, not a feed-forward processor conjoined with some sort of CPU (more on this theme in the next chapter).

6.5.2. Binding Solutions Revisited

How exactly would this new view affect hypothesized oscillation binding solutions? If entire cortical regions are considered to be one network system acting as a single resonating unit, then single-cell oscillations as a vehicle for separately uniting disparate feature-bits with previous memories of feature and object categories would be unnecessary. Instead, a higher level statistical aggregate of firing neurons would be all that is needed to explain how the brain unites disparate feature primitives. The different responses of our various firing neurons are entrained in higher level regularities just in virtue of higher level properties themselves; no lower level algorithm need direct the linkage. In other words, binding may not require, strictly speaking, a *process* at the level of the single cell to tie bits of perception together; instead, it might be determined solely by the connectivity among neurons between and across the various topographical maps in the cortical areas and the firing responses inherent in the neurons themselves.

Moreover, since our current techniques for single cell recordings do not allow us to chart the larger scale order as a function of smaller scale interactions, trying to separate the microprocesses which lead to a certain bifurcation in the informational phase space may not be possible in the first place. Indeed, since what we see on the larger scale reflects the statistical aggregation of underlying stochastic microprocesses, charting individual cellular behavior might be analogous to following the activity of a single particle in a Bénard cell in order to understand convection. Perhaps, as important as the lower level single-cell research is in understanding how neurons behave and how neural networks are actually constructed, it is not the appropriate level of analysis for perceptual experiences. Instead, the true story may be found in system dynamics. That is, the way to describe how visual perception occurs may be in terms of large scale network behavior (after perhaps some initial feedforward processing in the retina up to perhaps the lateral geniculate nucleus), and this sort of dynamical system cannot be decomposed any farther in any practical way.[198] The interaction of the neurons is what is crucial for the oscillations, and we can track the trajectory of the macro-patterns through state space in virtue of nonlinear mathematical functions.

6.6. Consciousness as System-Dynamic Oscillations

I admit that these hypotheses concerning higher level pattern recognition remain highly contentious. Nevertheless, I dare to extract some observations. Attractor dynamics and resonant frequencies entail a different conception of information processing than what we traditionally see using the descriptions of single cell interactions and individual connectivities as explaining changes in the system. In this case, the pattern of oscillation that emerges as we learn to recognize and categorize stimuli is the basic stuff of cognition, and the series of bifurcations through which the network goes just is a series of perceptual states (though the underlying microstructure does determine which pattern will emerge). In sum, we do not have to understand binding in terms of single cell interactions; instead, it could be a property inherent in our brain's "higher level" oscillations. At least, recent neurophysiological data point in this direction.

Moreover, using large scale network behavior to determine the "computational" space for neurobiological representations comprises a sort of Humean response to Kantian claims. Though the oscillatory dynamical system may not, strictly speaking, follow the law of association, it does rely on only a few simple principles (i.e., the low dimensionality) to guide its transitions in state space. Since periodic or chaotic attractors typically only occupy a fraction of the dimensions of phase space, we can generally describe their fairly complicated bifurcation path within multi-dimensional space using rather simple nonlinear equations. Order out of apparent disorder remains the calling card of nonlinear dynamical analysis.

The nonlinear system may also function as a modern mathematical interpretation of Hume's various "propensities of the imagination" which act to give the different ideas enough cohesion to be conjoined with related impressions. A winner-take-all "growth competition" among learned patterns to different inputs assures that degraded or brief sensory data trigger the proper impression-bundles and that these bundles then simultaneously resonate with the proper object-category pattern.

So then, here is one way in which Kant might be wrong in his claim that we "[add] different cognitive states [or their contents] to each other and ...[comprehend] their diverse [elements in a single representation]" (A77/B103). All we need for our impressions to call forth related ideas are the sensory data and the general structure underlying the oscillatory behavior, for individual neuronal computations wash out in the big picture and so tracing their individual functional contributions will not tell us how visual percepts work. Explicit Kantian synthesis becomes unnecessary in our explanation and simple Humean spatial-temporal contiguity of sensory impressions may be all that is needed to drive the dynamical pattern completor in our cortex. At least this remains an interesting possibility.

Taking this sort of perspective means that conscious states could be mapped to the transient firing patterns of groups of neurons whose behavior has a particular mathematical dynamical description.[199] To help make what I have to say about this alternative perspective a bit more concrete, let me give an example of how neural oscillatory patterns index at least very simple conscious visual perceptions.[200] Drug-induced visual hallucinations show a remarkable similarity in their early stages. Most generally experience simple geometric shapes, such as a gratings, lattices, checkerboards, cobwebs, funnels, tunnels, or spirals (Klüver 1967, Siegel 1977). These perceptions apparently originate cortically and are not a product of anything that happens to the eye or the retinal ganglion.[201]

Now, if we can find something occurring in cortices experiencing visual hallucinations absent in those that are not, we will have identified a neural correlate for the perceptual pattern. So: what is different about the cortex in organisms on hallucinogenic drugs? Obviously, there are ethical considerations in answering this question with humans.[202] However, EEG waves have been recorded over the cortex of hallucinating cats. They show the same sort of higher ordered, synchronous, oscillatory patterns that Freeman *et al.* had found in their rabbit experiments, with one important addition (Adey *et al.* 1962). *The patterns recorded over cat cortex are geometric transformations of the patterns seen.*[203] *Moreover, the transformations follow the same topographic transformations we find from retina to cortex.* That is, the projections from retina to cortex follow a topographic projection; however, this projection is twisted and distorted along its path. If we untwist and undistort the projection, we find that the patterns recorded moving over cortex (rolls and waves) exactly correspond to what we hallucinate (spirals and grids). (See Figure 6.8 for a schematic example.)

Of course, most of our visual experiences are much more complicated that these hallucinations, so naturally an EEG recording during normal perception should not show such regularities. However, the patterns that Freeman maps into attractor phase space are of the same type as the simple patterns found over hallucinating cat cortex. And these are the sorts of correspondences that are relevant to determining the proper neuronal location of conscious perceptions.

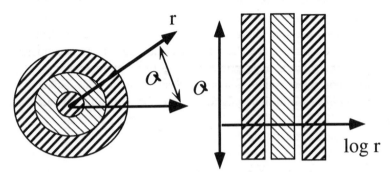

Figure 6.8. Schematic Example of Relation between Experienced Percept and Cortical Activity. (a) Pattern of a typical "white light" funnel hallucinatory pattern, which appears as a set of concentric circles. (b) Transformation of the funnel pattern as it would appear on cortex: a set of bars equal in size, arranged in parallel to the y-axis.

Identifications of this sort can ground psychological discussions of consciousness such that we can now consider exactly how consciousness is related to the SE memory system and now ask what the function of consciousness is. Indeed, tentative support connecting the higher level 40 Hz oscillations with SE interpretations exists. Basar-Eroglu and Basar (1991) have shown that the oscillations occur over the P3 waveform in the CA3 region of cat hippocampus. Moreover, the 40 Hz oscillations were largest in the hippocampal areas in which the P3 waveform was most pronounced. I have already noted that activation of SE memory depends in large measure upon the hippocampus, and in chapter 9, I will tie the P3 wave to the activation of the SE memory system. Much more research needs to be done, of course;[204] however, we have a bit of evidence relating oscillation behavior to SE mnemonic interpretations. At the least, this *sort* of formulation gives us a better handle on the question of consciousness than the introspectively slippery and intellectually suspect qualia.

Marr's Paradox is laid to rest, or, at least, it is set aside. Its oddness could be due solely to adopting a von Neumann-style model of computational perception, without adequate justification. If we take known neuronal architecture seriously, then we are forced to think in terms of recurrent processing loops in a continually active brain. Interpretations in SE memory become particular, activated, dynamic, oscillatory loops. Do these loops then *resemble* our phenomenal experiences? I would think that they resemble them as well as anything else one might find. Though serious mysterians may rest content gaping at consciousness's bizarre properties, if we assume materialism, then it follows that something in the brain is consciousness. And once we accept that conclusion, we should step aside and let science do its work (though perhaps with appropriate sniping from philosophers). *A priori* intuitions about what counts as a proper answer should not regulate scientific inquiry. *Informed* intuitions might, but thus far, our intuitions are far from that.

Refer to this chapter second p/49

Martian Pain and the Problem of Absent Qualia
Chapter Seven

There is a second sort of apparent "hard" problem in developing theories of consciousness, the problem of "absent qualia." One might complain (and indeed several have) that we can conceive of creatures constructed as described in the last three chapters, including multiple memory systems and semantic interpretations of inputs, and yet these creatures lack qualitative experience. If so, the argument goes, we don't have a proper theory of consciousness; we haven't unearthed the necessary conditions for being conscious and so have yet to tackle a "hard" problem.

I disagree. In what follows, I illustrate how the methodologies practiced in the cognitive sciences (and elsewhere) shed light on the philosophical problem of absent qualia and on how any theory of consciousness might go. As you may remember from chapter 2, there are limits to what a scientific theory can tell us about consciousness, especially concerning the quality of individual experiences. Nevertheless, we can still know a great deal about the location of consciousness in our own psychological and neuronal economies. Here I am stepping back from the explicit "location" problems that have engaged me in the last few chapters and returning to a broader conceptual concern: the proper location for difficulties associated with envisioning consciousness in others. In particular, after discussing more sophisticated versions of the simple intuitive problem of absent qualia, I argue that for persons or objects identical to us in the relevant way, absent qualia simply are not possible.

7.1 Supervenience and Absent Qualia

In a nut-shell, the traditional problem of absent qualia goes as follows: It seems that we can imagine a possible world physically identical to this one, but in which our possible-world twins, or "Döppelgangers," have no qualitative properties attached to any of their mental states. Or, put another way, it seems possible that we could be exactly the same as we are now physically, only that we would lack conscious awareness. But if our Döppelgangers need not be conscious, then our *prima facie* entirely reasonable assumptions of materialism and the corresponding token-token identity of mental states with physical ones are now suspect. Nothing about our physical world, it seems, is necessary for qualitative experience. Hence, there can be no theory of consciousness.

However, in his article, "Supervenient Qualia," Terence Horgan (1987) argues that putative imaginability does not necessarily imply metaphysical possibility. He invites us to consider the following question: can we really imagine the situation described above, or are have we fallen prey to some subtle fallacy? To answer this query, he reviews what we actually do when we imagine a possible world in which everything is physically identical to the real world, but in which our counterparts on that world have no qualia.

Here is how Horgan puts the argument.[205] First, "we imagine things from a 'third-person' perspective," and "we stipulate that things are physico-chemically just as they are in the actual world," including the neurochemical processes in the brains of the possible-world Döppelgangers having some sort of perceptual experience (p. 497). However, we do not stipulate what it is like for those people to have any perceptual experiences. Second, "we imagine things from a 'first-person' perspective," and we stipulate that when the Döppelgangers perceive something, there is not anything it is like to have that experience. That is, we pretend that these imagined people have no *qualitative* perceptual experiences (p. 497). However, "we do not stipulate what is going on in people's brains when they are having these...experiences" (p. 497). Third, "we suppose that since each of these two imagined scenes leaves unspecified precisely those aspects the imagined scene which are stipulated in the other imaginative act, the two acts can be 'fused' into a single complex act" (p. 497). In the case of absent qualia, this would be of a world physically identical to ours but in which qualia are absent from the inhabitants' mental life.

As Horgan concludes, this last supposition is mistaken. If we truly believe in a mechanistic universe in which physical laws fully determine all (physical) properties, then we cannot combine the two imagined situations on pain of inconsistency.[206] When we imagine the possible world from a third-person perspective, then when we imagine Döppelgangers with the same neurochemical processes as ours, "we are imagining people who *in fact* are experiencing the same...qualia we do — even though we do not imagine them as experiencing those qualia" (p. 498). And when we imagine the possible world from a first-person perspective, when we imagine persons without qualia experiences, then "we are imagining persons whose neural processes are *in fact* different from our own — even though we do not imagine those persons as being neurally different from us" (p. 498). Thus, Horgan concludes, the two imaginings are actually complete, even though they are supposed otherwise; and the two imaginings are incompatible, since one contains imaginary Döppelgangers with qualitative experiences and the other has imaginary Döppelgangers with no qualitative experiences. Hence, the putative imaginability of the absent qualia world rests on a fallacy and we cannot really imagine that possible world, despite its psychological plausibility.[207]

Indeed, if we take our commitment to a physically determinate universe seriously, then we have to conclude either that qualia supervene on the physical (that is, two states cannot differ mentally without differing physically) or that they are truly epiphenomenal. Horgan merely remarks that it is "wildly implausible" and "just too much" that epiphenomenalism could be true (p. 503-504), and so qualia supervene. In chapter 1, I enumerated several reasons why epiphenomenalism does not make sense. We concluded that a strict epiphenomenalist position is doomed and so we should agree with Horgan that qualia at least supervene on the physical.[208] And if qualia are supervenient, then absent qualia are not possible in worlds physically identical to ours. Regardless of how we can imagine the contrary, it cannot be the case that a being physically identical to me could have no qualitative experiences.

However, from these arguments we cannot conclude that absent qualia are impossible under any circumstances. Demanding that a possible world be strictly identical to ours is a stringent criterion and leaves open the possibility that a world with creatures made from different stuff — but still *psychologically* identical to us — may also have creatures lacking qualitative experiences. That is, if we disregard the fundamental stuff out of which we are made, but still preserve the relevant causal relations among the cognitive states, and if we take those causal relations as driving our mental life, then it is no longer clear how our thought experiments should fare.

7.2 An Argument Against Absent Qualia

Sydney Shoemaker (1975a) believes that absent qualia are necessarily impossible in creatures psychologically identical to us. His argument against absent qualia runs essentially like this: If absent qualia were possible, then the qualitative character of any mental state would necessarily be unavailable to introspection. Since it is absurd to suppose that we are talking about something that is in principle unknowable to anyone when we mention how we feel, and since we assume that the qualitative character of our mental states to be knowable in the same ways that our feelings are known,[209] then it is not logically possible for a state without qualitative character to have the same causal powers as a state that has it.[210]

Shoemaker's argument turns on the introspective accessibility of qualia, so let us work through a specific example to see how this first premise works. Let us return to the old philosophical chestnut of pain. If the story I have told in the last three chapters is correct, then if an organism interprets what it is feeling as pain in SE memory, that organism is aware of being in pain. More generally, if a state exhibits the proper causal etiology specified by the correct definition of (conscious)[211] pain, then the entity instantiating that state feels pain.[212] Causal relations of being in pain important for our purposes include its tendency to cause beliefs and judgments about itself (Dennett 1978b, Shoemaker 1975a).[213] Persons in (conscious) pain, generally speaking, believe they are in pain and have some notion of what the pain feels like.

A "friend of absent qualia"[214] would argue that some mental states psychologically identical to my mental states in SE memory can lack qualitative character.[215] That is, some mental states which exhibit the same casual powers and relations with respect to other mental states, stimuli inputs, and motor outputs as (conscious) pain might not feel like anything. Assume state P is pain corrected defined in some completed psychology (P may not include all attributes of pain) and that all tokens of pain are tokens of P. The "friends" would claim that some tokens of P lack pain's qualitative character. Call these states "ersatz pains."[216] Ersatz pains are psychologically identical to genuine pains — ersatz pains follow the same psychological etiology as real pains in the same or relevantly similar abstract physical system — but ersatz pains would form a different type than real pains nevertheless.

Now let us assume that ersatz pain and real pain are possible in the same entity. Then that entity cannot know by introspection alone whether the pain it feels at some time is ersatz or real, regardless of how detailed our psychological account of pain might be. Because ersatz pain is causally identical to real pain on the psychological level, there is nothing in the experience of the entity in virtue of which it could decide which of the two it is. Ersatz pain is caused by disturbing the endings of certain nerves and causes motor outputs designed to secure its cessation. It causes behavior identical to that caused by real pain. Of most importance is that even "on the inside," as it were, it has the same effects as real pain. It will cause the entity to believe that it is in pain and cause it to interpret that pain and judge how it feels just as it would with real pain. And whether it is in real pain or not cannot affect the interpretation that it gives — by hypothesis, ersatz pain and real pain have the same tendencies to produce any given judgment.

I take it that one's first reaction to this sort of example is that surely we would know that we are in real pain because it hurts, while it is like nothing to have ersatz pain. Wouldn't it be the case that the ersatz pain could cause the belief that we are in pain, bring about the desire to stop the pain, etc., and yet have it be a complete mystery to us how or why we are having these reactions, since we could find no source for our pain? If we are ever in this situation, wouldn't we know by simple introspection that we are in fact having ersatz pain?

As Lawrence Davis (1982) replies, we do generally know that we are in pain because we hurt, and that it is entirely possible to have the sort of nonqualitative state described above. However, that state would not be a breed of pain at all, ersatz or otherwise, since it is not psychologically identical to pain. It could not cause the higher-ordered judgment, "I am in pain because I hurt," as genuine pain can. Any sort of reaction different from that normally experienced with genuine pain would disqualify the originating state from being pain. If the qualitative state of pain is a psychological state, then we have to allow that the definition of pain includes the capacity to cause beliefs concerning the qualitative character of pain, regardless of whether the state actually has some qualitative character. Counter-intuitive as it may seem, any entity with both real and ersatz pains would not be able to tell them apart.[217] Shoemaker's first premise appears correct, and so the conclusion must follow: it is not possible for a state to lack qualitative character if it is psychologically identical to a state which has it. Absent qualia are not possible.

7.2.1. The Parochial Assignment of Meaning

There is one way in which this defense may not work though, and that relates to what Shoemaker (1981) calls a "parochial" assignment of meaning to mental terms. This semantic view follows from Kripke's and Putnam's discussion of natural kind terms (see also chapter 1). Roughly speaking, their idea is that the properties we common-sensically assign to referents of some terms may turn out to be merely contingent features of those objects. These characteristics are good enough to fix a referent and allow us to carry on discourse in our daily life, but the actual nature of the referent, which we would use to pick out that object counter-factually, has little or nothing to do with our common-sense property assignment. To take a standard example, we might normally describe "gold" as "the yellow substance in those rocks." However, the underlying essence of gold, that is, Au, is consistent with gold not being yellow. So being yellow is not necessary for being gold, even though it would seem otherwise given our common-sense semantic associations with gold.

Analogously, it might be the case that even though it seems that while our psychological descriptions of pain (exhaustively) capture the real nature of pain, its true referent is fixed by the physiological states which instantiate that psychological description. If "pain" actually refers to a physiological state (some pattern of neuronal firing, or some such thing), then it could be that no higher level psychological characterization is either necessary or sufficient for the occurrence of pain.

If we were to accept this *prima facie* reasonable view of mental states, then it would be possible to find some feature, namely, a physiological one, which would separate genuine qualia from ersatz states, even though the states are the same on the psychological level with respect to our cognitive economy. In this case, the first premise — if absent qualia were possible, then the qualitative character of experiences could make no difference to their causal consequences (and hence the qualitative character would be unavailable to introspection)[218] — is rendered dubious.

Shoemaker dismisses this view of semantics. He calls it a "parochial" view because assigning reference in terms of physiological states means that mental state terms would only apply locally to organisms with organically-based neural wetware (see also Block 1980a for a similar view). Any alien physiological realization of the same psychological description would not qualify for reference by these terms, thereby not being mental states.   And therein lies the rub, maintains Shoemaker.[219]

This parochial view means that (for example) silicon-based Martians would have merely ersatz pains.   We could discover this by comparing our neurophysiology with the physical realizations of their mental states and conclude that they differ in some relevant way.   However, if we could discover this fact about Martians, then presumably they could discover this same physical difference between us.   But, as Shoemaker asks, is "that they lack qualia and their pains are ersatz what *they* could conclude from discovering that they differ physically from us in some recondite way?   Why on Earth (or why on Mars) should they conclude *that?*" (1981: 594).   He concludes that "it would be preposterous to say that what we have, and what [the Martians] lack, are qualitative states" (p. 595):

> Is it plausible to suppose that the word "pain" and "qualia" in *their* language refer to states that only *we* have (or features which only our state have), and that the Martians are systematically mistaken when they claim to have what they call "pains" and "qualia?" It seems to me that this is not the slightest plausible....I think it obvious that if we mingled with the Martians, did business with them, struck up friendships with them, talked philosophy with them, and so on, we would use "pain" and the rest as if they applied univocally to them and us, and would have no inclination to give there words a parochial interpretation. (pp. 594-595)

It is far better and more natural to say that "pain" refers to a state in Martians that is causally connected in ways that make for reference. (If they were not so connected, then they would not be psychologically equivalent to us.)   But this position again entails that all pains are genuine and thus absent qualia are impossible.

7.2.2. A Scientific Assignment of Meaning

Let us leave aside the question whether the parochial view is correct. Let us just assume, as in chapter 1, that we have picked out certain aspects of qualia in our everyday descriptions of particular qualitative experiences as the important properties for identifying our sensations, and that we use those aspects as the tags for our folk psychological labels. But regardless of the way we use mental state terms in our everyday language, it may be the case that in our completed scientific theory of consciousness, the referents of mental state terms are fixed in virtue of physical properties. That is, the referents are fixed in virtue of neurophysiological mechanisms that instantiate the higher level description from psychology. Scientifically speaking, when you say, "I am in pain," it would actually mean that the neural firing patterns in your cortices are becoming entrained in a particular attractor basin (or something like that), even though the firing neurons and the attractor basin might have nothing to do with our *psychological* characterization of your utterance, "I am in pain."

What would these new scientific assignments then tell us about Shoemaker's Martians? On the one hand, if we interact with the Martians in our everyday lives, understanding them in terms of our common sense conceptual framework, then it would be legitimate and natural to assume they have qualitative experiences. On the other hand, the fact that Martians differ from us physically need not entail that they have no genuine qualia.[220] The referents of our terms for qualitative states could be a disjunctive set. Our scientific theory about how our conscious mental states arise could only give a sufficient causal history, not a necessary one, in which case, it would tell us nothing about the sufficient conditions in Martian physiology for qualia. At best then, our physiological differences would suggest that we should be agnostic about the nature of the mental states until we could conduct further empirical research.

Still, Shoemaker's argument has strong intuitive appeal. We accept that a sentient creature should be able to tell by introspection whether some of its mental states have a qualitative character. Moreover, it seems reasonable to accept further that we can determine whether an entity is sentient in virtue of the sorts of mental states it reports having and the types of mental states we posit it having. As Shoemaker remarks:

> [We should] ask whether anything could be evidence (for anyone) that someone was not in pain, given that it follows from the states he is in, plus the psychological laws that are true of him (the laws which describe the relationship of this states to one another and to input and output), that the totality of possible behavioral evidence *plus* the totality of possible introspective evidence points unambiguously to the conclusion that he [or she] is in pain? I do not see how anything could be....Here it seems that if the behavioral and introspective evidence are not enough, nothing could be enough....If we are given that a [creature's]...state is functionally identical with a state that in us is pain, it is hard to see how a physiological difference

between [it]...and us could be any evidence at all that [its]...states lack qualitative character. (1975a: 296)

Of course, this response is nothing more that an expression of a failure of imagination. Since no one has actually produced a detailed analysis of qualia either in folk-psychological terms or in scientific-psychological terms or in neurophysiological terms, then what is necessary for a true definition remains open. Our untutored intuitions cannot help us without a better conceptual framework to guide thought.

But having the referents of qualia turn out to be a disjunctive set would be fairly disconcerting. We expect our natural kind terms to be subsumable, and therefore partially definable, by some overarching general principles.[221] It seems that if we allow that qualia depend upon their physical instantiation and if what that instantiation is is not uniquely describable, then we are discounting the possibility of any overarching principles.

There are two possible responses to this difficulty. One is to bite the chauvinist's bullet and restrict the domain of scientifically defined qualia to organically based neural systems. Martians would then rely on a Martian definition of qualia, which could be similar to ours, but not identical. (Philosophers generally find this sort of response anathema, but I suspect that if we could successfully develop an exhaustive scientific analysis of human consciousness, even they would be properly impressed.)

The other line of response is to recall that theories of neural "instantiation" can still be part of the causal etiology of psychological events. Psychologists after all do rely on neurophysiological processes in their explanations. Think, for example, about the various neuropsychological pathologies one might experience. Alzheimer's disease is traced to a decrease in acetylcholine and an increase in cortical cell death. Schizophrenia is tied to abnormalities in the production of another neurotransmitter, dopamine. Autism is connected to an atrophied cerebellum. Aphasia, agraphia, alexia, hemineglect, stimuli extinction, Balint's syndrome...all are due to some cortical lesion. Indeed, one can only get psychology's binding problem from the last chapter off the ground in the first place if one knows a bit about how the brain processes visual information. Moreover, when neuroscientists wonder about how neurons process information or how neural assemblies recognize patterns or why lesioning particular lobes in the brain result in particular processing deficits, they are certainly worrying about the psychological aspects of wetware.[222] At the many points of investigation in neuroscience — membranes, cells, synapses, cell assemblies, circuits, networks, systems, and behavior — neuroscientists ask questions concerning the processes subserving some information processing capacity, as well as questions about the physical implementation of the psychological algorithm.

Not only causal relations on the (higher) psychological level, but also causal relations on the neuropsychological level — all the way down to the lowest level of biochemistry — might fall under the purview of a proper definition of some cognitive phenomenon. We can see that a scientific analysis of consciousness might include the relationships among mental states (as originally assumed) but (and perhaps more likely) it might include descriptions of the causal relations among neurophysiological components. In this case, Martians "psychologically" identical to us might not only exhibit the same behavioral and verbal patterns, and the same causal relations among mental states, but they might also have a (version of a) medial temporal lobe, a hippocampus, a limbic system, or whatever.

This sort of detailed multi-level story gives more bite to the "what else but a quale?" defense. If we incorporate neuroscience into our cognitive theories, then it does seem difficult to believe that some low-level structure which instantiates some neurophysiological algorithm is the sort of thing that would make a difference in whether Martians experience ersatz pain. That is, it seems difficult to believe that having XYZ channels instead of K^+ and Na^+ channels in a neuron's membrane is the sort of thing that qualitative experience turns on. It seems then that we would have sufficient reason to assert that Martian have mental states just like ours.

7.3. Epiphenomenalism Again

There is, to say the least, disagreement with this type of analysis. Ned Block, for example, argues that the first premise — if absent qualia were possible, then the qualitative character of any mental state would necessarily be unavailable to introspection — is at fault because qualitative character may not be a truly cognitive property after all, even though it does interact causally in very important ways in organisms who have them. His point is that ersatz pain "could be possible even though the qualitative character of genuine pain is crucial to producing the consequences that are produced *in another way* by ersatz pain" (1980a: 259, italics his). That is, it could be a *structural* property underlying our information processing, at whatever level.

The discussion sketched above is predicated on the assumption that if absent qualia were possible then qualitative epiphenomenalism for mental states as understood in cognitive science is real threat. To recapitulate: if absent qualia were possible, then we could have no introspective knowledge of our mental states. If absent qualia are possible, then the presence of the quale property could make no difference to the causal etiology for the mental states as abstracted for cognitive science. (Notice that this sort of epiphenomenalism is more restricted than the version discussed in chapter 1 and above. Here we need not assume that if absent qualia are possible, then qualitative character has no causal effects *whatsoever*. Rather, all we need to claim that it would have no effects *relevant to the accepted cognitive theory.*[223]) However, this assumption may be false. Block's point is that even though qualia may be relevant (and so not epiphenomenal) since they support the cognitive interactions for creatures who have them, this does not mean that they are relevant for all psychologically identical entities.

Consider Block's (1980a) analogy. Suppose a hydraulic computer. For this device, the "absent fluid" hypothesis may be true; that is, there may be another device process-identical to this one which lacks hydraulic fluid (because it uses electricity, say). But no one would argue that just because the absent fluid hypothesis is true, the presence of the fluid makes no difference to the operations of the hydraulic device. The hydraulic computer will have states that depend crucially on the causal properties of the fluid, even though states isomorphic to them in the electric computer would not depend crucially on hydraulic fluid. That is, the structure instantiating some processing algorithm is what allows the function to operate over its higher-level states. However, other structures with different physical properties could do exactly the same job with respect to the same processing algorithm.

Block suggests that the implicit assumption concerning an absent quale's (lack of) causal properties that drives the arguments above is wrong. These arguments will only work if, as Block suggests, absent qualia are like the colors of wire in a computer. He notes that our computers' wires are colored, but because the color makes no difference to the successful operation of the computers, they could have been some other color without making any relevant causal difference. If we could never look inside our computers, then we will never know the wires' color. He concludes that the color is thus epiphenomenal and we could have no knowledge about it. In contrast, Block does not believe that proponents of absent qualia need be committed to such a view. Instead, they could understand qualia as similar to fluid in a hydraulic computer — they are structural components crucial to the inner workings of certain creatures, but there could also be cognitively identical creatures who lack these particular components and hence lack qualia.[224]

7.4. A "Maximally Good" Cognitive Definition

The question now at issue is whether the causal differences that do exist between real pain and ersatz pain (at any level) are enough to allow us to distinguish between the two cases such that we can definitively claim that one case is real pain and the other is ersatz. Would we be able to do this? The answer has to be no.

Following Shoemaker, let us suppose that the true definition of pain is determined by a "maximally good" definition. We can develop a maximally good definition by following essentially Popper's method of conjecture and refutation. First we propose some definition of some mental state. We then look around for counter-examples to that definition. Once we find a counter-example, we refine our definition such that the example no longer contradicts our definition. And we continue this method of refinement until we can no longer improve the definition with further experimentation (either empirical or Gedanken). So a maximally good definition of some mental state is a definition such that it is not possible to formulate an alternative definition in such a way that there would be possible counter-examples to the proposed maximally good definition, but not to the alternative account, and the alternative account has no counter-examples that are not also counter-examples to the proposed definition.

The *proper* causal role of pain would then be the causal etiology that a maximally good definition assigns to pain (with respect to some physical system). This assignment would still be different from its *total* causal role, otherwise it would not be possible to have different instantiations of the same psychological definition, given psychophysical supervenience and the assumption of mechanism. Intuitively speaking, the proper causal role of pain would be what all the instantiations have in common. How could we tell real pains from ersatz pains? It could not be in terms of the proper causal role of pain, because that would be the same for each by definition. It would have to be some other causal difference, perhaps a low-level structural one.

But now suppose that we discover some property of mental states such that having that attribute entails that the state has a genuine quale and lacking that attribute entails that the state is ersatz. Having this (low-level structural) property of course would lie outside the purview of our definition. Or rather, having this property would lie outside the purview of our currently accepted definition. When confronted with this property, it seems that the natural move would be to adjust our definition to now include the newly discovered property. We should redraw the lines of causally relevant and causally irrelevant causal features so that this property is now important.

This discussion corroborates the previous suggestion that there is no principled division of labor between higher level psychological explanations and lower level neurophysiological explanations with respect to cognitive descriptions of some phenomenon. Our world, and we in it, cannot be neatly captured in two levels of description: computing algorithms and then physical implementation. Instead, the world is better explained in terms of a more complicated and interactive arrangement (Churchland 1986, Hardcastle 1992, forthcoming, Hatfield 1988, Lycan 1987). To put it more precisely, whether something counts as causally relevant depends on the type of questions asked and not upon antecedently decided boundaries for any given physical system. To be sure, the description of any physical system does determine how any phenomenon can be defined or explained. However, if the physical system does not meet the explanatory goals of the scientists who constructed it, then they should construct a different physical system. They should not declare that the problem is therefore not solvable by empirical inquiry.

To return now to our discussion of absent qualia, the discovery of an alleged low-level structural property that we could use to differentiate ersatz from real qualia would only show that our currently accepted definition is not a maximally good one and we should revise accordingly. And once we do have a maximally good definition, then there can be no property which we could use to distinguish genuine qualitative states from ersatz ones, and from this conclusion it does seem to follow that the first premise, that if absent qualia were possible, then the qualitative character of any mental state would necessarily be unavailable to introspection, must be true.

So even if we did discover that somehow, e.g., ionic transport were causally connected to whether a mental state had qualitative character, we could incorporate that fact into a multi-level cognitive theory. If our theory left no physical differences which could make a causal difference to the phenomena we are describing with respect to our physical system; that is, if we had a maximally good definition, then we would have to claim that the cognitively identical Martians feel genuine pain and that absent qualia are impossible. At least, from the perspective of science, we would have to accept that absent qualia are not possible.[225]

So insofar as we accept that we can adequately define our mental states in terms of a causal etiology, and since these theories are not restricted to any particular level of analysis or type of causal property, the defense of the impossibility of cognitively identical but qualitatively dissimilar mental states must go through. Indeed, if one is a physicalist of any stripe, then one would have to be committed to the impossibility of absent qualia. If we accept a token-token identity theory (each mental state is identical to some physical state) and the principle of supervenience, then insofar as we believe the difference between ersatz pain and real pain is a mental difference, we have to believe that they also differ physically.[226] And if they differ physically, then there has to be some difference in their respective causal powers. Since a cognitive definition is not restricted to any particular type of causal power, then whatever difference exists between ersatz pain and real pain must be capturable in a cognitive theory. So mental states psychologically identical to conscious ones, though lacking a qualitative character, cannot exist. At least, either we accept physicalism and that absent qualia are impossible, or we ascribe to some sort of dualism and assert that the qualitative character of mental states are epiphenomenal and beyond the pale of scientific theorizing.

Proponents of absent qualia are relying on an overly simple view of what counts as a psychological analysis. The level of something like belief ascription is not the only level at which one might perform a cognitive or information processing analysis. Indeed, I daresay that most cognitive theories are not at this level. All that is required for some description of a state in a physical system to be cognitive is that it be defined in terms of some physical system describing (some aspect of) cognition; what this state must ultimately look like is not specified.

So insofar as cognitive science is not restricted to a higher level of analysis such that any causal interaction could conceivably be found in a psychological description, then all empirically adequate theories of pain, or whatever conscious mental state you chose, will include whatever it is that makes that state have a qualitative character (in humans). Given the sorts of philosophical considerations presented here, we should expect a theory of conscious qualia to include several levels of description with causally connected components.[227] Indeed, the theoretical framework for explaining consciousness that I discuss above encompasses various levels of analysis, which in turn reflect different levels of organization in a single physical system. Specifying the relevant connections between the "programming algorithms" at different levels in the physical system leads us to a cognitive theory that mixes together "functions" and "structures" in a single theoretical model. It is my contention that any theory of consciousness will lead us to a computational model that looks very different from what philosophers of psychology had originally assumed. In particular, the level of beliefs and desires, and other traditional states, will not be the privileged level of analysis.[228]

In the end, what choice do we have but to assign consciousness to others in the basis of our best scientific theories? Intuitions about whether we can imagine something being conscious or not being conscious have their place, but surely they are not the best way to understand the ontology of our universe. Throwing our lot in with the materialists entails that some physical event in our brains *is* consciousness. Hence, locating that event and the proper way to abstract it tells us when others are conscious too. It really is as simple as that.

"Executive" Processing and Consciousness as Structure
Chapter Eight

In the last chapter I argued that if we take the decomposition and localization methodology of cognitive science seriously, then anything with the appropriate multi-level causal etiology has to be conscious. That is, if I am right, and if consciousness just is the appropriate dynamical patterns in cortex, then anything with these patterns over the equivalent of a cortex, would be conscious. (Notice though that I don't specify what counts as an "equivalent" of a cortex. I too am still searching for a maximally good definition.)

The perspective that I adumbrate, that conscious phenomena is aligned with the activation of memories in our SE memory system, stands in marked contrast to the approach currently in vogue in cognitive psychology. There consciousness is assumed to be aligned with some sort of supervisory system or executive processor that presumably takes the activated interpretations of our various memory systems and then manipulates them in some fashion so as to influence behavior. The most striking difference between these two approaches is that they assume that consciousness resides at different places in our psychological economies; the memory framework advocates that consciousness exists prior to what the "executive" theories postulate. In particular, a theory based on the framework of the previous chapters entails that conscious phenomena are components over which the executive or supervisory system operates. That is, I hypothesize that conscious phenomena themselves are one type of input to cognitive psychology's executive processors; these processors then compute over the inputted conscious mental states.[229]

This chapter is devoted to comparing my memory system framework with the popular executive theories of consciousness of contemporary psychology as a way of making more practical the arguments of the last chapter. Relying on a multi-level causal etiology is not only important for philosophical reasons, for it also impacts how to evaluate other theories of consciousness. Here, I address what the data from various levels of analysis tell us about consciousness as an executive processor and how we should use these data in constructing and supporting theories of consciousness.

Two conclusions will emerge from the following discussion. First, the phenomena of consciousness probably do not occur as a process at the higher (psychologically described) levels of cognition. If this be the case, then executive theories of consciousness will always miss their mark. Second, we should restrict the sorts of questions we ask about conscious phenomena until we know exactly when and of what we are aware. In particular, we should not focus upon the goals of conscious processing (as executive theorists are prone to do), nor upon the role consciousness plays in human cognition *tout court,* until we can better predict and localize the phenomena themselves.

8.1. An Outline of the "Executive" Theories

There are several respects in which the picture of the mind that executive theories assume agrees with the picture the memory system framework adumbrates. Generally speaking, both agree that perceptual input automatically activates relevant schemas for learned behavior from an ST memory system. These cognitive schemas are abstract representations of current and expected environmental regularities. They guide our perceptions, our interpretations of those perceptions, and the behavior resulting from our interpretations. These schemas are activated from any number of different sources in parallel and potential competition among them is resolved by a "winner take all" strategy. The schemas which are most active win, and their competitors are shut down through lateral inhibition.[230]

Beyond this rough sketch though, differences soon become readily apparent. The executive theories suggest that such brute force strategies cannot always work in choosing the "appropriate" behavior. One could be in a novel situation or the competition among schemas could be deadlocked. We need a second system that can act as a trouble-shooter when the first strategy somehow breaks down. In these cases, the specialized ST processors "require a 'central information exchange' in order to interact with each other" (Baars 1985: 41) and a supervisory system, analogous to an operating system, steps in and modulates the activity level of the schemas. This "additional system...provides one source of control upon the selection of schemas, [by operating]...entirely through the application of extra activation and inhibition to schemas in order to bias their selection" (Norman and Shallice 1988: 7).

Consciousness is then identified with or depends on some aspect of the operation of this second supervisory system.[231] Current theories in psychology are more sophisticated versions of earlier models that just identified consciousness with STS, then thought to be a central processing and decision-making system — the mental equivalent of a computer CPU (Atkinson and Shiffrin 1968, Dennett 1978a, Posner and Klein 1973). Contemporary theories now envision consciousness as a central information broadcasting station (though what that "station" actually comes to differs across the theorists), and they maintain that consciousness serves a definite and important processing function: consciousness is activated whenever we need to solve a comparatively difficult cognitive problem. In these theories, consciousness is a process that our minds use in special situations in which applying an action schema without some sort of control would probably lead to error. For example, we would most likely use conscious processes when acquiring new knowledge, making choices, or exercising judgments.

Executive theories then understand conscious contents as "a special operation mode of a global data base, namely one in which there is a stable and coherent global representation that *provides* information to the nervous system as a whole" (Baars 1985: 42, italics mine). These global representations — our conscious states — are created from preconscious structures (from ST memory presumably) in response to the immediate cognitive processing needs. As do I, cognitive psychologists think of the resulting qualitative experience as our mind's attempt to make sense out of as much data as possible, given the intentions of the individual and the demands of the environment.

According to these models, we are conscious only of "experiences" that we *construct* out of previously activated schemas from various modules; George Mandler writes: "Consciousness is a constructivist process in which the phenomenal experience is a specific construction to which previously activated schemata have contributed" (1988: 35-36). However, we are not conscious of the actual constituents of any of the activated schema in any individual modules. Borrowing heavily from the computer metaphor, Phillip Johnson-Laird explains that the "contents of consciousness are the current values of parameters governing the higher-level computations of the operation system, [which] can receive such values from other processors, but...cannot inspect the internal operations of these processors" (1983: 465).

Finally, these conscious states (the global representations) do not control behavior directly because mechanisms in the individual modules actually select the behavioral responses of the organism. Instead, the conscious state indirectly controls action by setting some of the parameters modules use in choosing a behavior.[232] In bringing together two or more previously unconscious mental outputs, consciousness redistributes schema activations in modules so that the revised values now determine motor output. That way "consciousness controls only activation and inhibition values, not selection itself" (Norman and Shallice 1988: 7). We can think of conscious representations then as merely "[triggering] adaptation in the system as a whole" (Baars 1985: 49).

Executive theories then tie consciousness to a centralized mechanism within long-term store that is designed to adjudicate conflicting bits of information, as well as to process new or surprising information. This informational "depot" services different modular processors by producing a coherent representation of some aspect of the environment which each of the relevant specialized modules can then use to help process whatever data currently occupies the modules. As a central "decision-maker," it indirectly controls behavior by influencing the processes within other specialized modules. In sum, the executive theories maintain that consciousness is an information process (as defined by cognitive psychology) and serves a definite and well-defined goal. Below I question both of these *prima facie* reasonable positions.

8.2   The Neurophysiological Evidence

The basic form of the neurophysiological argument that cognitive psychologists use to support their theories of consciousness is as follows:

(P1) Consciousness is a processing unit U which has attributes $A_1..., A_n$.
(P2) The neurophysiological structure S demonstrates processing
          attributes $A_1..., A_n$.

(C1) S is the neural equivalent of U.
(C2) Consciousness just is S.

The goal of these arguments is to elucidate the underlying neurophysiology of conscious processes. In particular, they attempt to support the information processing account of how mental states are manipulated consciously by using neurophysiological data to describe and predict the appearance of consciousness.[233] In what follows, though, I show that even if cognitive psychologists can use neurophysiological evidence to support and extend their theory by supporting C1, they still fail to demonstrate C2 and so fail to develop a meaningful connection between consciousness and some part of the brain.

8.2.1. The Frontal Lobe as an Executive Processor

As outlined above, information processing theories of consciousness postulate two types of schema selection in a cognitive system: automatic and controlled, with consciousness being aligned with the second.[234] Donald Norman and Tim Shallice argue that "possibly the strongest evidence for the existence of both levels comes from neuropsychology" (1988: 8) and that the processing functions they have assigned to consciousness correspond to the processing functions neuroscientists have assigned to the prefrontal region of the brain. Hence, they conclude, the prefrontal lobe is the structure underlying conscious processing and neuropsychological and neurophysiological evidence concerning the prefrontal lobe helps to support a psychological information processing theory of consciousness.

Norman and Shallice discuss two points of convergence between their psychological theory of consciousness and neuroscientific data: predictions of behavior based on impaired or absent conscious processing (on a lesioned or oblated prefrontal lobe), and predictions of the processing prerequisites for consciousness (the functional connections the prefrontal lobe has with other processing centers in the brain). They claim that, in both instances, the properties of consciousness are the same as those of the prefrontal cortex.

What sort of behavior would we expect to find if one had an impaired conscious supervisory system? Cognitive skills that have been well learned do not need the supervisory system to become activated; rather higher level control only becomes necessary in novel situations, in correcting errors, and in planning. In these cases, because essentially only automatic control would be left, the organism would have no way to decide upon one schema if several schema were "tied" in their activation values, nor could it prevent one strongly activated schema from controlling behavior. Hence, with an impaired supervisory system, we should see impairments in tasks that require constant monitoring or advance planning. Norman and Shallice conclude that the organism should either show increased distractibility (poor or no planning) or increased perseveration (poor or no error correction), depending upon the schemas activated. If only one schema were activated, then the organism should act upon that schema, regardless of any environmental contraindications. If more than one schema were activated, then the organism would be confused and unable to settle upon one interpretation or pattern of response.

Interestingly enough, both sorts of response patterns are observed in patients with various parts of their prefrontal lobes oblated, though they lurk under an array of behavioral deficits. As Patricia Goldman-Rakic (1987) notes, damage to significant portions of human prefrontal cortex results in disturbances of attention, in synthetic reasoning and planning, in being able to regulate behavior through verbal instruction or through manipulating past experience, in initiative, restraint, affect, and personality. Patients are also impaired in tasks which require that they remember the recency or order of their previous responses, that they decompose their ultimate goal into subgoals which must be sought in a certain order, or that they generate new responses.

One prominent feature of the frontal lobe syndrome is appearing trapped by immediate environmental contingencies. Patients appear to be unable to pay attention to some particular task at hand for any length of time; instead, irrelevant stimuli constantly distract them. Objects or events in their immediate surroundings cue their behavior; stated goals or plans do not. For example, in tasks requiring monkeys to remember where a food reward is hidden over some distractions (similar to the Piagetian AB task), prefrontal monkeys cannot chose the correct location of the hidden food. Rather, the external stimuli controls their behavior: they chose the first item they see. Bartus and Levere's description of these monkeys as "animals of the moment" (1977) is quite apt. In addition, these monkeys perseverate, just as infants and amnesics do. If they have been rewarded for choosing a particular food well, then they will continue to chose the same food well, even though food is now clearly placed in a different well.[235]

Goldman-Rakic argues that being easily distracted and persevering in previously rewarded behaviors are symptoms of a single "more basic" defect in mnemonic processing (1987: 379). She suggests that the frontal lobe accesses and picks events in "representational memory" which it then uses to guide behavior, irrespective of immediate environmental cues. Hence, the prefrontal cortex is necessary for more than automatic, externally-driven control of response. "The integrity of the prefrontal cortex...may be necessary to override the tendency to behave strictly from reinforcement contingencies or to reflexively respond on the basis of stimulation present at the moment of response" (p. 379).

At first glance, this account dovetails nicely with information processing theories which claim that the supervisory mechanism can access and pick schemas from long-term store, which it then uses to help guide behavior, irrespective of other activated schemas. It also fits well with the data concerning the underdeveloped prefrontal cortices in young infants, for in these infants automatic behavioral patterns predominate. (Notice that according to executive processing theories of consciousness which identify phenomenal experiences with the processes of the prefrontal cortex, infants are not conscious either.[236])

However, Goldman-Rakic's interpretation of the data is not uncontroversial. Joaquin Fuster argues that frontal lobe syndrome reflects the patients' inability to integrate temporally discontiguous items of information. The prefrontal cortex then would be engaged crucially in the "temporal structuring of behavior" (1980: 144); it would "[synthesize] cognitive and motor [schemas]... into purposive sequences" (p. 144). As part of its integrative task, it would suppress or gate irrelevant environmental cues and override competing schemas. *Prima facie*, this interpretation also fits nicely with the theories which assert that consciousness helps in devising responses to novel situations.[237]

Nevertheless, regardless which accepted interpretation ends up being correct, cognitive psychology is still in solid position because both interpretations coincide with, and hence support, cognitive psychology's explanation of consciousness.[238] Of course, cognitive psychologists are not in a position to adjudicate the disputed interpretations (nor can they simply pick the description that best suits their goals[239]). Still, they can use the extensive data about which neuroscientists do agree to support and extend their computational theories[240] — neuroscientists do not contest descriptions of the phenomena involved in the frontal lobe syndrome; they agree among themselves what the results of the testing *are*; they just disagree over what the results *mean*.

We could think of the test results in conjunction with a description of the tests themselves as a way to define the capacities of an executive processing system operationally; as such, it would a decomposition of Goldman-Rakic's and Fuster's neurophysiological descriptions. That cognitive psychologists have some way of describing the behavioral and cognitive processes which the frontal lobe affects is all they need to be able to use neurophysiological data. Executive theories of consciousness try to list the processing attributes of consciousness; whether these attributes can be subsumed under one label is really beside the point. Granted, an unwieldy list of operationally defined capacities is not as nice as a predictive general description, but it is better than any available purely psychological description, and it is all cognitive psychologists would need to help support their theory of consciousness.

A second sort of correspondence between the executive theory and neuroscience concerns the processing prerequisites for carrying out the duties of the supervisory system. Norman and Shallice list some of the types of information the system would need access to in order to fulfill its functions: it would require at least "representations of past and present state of the environment, of goals and intentions, and of the repertoire of high-level schemas it could activate" (1988: 14). Both Goldman-Rakic and Fuster argue that the prefrontal system accesses just that sort of information. Knowing the connections the prefrontal cortex has with the rest of the brain and the function of those connections would give us one indication of how the frontal lobes should behave as a whole.

Three sorts of connections are relevant for cognitive psychology: connections with the parietal cortex, which process current perceptual stimuli; with the hippocampal system, which is related to long term store; and with the motor areas, which, of course, are responsible for behavioral responses.[241] (See Figure 8.1.) The posterior parietal cortex sends topographically organized inputs to two-thirds of the principal sulcus in the prefrontal lobe, whose organization is probably continued in the frontal lobe itself. Moreover, the hypothesized topographical units in the frontal lobes feed back to the parietal cortex both within and between hemispheres. Goldman-Rakic suggests that this reciprocal circuitry "provides a regulatory mechanism for selecting, adjusting, and maintaining a flow of relevant information from the parietal to the prefrontal cortex" (1988: 388). The prefrontal cortex then helps regulate the flood of sensory information processed in the parietal cortex. Neurophysiological data suggest that, via connections with parietal cortex, the frontal lobe may pick appropriate information out of the mass of incoming data, and this choice presumably helps determine behavioral response by altering how sensorimotor integration proceeds in the parietal cortex. Thus the prefrontal cortex influences the parietal cortex such that the prefrontal cortex also influences an organism's choice of behavior.

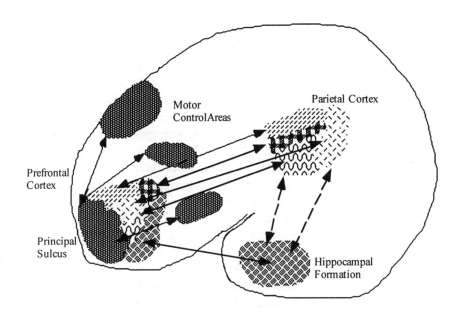

Figure 8.1.   Frontal Lobe Connections.   This brain schematic illustrates the following reciprocal relations: (1)   topographical connections between parietal and prefrontal cortex, which may be important for gating incoming information; (2)   prefrontal connections to the hippocampal areas, which is used in creating long term memories; and (3)   principal sulcus connections to the major motor control areas, which might be used in executing appropriate behavior.

The prefrontal cortex is also directly and indirectly connected to the hippocampal formation, a part of the brain affiliated with LTS.[242] Whereas the parietal-prefrontal circuits are probably used to access and hold relevant information "on line," the prefrontal-hippocampus circuits are probably used for tracking the context in which this information is used so that if similar circumstances ever arose again, the contextual information could be retrieved. In other words, the prefrontal-hippocampal circuits are related to accessing appropriate schemas stored in long-term memory.

But once irrelevant information is gated and relevant data are processed, the prefrontal cortex also needs to be able to act upon its decisions. The principal sulcus has good connections with the basal ganglia, tectum, and premotor cortex; hence, the prefrontal cortex is in a prime position to issue or regulate motor commands. Although probably not able to generate motor responses directly, the principal sulcus may nonetheless initiate, facilitate, or cancel commands to the structures which compute and execute motor behavior.

However, different areas of the prefrontal cortex do have different connection patterns. For example, the orbital prefrontal cortex is primarily connected with the medial thalamus, hypothalamus, ventrolateral caudate, and amygdala, while the dorsolateral prefrontal cortex is primarily connected with the lateral thalamus, anterodorsal caudate, hippocampus, and neocortex.[243] Moreover, the orbital areas mature faster than the dorsolateral areas, indicating a different developmental path and possibly a different genetic origin (Nonneman et al. 1984). Neurophysiological data also suggest that the orbital areas have access to a different knowledge base than that of the dorsolateral regions, e.g., interoceptive versus olfactory stimuli. We are getting hints that the prefrontal cortex may not just be one unified system with a single purpose; rather, its topography and developmental history imply that it is several independent processing systems lumped together.

The divisions do not seem to be limited to just dual processing structures either. Rather, neuroscientists consider the prefrontal cortex to be highly differentiated with many anatomical and functional subdivisions. For example, electrophysiological data show that "the inferior prefrontal convexity [below the principal sulcus] appears to be specialized for *visual feature* processing as the caudal principal sulcus is for *visuospatial* processing" (Goldman-Rakic 1987: 401, italics mine). The story about exactly what the function is of each sub-area is complicated by the fact that lesions in each of the sub-areas lead to similar patterns of deficits. Patients with any sort of frontal lobe lesion have difficulty focusing attention, controlling their behavior, and recalling previous events. So, we cannot yet precisely specify the actual purpose of each sub-area, even though we know the modality of information processed differs. Still, we may conclude that not only are there different interpretations of what the prefrontal cortex does as a whole, there may also be different processes carried out within the different areas of the frontal lobes.

Nevertheless, even though there are anatomical structural differences in the frontal cortex, and the corresponding processing functions splinter, cognitive psychologists can still use these data to support their psychological theories of consciousness. Cognitive psychologists are generally concerned with a broader description of processing phenomena than are neuroscientists, and as long as the many different processors of the prefrontal cortex are nothing but a decomposition of the larger processing unit U — regardless of how the lower level functions are eventually defined (if at all) — then cognitive psychologists are safe in using the neurophysiological evidence to support the existence of U in humans (and primates). How the higher level description is decomposed and analyzed in the lower level is not entirely relevant to the explanatory goals of the higher level theory; that it can be decomposed *somehow* is all that is needed.

8.2.2. The Relationship Between Consciousness and U

Let us grant that neuropsychological and neurophysiological data concerning lesions in and the connectivity of the prefrontal cortex do support the existence of the supervisory system U in psychology. That is, the data support (C1), that S is the neural equivalent of U. Can we now conclude that the data also support (C2), that consciousness just is S, and the concomitant theory of consciousness? The answer must be no, for there are problems with the first premise and identifying the processing attributes of consciousness. Remember, executive theories align the phenomena of consciousness with a particular type of executive processing system. Therein, I maintain, lies the rub. Neuropsychological and neurophysiological data may support the existence of a particular psychological processing system, but they also establish that this system is divorced from phenomenal experience.

Over one hundred years ago, scientists observed the somewhat contradictory effects of a prefrontal lesion: *cognitive processes deteriorate while sensory experiences remain the same.* For example, Ferrier wrote in 1886:

> An animal deprived of its frontal lobes retains all its powers of voluntary motion unimpaired and that it continues to see, hear, smell and taste and to perceive and localize tactile impressions as before....And yet, the facts seem to warrant the conclusion that...[the animals] generally appeared to have lost the faculty of intelligent and attentive observation. (pp. 231-232)

Today we know that monkeys with lesions in the (orbital) prefrontal cortex can perform normally on a wide variety of tests, including visual-pattern discrimination problems, object learning sets, object discrimination reversal, object alternation, matching to sample, and cross-modal matching.[244] This list provides powerful evidence that the impairments they do have are not caused by sensory problems, motor problems, task difficulty, or memory loss. And just as with monkeys, none of the deficits found in human frontal lobe patients are purely sensory either; they too can easily discriminate the spatial arrangement of stimuli. Instead, as discussed above, the problem appears to lie with the ability to *manipulate* the internal schemas in some fashion. As Fuster writes, the "deficit...is supramodal, largely related to task formalities, and not the nature of the *discriminanda*" (1980: 72). In fact, as Eslinger and Damasio (1985) point out, patients can even lose their entire frontal lobe and still be conscious.

The neuropsychological and the neurophysiological evidence suggest that wherever consciousness as a whole lies, it is not within the prefrontal cortex. For this reason, we must conclude that whatever properties consciousness has cannot be captured in the higher level psychological description of the function of the prefrontal supervisory system. Hence, (P1) appears false, and the neuropsychological and the neurophysiological data fail to support the psychological explanation of consciousness (though it does support (C1)).

Notice though that the memory system framework I support remains unaffected by this discussion. Since I do not align consciousness with any sort of supervisory processor, that these processors are not conscious can only count in my favor. Moreover, my framework also explains why cognitive psychologists might assume that executive processes are relevant to explaining consciousness. If conscious phenomena formed a subset of the components that the executive system manipulates, then that fact would account for the obvious close alliance between conscious states and our more sophisticated cognitive decisions. But aside from explaining away cognitive psychology's mistaken vision, the structure and the function of the frontal lobe system are orthogonal to consciousness.

8.2.3. Consciousness as a Global Broadcaster

On the other hand, it is also still possible that the frontal lobe and the executive processor form only *one component of* conscious processing. That is, the psychological description of the frontal lobe would be but a description of some component within conscious processing. In this case, oblating the frontal lobe would not mean that consciousness *per se* would be lost, but only that aspects of processing relevant to a complete conscious percept would be missing.

Clearly, a difficulty in trying to develop theories of consciousness today is that we do not have a clear notion of what the proper location for analysis and description are. At least, though, we know that it is not at the executive system *qua* frontal lobe. In this section, I examine whether consciousness can be found at a different level of organization in which the frontal lobe is but one component of a larger processing system. I shall conclude, however, that investigating conscious phenomena at this location is not the correct path to take either.

It is possible that the prefrontal cortex could underlie only part of the supervisory system U, a part which does exhibit attributes $A_1,..., A_n$, but which fails to exhibit the phenomena of consciousness. In this way, U could be a processing system that encompasses both the frontal lobe and some other system that together have $A_1,..., A_n$ and are conscious. Bernard Baars and James Newman (1988, 1994) explore that possibility.[245] They accept that the prefrontal cortex forms (part of) the supervisory system, but they also argue that this area is only a portion of the story behind consciousness. They take the lessons outlined above seriously and try to define a neural instantiation for the entirety of their information processing theory of consciousness.

Baars and Newman grant that the prefrontal cortex, via its connections with the nucleus reticularis of the thalamus, acts as the "supervisory" system by focusing "attention upon highly relevant stimuli, not just in terms of immediate perception and needs..., but [also in terms of] purposes and plans...over time" (1988: 52). However, they are more interested in the "broadcasting" capabilities of the centralized processing system, *viz.*, the ability of the processor to forward its supervisory decisions to the relevant specialized modules, for they believe that we derive our phenomenal experience out of the information that is sent globally throughout the brain.

They argue that there are two components to this broadcasting system: what they call the "reticular formation," which includes the nucleus reticularis, and the intralaminar nuclei, both of which are part of the diffuse projection system of the thalamus. (See Figure 8.2.) They hypothesize that the reticular formation acts as an attentional filter for inputs converging on the thalamus from all over the brain. This forms the first step in the broadcasting portion of their executive theory. The intralaminar nuclei then take the highly processed multimodal inputs from the nucleus reticularis (NR) and the reticular formation and forward them to widespread areas of the cortex. The nucleus reticularis forms an outer shell over most of the thalamus and so most of the projections running between the cortex and the thalamus must pass through the nucleus. These fibers give off collaterals to cells in the NR itself (Scheibel 1980). Apparently the NR functions as a set of gates which can regulate information through the sensory relay nuclei of the thalamus by selective inhibition. Each gate of the NR is tied to some specific receptive zone, with each zone being under the influence of specific sensory input and its integrated feedback from sensorimotor cortex; the mesencephalic reticular core, with its general and fairly primitive concern for danger; and the prefrontal-medial thalamic system, which is connected to the higher level strategies of the organism (Scheibel 1980, Skinner and Yingling 1972). These connections entail that the NR is a structure centrally involved in regulating selective attention, and so, (as Baars and Newman argue) it must also be centrally involved in regulating input to the centralized processor. This system determines "which of the thousands of messages generated by the specialized processors gain access to consciousness" (Baars and Newman 1988: 47). That is, it helps determine the contents of consciousness.

Information about the broadcasting structure of Baars and Newman's theory is much more limited than the information we have about the nucleus reticularis. Nonetheless, Baars and Newman argue that what we do know about the intralaminar nuclei and the diffuse projection systems of the thalamus make them ideal candidates for the broadcasting position. Generally speaking, these areas receive a greater diversity of inputs than any other region of the brain and they show no well-delineated sensory or motor function; rather, they have more generalized effects upon neural activity in portions of the nervous system. In particular, the intralaminar nuclei send polysensory projections to most of the "association areas" of cortex. Activation of these projections appear to be largely independent of current sensory input (Jones 1985). Baars and Newman hypothesize that the intralaminar nuclei send contentful information that they have received from diverse areas of the brain back to the cortex and its parallel processing modules so that they can complete their processing tasks. Through this relay, the intralaminar nuclei and the messages they broadcast help determine the phenomenal "feel" of consciousness.

Moreover, anatomical and physiological evidence suggest a close connection between the nucleus reticularis and the intralaminar nuclei. For example, if we stimulate the NR, we get activity in the cortex, even though the NR itself has no projections there (Scheibel and Scheibel 1967). Baars and Newman argue that the effects may well be transmitted via the intralaminar nuclei. Hence, they conclude:

> the selective qualities of consciousness result from competition for access to the neural...["workspace"], as mediated through the converging influences of the midbrain reticular formation, posterior cortex, and prefrontal cortex

upon the nucleus reticularis of the thalamus. Widespread activation follows from the broadcasting of whichever processor (or group of processors) gains access to the...["workspace"]. Broadcasting is mediated through the...intralaminar nuclei of the thalamus which send diffuse projections upon the cortex. (1988: 61)

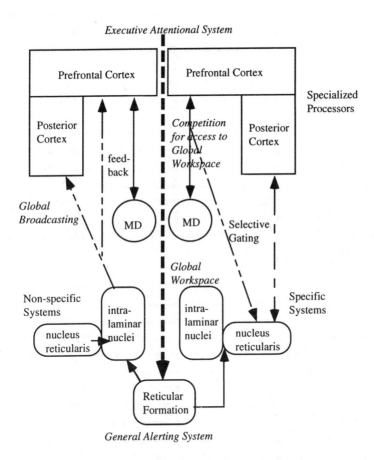

Executive Attentional System

General Alerting System

Figure 8.2. Possible Neuronal Configuration for a Global Broadcasting System. A combined cognitive-neural model of Baars and Newman's Global Workspace system. The cortex forms an arch above the thalamus. The midbrain reticular formation is the general alerting system, receiving input from the perceptual systems in posterior cortex. The entire system is under executive control from the executive attentional system, which is correlated with the prefrontal cortex-nucleus reticularis circuit (based on Baars and Newman 1988).

So then, if Baars and Newman are correct, the prefrontal cortex would be only part of a larger processing mechanism that supports conscious phenomena. Descriptions of frontal lobe's function would actually be descriptions of a particular component within the more complicated processing interactions that comprise consciousness. Conscious phenomena are hypothesized then to exist at a higher level of organization than particular brain areas. To be conscious would require the interaction of several brain systems (including the SE system), each with its own function, and each acting as a component in the higher level process.

8.2.4. Difficulties With Higher Level Theories of Consciousness

However, Baars and Newman's hypothesis is not without difficulties. The problems are two-fold. First, there are other brain systems that appear have the same processing attributes as those of the nucleus reticularis and the intralaminar nuclei. If this be the case, then Baars and Newman may have not outlined the neural structures necessary for the executive theory.[246] Second, and more important for our purposes, the qualitative "feel" of consciousness seems to occur independently of the inputs from the intralaminar nuclei *qua* broadcaster. Baars and Newman probably have not outlined the structures sufficient for consciousness either.

The first difficulty with Baars and Newman's attempt at supporting an information processing view of consciousness is that it is simply not the case that the properties of the intralaminar nuclei outlined above are unique for that system. For example, the noradrenergic neurons of the nucleus locus ceruleus (LC) have as widespread, if not wider-spread, connections as the intralaminar nuclei of the thalamus. The LC projects to the neocortex, hippocampus, amygdala, olfactory bulb, thalamus, hypothalamus, various nuclei of the midbrain, and the spinal cord. Moreover, evidence concerning the afferent inputs clearly suggest that the LC is not merely a relay nucleus for primary sensory or motor information. Neurons in these nuclei are activated relative to internal and external sensory stimuli and the affective state. The bottom line appears to be that the locus ceruleus becomes active during alerting or arousal and then acts to enhance the selectivity or vigor of its target neurons (Foote 1985, Foote *et al.* 1983), just as the intralaminar nuclei are supposed to. The other monoamine systems have similar effects as well. They all appear to be tied to the specific enhancement or impairment of activity in certain stages of information processing, and exactly how they behave depends upon the current physiological state of the target neuron (Foote 1985).[247]

Exactly how to sort out these data is not clear, for too little is known about the synaptic relationships and the properties of the neurotransmitters of the thalamic diffuse projection systems to draw any specific conclusions about that system (Sapir 1987). We do know that the diffuse projections from the intralaminar nuclei to layer VI in the cortex may be important in maintaining a state of cortical arousal (Hyarinen *et al.* 1980). However, this hypothesis remains to be conclusively tested; it is also possible that other sources of diffuse projections from the basal forebrain, the hypothalamus, or the brain stem may underlie the cortical arousal observed. For example, cortical responsiveness can be facilitated independent of thalamic facilitation, and midbrain reticular facilitation enhances cortical response even after the thalamic relay nuclei are destroyed.[248]

Finally, we cannot be sure that the intralaminar nuclei are involved in any sort of contentful global broadcasting. As first shown by Evarts in the 1960's, the increased responsiveness of the cortical neurons during arousal really amounts to the ratio of evoked to spontaneous activity becoming greater. That is, the ascending brain stem systems (especially the locus ceruleus), as well as the intralaminar nuclei, may work simply to increase the signal-to-noise ratio of the neurons firing in the various cortices. The nuclei themselves may not carry any particular semantic information at all, as Baars and Newman assert; aside from maintaining a minimal level of arousal, they simply may help the cortices to be more efficient at their duties than otherwise possible. The bottom line is the data are not yet available to support Baars and Newman's particular theory.

The second difficulty concerning Baars and Newman's hypotheses comes from data concerning disorders with consciousness. We see one such example in simultanagnosia, a difficulty in sustaining visual attention such that stationary objects in the visual field seem to "disappear" from view. Patients with this disorder have only a fragmentary perception of their visual environment. This disappearance of visual objects does not result from interference from other ongoing cognitive functions, such as listening, hearing, speaking, performing motor tasks, or mentally solving problems. Moreover, there is no evidence that there is any impairment of arousal, alertness, or cognition; the patients can still shift their gaze accurately and voluntarily, despite the intermittent loss of visual awareness.

What we are seeing here is a fairly clear dissociation between cognitive processes such as arousal, attention, performing motor tasks, problem solving, and cognitive control, on the one hand, and conscious experience, on the other. Further, the anatomy of the disorder supports this division. Bilateral lesions of the superior visual association cortex in the occipital lobes are correlated with simultanagnosia; the projection systems are not involved in any way. (See Figure 8.3.) Even if we grant for the moment that the diffuse projection systems of the thalamus help in cognitive processing by linking together specialized modules, we have no reason to believe that this centralized information exchange is in any way connected to the actual qualitative experience.

Other dissociations associated with the cortices also support a general dissociation between cognition and consciousness.[249] Bilateral lesions in the ventral and mesial portions of the occipitotemporal visual areas are associated with visual object agnosia, a condition in which patients are unable to recognize the class to which an object belongs. (See Figure 8.3.) This again appears to be a purely perceptual deficit, since these patients can recognize the objects through other modalities. Severe bilateral damage to the visual association cortices and the optic radiations can lead to Anton's syndrome. In these cases, the patients are in fact blind, but they insist that they can see perfectly well. Finally, focal damage of the visual association cortex or its subjacent white matter causes the central achromatopsias, a set of color perception disorders in which perception of visual form is preserved.[250] It seems that the neurophysiological structures that Baars and Newman take as an instantiation of the information processing theory may be neither necessary nor sufficient for conscious qualitative experience.[251]

We must conclude that evidence for Baars and Newman's hypothesis is inconclusive at best. We cannot assign an exact function to the intralaminar nuclei and it appears that other diffuse projection systems operate using similar "algorithms." At least, we have no principled way to distinguish them functionally; so far we only have differences in structure (e.g., projection targets) which tell us little about the corresponding function.

Moreover, even if the function Baars and Newman assign to the nucleus reticularis and the reticular formation were correct, such cognitive processing is divorced from actual experiences of consciousness, as seen in some lesion patients. The disassociation between qualitative experience and the larger executive processing system, as well as most cognitive functions, suggests that this is not the appropriate place to search for consciousness. If correct, this can only mean that consciousness is part of the decomposition of the more general description.

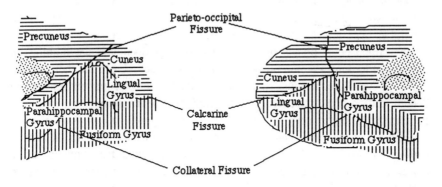

Figure 8.3.   Mesial View of Visual Areas.   Patients with visual agnosia (including prosopagnosia) have lesions in bilateral structures of the occipitotemporal region (vertical hatching), comprising the lingual, fusiform, and parahippocampal gyri.   Patients with simultagnosia have bilateral lesions in the occipitoparietal region (horizontal hatching), which is composed of the cuneus and precuneus.   Unilateral lesions of either occipitotemporal region can produce visual defects (contralaterally) and hemichromatopsia (also contralaterally). Unilateral lesions of the left occipitotemporal region often produce the syndrome of pure alexia (based on Damasio 1987).

In addition, these lesion data provide some support for the multiple memory system view by dovetailing with the hypothesis that consciousness is located in diverse areas of cortex. If these systems were located in part in posterior cortex, as chapter 4 argued, then damage to this area would affect aspects of our mnemonic interpretations.   And if conscious states just are the active interpretations of SE memory, then we would expect that were this system degraded, aspects of the qualitative experiences would be lost.   The sort of clinical evidence discussed above helps better to localize the areas of the brain responsible for our semantic interpretations of incoming perceptual stimuli and for our phenomenological "feels."

8.3   Consciousness as a Decomposition

I conclude that cognitive psychologists who advocate executive theories of consciousness are guilty of assuming that consciousness operates at a more general level of description of our cognitive processes. It could be the case that all the supposed attributes of consciousness they document are nothing but artifacts of looking at consciousness in the wrong place. From the more general point of view, conscious states may actually be part of the underlying decomposition of our psychological descriptions of our information processing. Psychology's supervisory system would be orthogonal to the phenomena of consciousness entirely because it is described in a physical system that cannot capture the processes of consciousness (i.e., the particular activations in parietal cortex). A conscious percept may be a component over which a supervisory system, and other systems of the brain, operate. The cognitive psychologists' basic mistake is to assume that consciousness is identical to some box or other in a psychological model of information processing in the first place. Such unilevel models abstract over the more complex descriptions of the component pieces that may form the true explanatory bases for mental activity. From psychology's perspective of the mind, consciousness may therefore always drop out of the picture.

I take the moral of psychology's pseudo-reductive failures to be that if we want to refine our psychological theories further or if we wish to connect them ultimately to neuroscience, we would do well to divorce the phenomena of experience from theories concerning supervisory systems. We need to do a better job of predicting the occurrence of qualitative experience and localizing it in the brain before we can begin to construct hypotheses about the *purposes* behind the experiences. We really don't know enough neuroscience to attempt this sort of explicit reduction of conscious experience or to rely on neurophysiological data to justify the higher level computational theories of cognition. The lesson here is that instead of fairly sweeping executive theories, one should pursue a theory of consciousness that tries to locate consciousness in the brain and to outline the processes of that particular spot (or the relevant interconnected circuits) before attempting to explain how those functions fit into our information processing picture of the mind.

As in the last chapter, I advocate looking more closely at multi-level descriptions as a way of overcoming difficulties (intuitive or otherwise); in this case, we should define a multi-level physical system in order to understand consciousness as but a component piece with respect to higher level information processing models of cognition. Methodologically, this approach means that instead of just looking for the higher level information transformations that are necessary or sufficient for consciousness, we should be focusing on what we are conscious *of* — both the kinds of representations we can perceive consciously and the sorts of neural activity underlying those representations — and how the psychological and neurophysiological structure of conscious events differs from those of unconscious events.[252]   We could then be free to tie consciousness to certain types of lower level functional components or neuronal structures, instead of being confined to the more general input-output processing functions of cognitive psychology. A theory thus responsive to neuroscientific and psychological data would be more "bottom-up" than "top-down" — perhaps to the detriment of the grandeur of the story, but certainly not to its testability.

The Moment of Consciousness
Chapter Nine

I have been circling around an apparent dilemma in explaining consciousness in the last few chapters: If we view the mind as serious materialists then consciousness as appreciated intuitively seems to disappear. Nothing in any physical system appears to be either necessary or sufficient for our rich conscious experiences. How can we develop a scientific theory of consciousness if we can't develop of plausible third person account of it? We seem forced to the conclusion that the phenomena of consciousness has no place in materialist theories of the mind. But, as I have maintained throughout, the solution to this difficulty is to realize that our commitment to materialism is more fundamental than any intuitions we have about what conscious experience is or is like. Once we do that, then all we need to is search for things in the mind/brain that differentiate conscious events from unconscious ones.

To that end, I constructed a framework for locating consciousness using detailed converging evidence for multiple memory systems. To review: I conjectured that the hippocampus and surrounding areas are responsible for laying down unitized memories into a long-term SE store which are later explicitly accessible in something resembling declarative form. The memories themselves reside in distributed but perhaps modularized form throughout neocortex. Of course, manipulating these memories (or any original percepts) in some fashion — including simply rehearsing them — requires processing mechanisms outside the neocortex. (For example, in normal adults, executive control over the memories resides in the frontal lobe-parietal cortex-limbic system circuit.) However, all that need be active to have some conscious perception, either as an original (interpreted) experience or as a memory, are the relevant neocortical areas. Exactly what that conscious percept is depends upon the interpretation we give incoming stimuli, and that depends upon the stimulus itself, priming from the ST system, and previous activity in SE memory.

Philosophers may lament, but this sort of narrow explanatory strategy is needed before we can begin to paint the story of conscious processing in broad strokes, if for no other reason than it tells us where among the various levels of membranes, neurons, cell assemblies, circuits, networks, systems, intentional states, and sets of intentional states that we should locate the qualia of experience.[253]

This story links disparate animal models together into a single explanatory system. We have amassed a plethora of data from cognitive psychology, clinical neurology, developmental psychology, neuropsychology, and neurophysiology, all of which seem somehow relevant for building a story about conscious experience.   Our investigation has left us with lots of messy details lumped together from different levels of analysis, different theoretical frameworks, and different investigative questions. Certainly what we are left with is nothing like the neat deductive-nomological theories we find in physics or mathematics. Nevertheless, I have maintained that what we are left with is a solid theory, or, at least, a solid interdisciplinary framework in which to develop a theory.

I have claimed that a multi-level theory will be needed in order to explain consciousness. This theory would operate over several levels of description and analysis (with no single level privileged). Arranged properly, the different levels should act as a decomposition of the relevant causal factors, thereby exhibiting the systematic dependency relations between higher and lower level mechanisms. And it is this sort of approach that should help overcome the uneasiness one feels when confronting the explanatory gap or Marr's paradox or the problem of absent qualia.

However, the success of this approach depends upon how well neurophysiological properties correspond to (or reduce) psychological ones. As one might suspect, the problem of psychophysical reduction within the cognitive sciences is not trivial. Indeed, the different time courses between neuronal and qualitative phenomena may be great enough to preclude any correspondence in actual practice. In this final chapter, I examine one argument to the effect that the general framework principles were drawn too hastily. We can understand Daniel Dennett and Marcel Kinsbourne (1992) as arguing (among other things) that experimental paradigms in psychology are too crude to allow us to tie psychological models to those in neuroscience successfully.

This again is but another formulation of the same dilemma (though with a slightly different twist): Our intuitions about consciousness and what science tells us about the mind are fundamentally incompatible. Hence, at least one must go, though both are exceedingly well-entrenched and much beloved. Dennett and Kinsbourne agree that our intuitions are the losers in this contest; however, they also conclude that my project of locating consciousness is wrong-headed as well. Our science of the mind isn't good enough to pinpoint conscious experience, so even though our intuitions should be ignored, we can't have a proper theory of consciousness anyway. And the answer I give should seem familiar: a multi-level approach to understanding consciousness goes a long way in smoothing over our intuitions concerning what counts as explanatory, even (maybe especially) when consciousness is concerned.

9.1. The Problem with Psychological Techniques

My sketch of the theoretical framework for multiple memory systems gives the impression that there is no one place into which all information funnels — cognitive processes are distributed throughout the brain — and that everything is happening more or less at once — firing patterns are entrained into attractor basins. If this impression is accurate, then we will have great difficulty picking out a point in neuronal or psychological time at which phenomena become conscious. If so, then trying to point to one place in which we are conscious of a particular event seems a fool's errand.

Dennett and Kinsbourne (1992)[254] express the problem in the following way: In psychological experiments (like subliminal priming studies from chapters 3 and 4), behavioral measures (like mean reaction time) are used to determine the differential speeds at which information is processed. We assume that our actual conscious experiences occur between the time information stimulates the retina and the later behavioral reaction. For large time intervals, we can categorize events into "already observed" and "not yet observed," but since we are working with relatively short time intervals in these sort of experiments, we run into a "*logical* difficulty" if the moment of consciousness is "spread over a rather large volume in the observer's brain, the observer's own subjective sense of sequence and simultaneity *must* be determined by something other than a unique 'order of arrival' since order of arrival is incompletely defined until we specify the relevant destination" (p. 184).

In particular, Dennett and Kinsbourne insinuate that we have no way to determine when various priming effects occur in a processing stream. The theoretical framework I suggest above postulates a place in the head in which

activated interpretations or schemas or feature-representations constitute
conscious experience. This implies that we could define or locate all (or most)
cognitive processing relative to this place. Nevertheless, Dennett and
Kinsbourne claim that this intuitively pleasing implication is false.

Consider how our minds play tricks on us. On the one hand, we can
falsely remember something later that we sincerely believed occurred earlier, but
which never in fact actually happened. For example, on Monday we may
remember Maude from the party we attended Friday night, even though she was
never there. We are all aware of this sort of common post-experiential revision
of memory. On the other hand, we could have caught a glimpse of someone
who looked like Maude at the party on Friday so that on Monday we would
swear Maude was there. If there were no way to check on the actual facts of the
matter, then we have no way of knowing which type of ersatz experience we
were having — a later fabrication of history or the fabrication first of a
nonexistent event.

Now consider the same sort of problem on a shorter time scale:

Suppose a long-haired woman jogs by. About one second *after* this, a
subterranean memory of some earlier woman — a short-haired woman with
glasses — contaminates the memory of what you have just seen: when asked
a minute later for details of the woman you just saw, you report, sincerely but
erroneously, that she was wearing glasses. Just as in the previous case, we are
inclined to say that your original *visual* experience, as opposed to the
memory of it seconds later, was *not* of a woman with glasses. But due to the
subsequent memory contaminations, it seems to you exactly as if at the first
memory of when you saw her, you were struck by her eyeglasses....[A] post-
experiential revision has happened: there was a fleeting instant, before the
memory contamination took place, that it *didn't* seem to you she had glasses.
For that brief memory, the *reality* of your conscious experience was a long-
haired woman *without* glasses, but this historical fact has become inert; it has
left no trace, thanks to the contamination of memory that came one second
after you glimpsed her.

This understanding of what happened is jeopardized, however, by an
alternative account. Your subterranean earlier memories of that short-haired
woman with the glasses could just as easily have contaminated your
experience *on the upward path*, in the processing of information that occurs
"prior to consciousness" so that you actually *hallucinated* the eyeglasses

from the very beginning of your experience. (Dennett and Kinsbourne (1992: 191, italics theirs)

We can easily apply this sort of analysis to the masked priming paradigms of chapter 3, for example. If a stimulus is flashed briefly on the screen, followed a short time later by a "masking" stimulus, subjects will report only seeing the second stimulus. The usual account of this phenomena, and the one upon which I rely, is that the second stimulus prevents the first from becoming consciously experienced. That is, it interferes with cognitive processing before the second stimulus can become conscious. But it is possible that subjects do indeed consciously experience the first stimulus, but their memory of this experience is "blanked out" by the second stimulus, and we have no way of telling the differences between the two accounts as long as we are forced to rely on only verbal reports or other behaviors for data. As Dennett and Kinsbourne point out, both accounts are entirely adequate to the data.

One account claims that we are reporting "mistaken" experiences accurately, while the other claims that we are mistaken in our reports of actual events. Another way of understanding the difference between the two hypotheses is to see that they agree about where in the processing stream the masked content enters, but they disagree about whether that location is pre- or-post-consciousness: "they tell exactly the same story except for where they place a mythical Great Divide, a point in time (and hence a place in space) whose *fine-grained* location is nothing that subjects can help them locate, and whose location is also neutral with regard to all other features of their theories" (Dennett and Kinsbourne 1992: 193-194).

Dennett and Kinsbourne draw a rather strong conclusion from their arguments. They decide that since there are no psychologically defined differences to tell us which stages of processing occur prior to conscious experience and which occur after, deciding on the moment of consciousness itself has to be arbitrary. Any distinction between the two falls apart under close scrutiny. (Stevan Harnad, on the other hand, understands the dilemma as an insoluble problem of measurement. Though he believes that there is no independent way of determining the precise timing of the actual events, he sees this "incommensurability as a methodological problem, not a metaphysical one" (1989: 183).) In either case, our proposed theoretical framework for consciousness based on different memory systems is in trouble. Does the output of the ST system only influence the processing of SE, as I suggest it does, so that the output is never consciously perceived? Or does ST operate alongside or after SE, with its outputs rapidly forgotten? Our psychological window of investigation is simply too crude to tell us exactly what is consciously perceived when.

Dennett and Kinsbourne's point is important because they have found a psychological phenomenon (*viz.*, consciousness) which cannot be explained using purely psychological methods. This is more radical than the simple underdetermination of theory by evidence which holds that, as a practical matter, we can't collect all of the pertinent evidence; however, for each pair of possible interpretations, there is some evidence which can adjudicate between them (*cf.*, chapter 7). Dennett and Kinsbourne are claiming that there is no (psychological) evidence which could adjudicate the matter *at all.* The underdetermination is ubiquitous and cannot be overcome even counterfactually.

Dennett and Kinsbourne present informational processing models of the mind as landing us in an empirically unresolvable difficulty, and as long as we are restricted to data from only one level of organization in psychology, I fear the problem will remain. The problem is one of tying psychological phenomena to neurophysiological events; in this case, tying the psychological descriptions of the properties of the ST and SE systems to underlying neurophysiological structures. If we cannot resolve the question of when each system becomes active (on a psychological level), then we have no way to link our psychological model to occurant neurophysiological events. And if we cannot overcome this fundamental problem with measurement, then the framework outlined in chapters 4, 5, and 6 cannot work because we have lost all except the vaguest connections between psychological and neurophysiological descriptions.

But we do have one investigative path open to us which can tell us about the time course of psychological events with greater accuracy than most psychological experiments, and that is using measurements of event-related potentials (ERPs) to cognitive stimuli. Dennett and Kinsbourne accept verbal reports as indicators of conscious experience, but they do not argue that these reports are the only such indicators, nor that neurobiological activity could not be an indicator as well. *Prima facie*, there is no reason why neurobiological evidence could not prove a robust index of qualitative experience. Indeed, as I shall indicate below, evidence is already on hand.

9.2. ERPs, Priming, and Temporal Windows

As one might have gathered from the previous discussions, much research in cognitive psychology focuses on the influence the semantic properties of one word have on the recognition of later words. Repeatedly, it has been shown that words are recognized faster if they have been semantically primed by an earlier presentation of a related word. The question before us now is whether subliminal priming occurs before conscious access to the second word, so that we actually are conscious of the stimuli faster, or whether it occurs after conscious access so that only our motor responses are affected. If we can answer this sort of question, we will learn something about the processes leading to (and coming after) a conscious experience, thereby providing additional support for the theoretical framework. If we cannot answer this type of question, then Dennett and Kinsbourne are right, and we cannot have a theory of consciousness of the sort I propose.

9.2.1. Unmasked Semantic Priming

One avenue of investigation in semantic priming paradigms has been through using event-related potentials (ERPs) to visual and auditory stimuli, which can give a much higher temporal resolution to cognitive processing than do any purely behavioral measure. ERPs are electroencephalograph recordings time-locked to a series of stimuli and then averaged across like trials. Simple EEG waves contain much noise, but if several trials of the same stimulus are averaged together, most of the noise drops out and a waveform distinctive for that stimulus remains. Manipulating the conditions under which stimuli are given can suggest, among other things, the various time sequences for different types of processing.

Semantic priming has been studied using ERPs to visual and auditory stimuli. In general, when we compare the waveforms for semantically related pairs of words with semantically different words pairs, we find a difference in a late negative component that onsets at around 200 msec, peaks near 400 msec after the stimulus presentation, and is bigger over the right hemisphere than the left (Bentin *et al.* 1985, Holcomb 1988, Holcomb and Neville 1990, Rugg 1985). The waveform is generally referred to as the N400 wave. (See Figure 9.1 for an example.) Study of this waveform under different probability conditions for semantic relatedness suggest that the N400 is sensitive to "the

degree to which a word has been primed" (Kutas *et al.* 1984: 237). The more
two words are *unrelated*, the *larger* the N400 waveform.

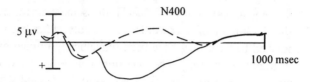

*Figure 9.1. The N400 Waveform. A schematic of grand mean target ERPs to semantically
related words (solid line) and semantically unrelated words (dashed line) for the visual modality.
Stimulus onset is the vertical bar.*

This type of paradigm has been repeated in the auditory domain, with
similar results (Holcomb and Neville 1990, McCallum *et al.* 1984), although the
negativity had an earlier onset, a later peak latency and a somewhat different
scalp distribution. The N400 effect, and the differences between the modalities
for this effect, are most clearly seen in ERP "difference waves," formed when
the waveform for one experimental condition is subtracted from the other and the
results plotted. (See Figure 9.2.) The N400 has also been studied with respect
to pseudo-words and nonwords in an effort to understand with what *level* of
processing (e.g., semantic, lexical, graphemic) it is correlated. We find an
N400 wave for pseudo-words (words which are pronounceable and follow
standard English phonemic rules, but which are nonsense), but not for true nonwords (letter strings which are not pronounceable). Instead, the nonwords
elicited a large positive component (a P3) during the period in which words and
pseudo-words produced the N400. (See Figure 9.3.)

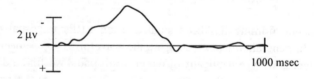

*Figure 9.2. The N400 Difference Wave. A schematic of difference waves calculated by
subtracting the ERPs for semantically related words from the ERPs for semantically unrelated
words. Stimulus onset is the calibration bar.*

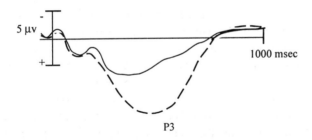

Figure 9.3.   The P3 Effect.   A schematic for grand mean target ERPs to identity primed pronounceable nonwords (solid line) and identity primed backwards nonwords (dashed line) in the visual modality.   Stimulus onset is the calibration bar.

These results suggest that the N400 is specific to events which are members or potential members of a subject's language system (Holcomb and Neville 1991).[255] It is possible that the N400 indexes some aspect of the lexical search process and that its amplitude and duration are a function of the extensiveness of the search.   In this case, the N400 component may be smaller when the target is semantically related to the preceding prime because the search required for locating the target within a subject's lexicon is helped by the activation of the prime; it would then be larger with unprimed words because these words cannot facilitate the processing and so a more extensive search is required.

Related ERP measurements also indicate specialization for other domains. For example, Barrett and Rugg (1988, 1989) examine identity and semantic priming in faces.   They found an early negative component similar to the N400 indexes primed versus unprimed faces.   However, this waveform, an N250, is larger over the frontal and parietal regions, whereas the N400 is larger over the centro-posterior regions, and the N250 shows no hemispheric asymmetries, while the N400 is larger over the right hemisphere (Knaudt 1990). These results suggest that the N250 and the N400 are elicited by different brain systems even though they both can be primed by the previous context.   (When ERP results display different distributions (anterior versus posterior or right hemisphere versus left hemisphere), then they are generally taken to be generated by non-identical neural systems.)   Indeed, non-identical brain systems may carry out the processing and priming of words and faces, even though behaviorally the results are virtually indistinguishable.

ERP research is proving to be a useful methodology for teasing apart different processing systems in the brain — systems that we are able to identify functionally within cognitive psychology, even though behavioral results alone cannot easily separate them. This sort of investigation also indicates the relative time-course of various cognitive events. For example, we can argue that the brain can recognize the semantic-relatedness of two words after only 200-300 msec or so of processing. Though we may not be able to conclude conclusively when any specific processes occur, we certainly can compare the differential processing of two types of events and argue that one occurs before the other. For example, we know that the brain can recognize the semantic-relatedness of spoken words faster than it can in the visual modality.

9.2.2. Masked Priming

Researchers are now starting to gather data from ERP studies which suggest that accessing an implicit memory system gives rise to a qualitatively different kind of ERP wave than does accessing the memory system which apparently underwrites explicit conscious experience (Leiphart *et al.* 1993, Neville and Weber-Fox 1994, Neville *et al.* 1989, Paller 1990, Paller and Kutas 1992). In particular, Neville, Pratarelli, and Forster's investigation centers on the debate concerning whether there are systems specialized for rapid linguistic analysis which are automatically accessed prior to consciousness and whether these systems are separate from our more general information stores. These domain-specific ST sub-systems would stand in contrast to the more general SE system which represents words, along with other types of knowledge about the world.

As before, subjects rapidly decided whether a string of letters was a word. In half of the trials, this "target" was preceded by an identity "prime" (e.g. sun-SUN, gif-GIF) or by semantically related primes (e.g. cat-DOG). Neville and her colleagues examined the ERP waves for distinct patterns of priming in cases in which the subjects were aware of the primes and so presumably the SE system was activated, as contrasted with trials in which the primes were masked and subjects were hence unaware of them. As has been well documented, they found that ERP waves correlated with the explicit semantic priming onsets at about 300 msec after target presentation, lasts about 300 msec, and is concentrated in the centro-posterior portions of the brain. They also found that word and nonwords displayed a similar N400 effect with repetition priming.

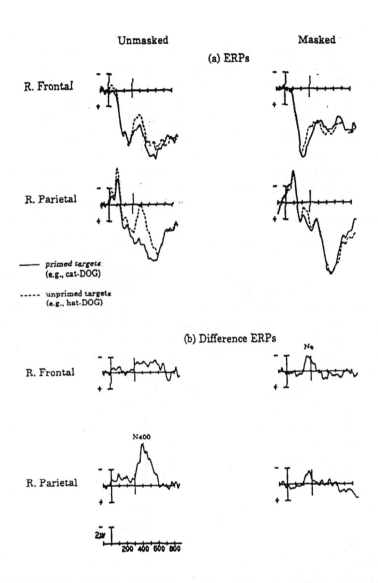

Figure 9.4. Masked Versus Unmasked Priming. Effects of semantic priming when subjects were able (unmasked; left) and were not able (masked; right) to report the prime. (a) Event-related brain portentials (ERP) elicited by primed and unprimed targets. (b) Difference ERPs formed by subtracting ERPs to primed targets from those to unprimed targets (from Neville and Weber-Fox 1994, reprinted with kind permission by the publisher and Dr. Helen Neville).

There were also consistent ERP effects under the masked conditions. However, in these cases, the ERP component which marks the masked semantic priming effects is an enhanced negativity that occurs earlier (around 200 msec after target presentation), lasts only 120 msec, and has a centro-anterior distribution. As can be seen in Figure 9.4, this distinction shows itself clearly in the difference waves. The different timing and distribution of the masked and unmasked effects suggest that non-identical sets of neurons are being activated in the two conditions. And, interestingly enough, though one can get the N400 priming effect for both words and pseudo-word letter strings in repetition priming, Neville *et al.* saw no ERP effect for pseudo-words in the masked condition. This result is compatible with the hypothesis that the earlier anterior priming effects seen in the masked condition does in fact index activity of a system specialized for words, while the later posterior N400 priming effect indexes access to or decisions about general, episodic representations of words.

In any event, we can conclude that the different timing and distribution of the unmasked and masked effects suggest that separate perceptual and declarative representations of words exist in different brain areas. Conscious access (allied with the SE system) shows a large negative effect with a posterior distribution at around 400 msec after target presentation. On the other hand, masked priming (allied with the ST system) shows a smaller anterior negative effect at around 200 msec after target presentation.[256] Hence, the results also suggest that the early anterior priming effect may indeed index access to a more specialized structural representation of words in some sort of lexicon *before* the more general SE system is activated. At the least, the two priming effects point out distinctly identifiable temporal processes within our language processing system — Dennett and Kinsbourne are simply wrong when they claim that we cannot narrow our investigative window enough to distinguish when masked priming effects occur. There is some evidence that the effects occur (and the ST system is activated) before conscious access. The hypothesis of a processing stream *from* the ST systems *to* the SE systems remains plausible.

Nevertheless, even if using ERPs does overcome the methodological version of Dennett and Kinsbourne's objection, we still have to address the question of whether it will help counter their metaphysical skepticism (Lloyd, personal communication). Dennett and Kinsbourne could respond that ERPs are not the process itself, so we still do not know when consciousness itself occurs. In particular, we do not know whether *it* occurs before, alongside, or after our memories are activated. The skepticism remains, for all we have are suggested correlations, not positive identifications.

However, we must keep in mind how science works (*cf.*, chapters 1, 2 and 3) and we should not expect a theory of consciousness to be any more or less supported than any other scientific theory. We never (or rarely) capture the "process itself" in all its glorious detail for any process putatively measured. All we can do is collect evidence that points in the direction of the physical system we have posited as adequate to our data and to our particular circumscribed conception of the phenomenon we are investigating. Consider, for example, the relationship between mean molecular kinetic energy and heat. We have little difficulty claiming that heat (properly understood) just *is* MMKE. We have devised an empirically adequate abstract physical system in which we can model the important properties of what we commonsensically refer to as 'heat'. And that is all that science is required to do in order to make an identity claim. Likewise, I submit that the majority of data collected today implies that consciousness (properly understood) occurs as the activation of our SE memories. That is, a proper model of our SE system, including its interactions and causal history, will also allow us to identify conscious phenomena just as something like the perceptual activations of our SE memories. And this type of educated "guess" is as good and as much as we can ever do.

Hence, I conclude that results like these show how it is possible to parse psychological events finely enough in (neuro-)psychological investigations to determine when particular psychological events do occur in the head. If we could align consciousness with some psychological event or (perhaps some other sort of neural process), then we should be able to articulate definitively when that event occurs in the processing stream (relative to other events) as long as that event can be correlated with an ERP waveform. Hence, we should be able to locate the moment of consciousness for any particular (set of averaged) cognitive processes.

9.2.3. Priming with Novel Visual Stimuli

But on the other hand, if the picture I sketched above for the different memory systems is correct, then the data I recounted so far cannot be the entire story, for I claim that the early ST system can access and process *non-word* material. Fortunately, though, there is now evidence for implicit priming effects using completely novel visual stimuli (Gabrielli *et al.* 1990, Haist *et al.* 1991,

Holcomb and McPherson 1994, Musen 1989, Musen and Squire 1992, Musen and Treisman 1990, Schacter *et al.* 1991). In these studies, however, subjects showed implicit priming effects for the nonverbal stimuli only if the instructions for encoding forced them to form a structural description of the objects. (These results buttress Schacter *et al.*'s suggestion that implicit priming is due to a perceptual memory system specialized to represent an object's form.)

The lexical access mentioned above could thus be tapping into just one specialized sub-system within larger perceptual memory. The reason that the masked paradigms involving pseudo-words show no implicit priming effects is that the tasks use stimuli too complicated for an early automatic system to encode rapidly. Masked priming effects for novel stimuli then should be seen immediately with simple input patterns. To test this hypothesis (as well as to try to differentiate the supposed early lexicon from other sorts of early access memory systems and to characterize more fully the capabilities of these early systems) I designed a series of experiments to compare the ERP waveforms in unmasked and masked priming conditions for simple 5-line visual patterns (Hardcastle 1993b). Patterns consisted of five connected lines joining dots in a 3 x 3 dot matrix. Most of the patterns were variations of the patterns used in Musen and Treisman (1990) (with the exception that the dots of the matrix were not shown in this series of experiments). Patterns were sorted into three categories: *closed*, in which some part of the patterns formed an enclosed area; *continuous*, in which no portion of the patterns formed a closed area and in which the lines form a continuous shape; and *hatched*, in which patterns were neither closed nor continuous. Only closed and hatched patterns were used in these experiments in order to maintain consistent shape complexity. The targets were proceeded by primes either identical to, the mirror image of, in the same category as, or unrelated to the target. (See Figure 9.5 for examples.)

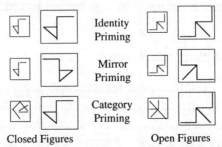

Closed Figures   Open Figures

Figure 9.5. Examples of the Novel Visual Stimuli Priming Conditions.

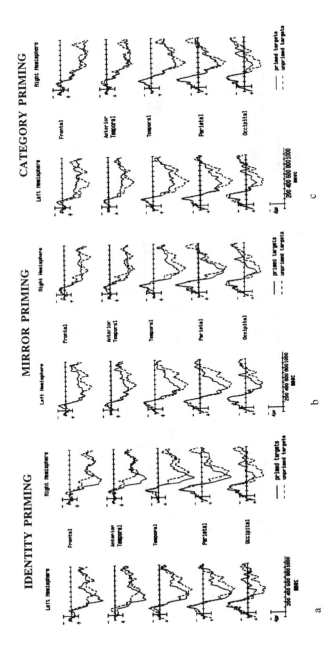

Figure 9.6. ERP Waveforms for Unmasked Novel Visual Stimuli. (a) Grand mean target ERPs for identity primed versus not primed simple novel shapes. (b) Grand mean target ERPs for mirror primed versus not primed simple novel shapes. (c) Grand mean target ERPs for category primed versus not primed simple novel shapes. Time is in msec; each tic mark is 100 msec. Stimulus onset is the calibration bar.

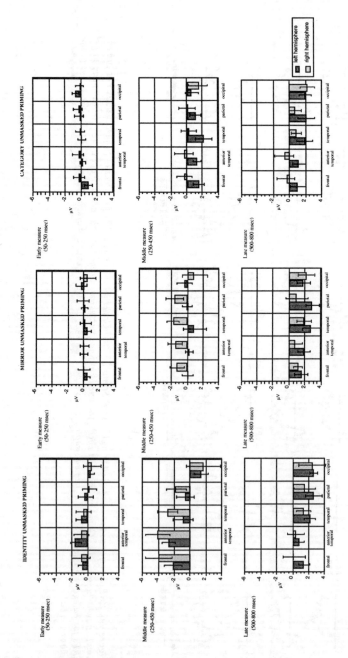

Figure 9.7. Early, Middle, and Late Measures for Priming Effects Using Novel Visual Stimuli. These charts show no early effect in any priming condition, a negative effect for identity and mirror priming in the middle measures (the N400), and a late positive effect in all three conditions (the P3).

Under the unmasked conditions, as one would expect, subjects were faster at deciding whether a shape is closed if that shape is preceded by a prime identical to, the mirror image of, or the same category as the target.[257] As illustrated in Figures 9.6, there is a negative effect with identity and mirror priming similar to the negativity seen in the semantic paradigms discussed above.[258] These effects are followed by an amplitude and latency shift in the P3 component, similar to the effects of the non-word priming paradigm above (cf., Figure 9.3).[259] (In the category priming condition, all we find is a modulation of the P3.) Figure 9.7 summarizes the ERP effects for the three measured epochs in the difference waves and it indicates a negative effect for both identity and mirror priming, as well as a P3 modulation in all three conditions.[260] [261] In summary, the ERP results are fairly consistent with what one would expect given the priming data for words.

The reaction time results in the masked condition are what one would expect as well. Schacter predicts that subjects who have no previous structural memory of some shape should show no priming effects and should not to be faster in deciding whether a target stimulus was closed. And there were no significant differences in the behavioral data.[262] However, the ERP data do not corroborate this hypothesis. Though there were considerable individual differences, I also found some significant masked priming effects in both the identity and mirror conditions when the subjects were averaged together, even though these effects were not reflected in reaction time.[263] With both identity and mirror priming, there was a priming-induced positivity onsetting at about 100 msec and continuing essentially for the duration of the recorded epoch.[264] (There were no significant changes however in the category priming condition.) (See Figure 9.8.)

That there are effects at all suggests that the masked priming positivity with novel visual stimuli indexes something other than specialized representation of words in a lexicon. However, because these effects are substantially different than those of semantic priming, the specialized early lexicon may still exist. These results only demonstrate that more than a lexicon operates prior to conscious processing. At the least, we are able to recognize simple nonsemantic visual information as the same as or different from other stimuli prior to conscious access.

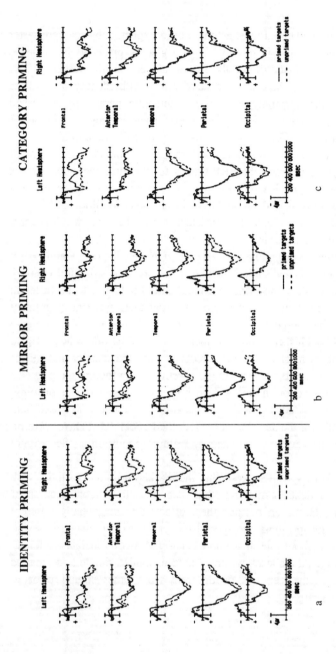

Figure 9.8. ERP Waveforms for Masked Novel Visual Stimuli. (a, b) Shown here are ERP waveforms for identity and mirror priming using simple novel visual shapes. In both conditions, we find an enhanced positivity onsetting at approximately 100 msec and continuing essentially for the duration of the recorded epoch. These effects are very different from the effects seen in the unmasked paradigm using the same stimuli. (c) There are no ERP priming effects using the masked category primes.

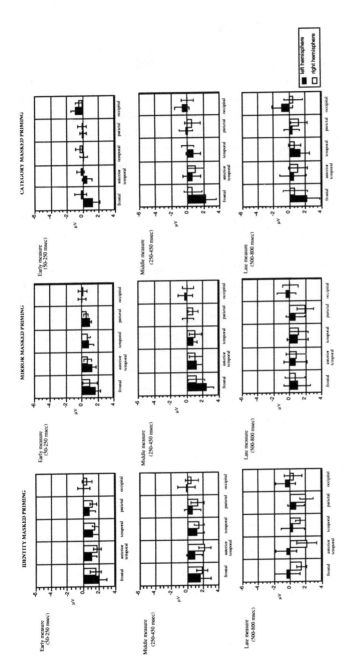

Figure 9.9. Early, Middle, and Late Measures for Masked Priming Using Novel Visual Stimuli. These charts indicate that there is an early, middle, and late positive enhancement of the masked primed condition with both identity and mirror priming, but few effects with masked category priming. We can compare these effects with the early, middle, and late measures for the unmasked paradigm and see that masked and unmasked priming with novel visual shapes give rise to radically different effects across all conditions.

If we compare Figures 9.7 and 9.9, it is clear that the masked priming effects are very different from the unmasked effects, again suggesting that masked and unmasked priming activate non-identical systems. The system which underwrites masked priming seems to be activated automatically and accessed quite early in cognitive processing. Though it can perform rather sophisticated analyses (i.e., recognizing a stimulus as the same as or different from a previous stimulus), it is not capable of categorizing stimuli based on higher level distinctions, such as arbitrary category definitions. The conscious processing which supports unmasked priming, on the other hand, occurs later, and appears to be sensitive to the more "abstract" properties of stimuli.[265] At least, it can be primed with information relative to the task at hand.

As we saw in the ERP semantic paradigms, the different timing and distribution of the unmasked and masked effects point to early and late processing systems which are consistent with the hypothesized ST and SE memory systems. The systems have different processing capabilities, operate under different time-frames, and use different nets of neurons. In the unmasked condition, we saw differential responses for both words and nonwords and for all three priming possibilities with novel visual stimuli. These effects began relatively late in the recorded epoch and were posteriorly distributed. In contrast, in the masked conditions, we only saw differential brain wave responses for repetition priming using meaningful words and for identity and mirror priming using completely novel visual shapes. These effects began earlier in the anterior portion of the brain. These data concerning the processing capacities of the two systems lend support to the hypothesis that the early system is more structural, while the later also includes "higher level" semantic analyses.

The fact that the behavioral data showed no masked priming effects only underscores the need for psychology to extend its theories via neuropsychological and neurophysiological data. While it shows that Dennett and Kinsbourne are quite right to argue that psychology alone may not be enough to answer all the questions we have about cognitive processing on the psychological level, we cannot thereby conclude that some psychological questions cannot be answered. ERPs can narrow the temporal window in which we have the power to distinguish various processes, and it can increase the resolution enough to determine whether the ST system is activated before the SE system.

9.3. Conclusion: Mind as Brain

Well, I am just about finished. While I do not pretend to have listed everything that psychology and neuroscience can tell us about consciousness, I do think that I have made a fair start. There are interesting parallels between certain phenomenal experiences (or their absence) and twitches in the brain. These parallels then can serve as a basis for postulating the location of consciousness in and among our various processing streams. Another way of putting this point is that these parallels can ground the construction of an abstract physical system which would refine, regiment, and clarify our intuitive ideas about what consciousness is and is like. We could use then this physical system to explain, predict, and control the appearance of our phenomenology.

Of course, not all of our folk notions of consciousness will be decomposed in the physical system. (This fact should surprise no one.) For example, our conscious states do not give us reliable and transparent information about our motives or our experiences. Moreover, some well respected facts about conscious experience probably won't be used either. (This fact can now serve as grist for the skeptic's mill, though it is how science proceeds, warts and all.) For example, individual differences among qualia not accounted for in my model. Nevertheless, I did extract a core set of properties that matched a subset of our intuitive notions of conscious experience and I used these to build a more streamlined conception of consciousness. The most important property for my purposes here: conscious perceptions (as understood in terms of later reportability of qualia) affect behavior differently from unconscious ones. Hence the central question of this text: With what else can we identify this difference? The short version of the answer is: activations in SE memory versus activations in our other memory systems.

Activated SE memories offer unique and rich semantic interpretations of input, be they perceptual stimuli or internally generated neuronal patterns. These interpretations unify the input, put it in a context, and (to speak wildly metaphorically) present it to the perceiver as a bound bundle of information. To speak not so metaphorically, we might be able to understand these bundles in terms of bifurcations in a complex dynamical system. Each bifurcation, composed of higher level activity patterns over cortex, would correspond to a single complex SE interpretation. That is, a relatively stable attractor pattern in an informational phase space and located in the appropriate place in the brain just is a conscious experience. If we lose the appropriate places in the brain, or if we are unable to entrain inputs into attractor patterns, then we lose (some of) our conscious experiences. Malfunctions in the cortex by and large translate to a loss of phenomenology, which is more or less what one would expect if one is a materialist.

I want to be clear about what I am claiming. When we use a memory laid down in parietal cortex by the medial temporal lobe to interpret some incoming stimuli, we experience something phenomenally. If we can't use these memories to interpret incoming stimuli, then we do not experience anything at all. These conditionals entail that phenomenal experience is inextricably tied to what information we can access in our brains and how we can access it. *Contra* Ned Block (1991, forthcoming), it does not make sense to talk about "phenomenal consciousness" apart from "access consciousness." For a certain type of "access" just *is* phenomenal awareness.

Is this a radical claim? Yes and no. It is in that it immediately suggests how one might go about falsifying it. Find someone who has activated SE memories without being conscious of them or find someone who by all other reasonable standards is conscious, but lacks the correlative SE memories. It is too in that I am not hedging bets; this is my best guess about how to locate consciousness in our processing streams, given what we know today, and, for now, I am willing to stand by my bet unequivocally and unashamedly. It is *not* a radical claim (contrary to what a skeptic might think) because I *identify* consciousness with something in our heads. For it is exactly the sort of claim one must make if one is to be an earnest, anti-epiphenomenalist, materialist. The mind just is the brain (plus maybe some connections to its environment), so all mental phenomena must be identified with some brain phenomena.[266] For an already converted naturalist, the question is which phenomena to identify...and nothing more.

NOTES

1. Many of these connections are discussed later in the book.

2. David Chalmers (forthcoming) might be an exception.

3. Reliabilist theories of knowledge do not require causal interactions; see, for example, Dretske (1981, 1989), Fodor (1987). In these theories, one knows something if some internal occurrence (like a belief) is reliably correlated with some external event or state of affairs. However, it is not clear that these theories don't implicitly require on causal connections once the particular sorts of relations that hold in our world are taken into account. (Gary Hardcastle pointed this out to me.)

4. In the end, I have to take back a strict distinction between perceptions and judgments (see chapters 5 and 6). However, incorrectly interpreting our perceptions remains a distinct, indeed, likely, possibility.

5. I get this line of reasoning from John Searle, though others have made the same point (e.g., Dennett 1988, 1992).

6. Paul Churchland (1984) makes a similar point.

7. See also Watkins (1989).

8. Roger Sperry (1965, 1969, 1987, 1991) and other emergentists, e.g., Alexander (1920), Morgan (1923), hold this sort of view.

9. Joe Levine coined the term "explanatory gap;" see his (1983, 1993).

10. See also chapter 7 for elaboration of this point.

11. Others who express similar worries include Kripke (1980), Jackson (1982, 1986), McGinn (1989, 1991), and Searle (1980, 1984, 1987, 1990a, 1990b).

12. Flanagan suggests that the skeptics' question would not be begged if the naturalists admit that we use token reports of phenomenal experiences to develop an objective type (Flanagan, personal communication). However, I maintain that the skeptics' point is stronger: naturalists who believe that they can build objective types from first person reports are mistaken (see especially McGinn 1989).

13. The strictest case of translation of course is a *reduction* between theories. In this case, each primitive predicate of the reduced framework would be associated with an open sentence of the reducing scientific theory via a bridge law such that if each predicate were satisfied by an n-tuple, then the open sentence would be satisfied by the same n-tuple. We would then be able to derive the reduced conceptual framework from the union of the

reducing scientific theory and the bridge principles. Elsewhere I have dismissed the possibility of reduction among theories in the disciplines which comprise the cognitive sciences as a useful methodological goal. Here though all we need concern ourselves with is the weaker notion of translation between frameworks. The concept translation I discuss here is concerned only with preserving causal powers; the types of the explanation each domain gives and the questions they try to answer are not relevant (see Hardcastle 1992).

14. See Churchland (1989) for a similar position.

15. I should note that I am not suggesting a formula for scientific investigation. That is, I am making no claims about how science proceeds, whether seeking these sorts of identities drives theories, whether theories drive seeking identities, or whether science should even be concerned about such correspondences. Rather, I am simply pointing out that with science we get these sorts of identities and that these identities are useful for extending and explaining our folk notions.

16. An anonymous reviewer pointed out that this skeptical concern is not one over causal powers, hence, I misconstrue the skeptic in the passages above. However, notice that the only way the skeptic could run this argument *modulo* the considerations mitigating dualism and epiphenomenalism is to assume that the qualia of perceptions possess some causal power or other (otherwise, how could we know what it is like to experience some experience?). Presumably this causal power (the power to cause us to know that we are experiencing some state) is not captured by a purely neuronal description. That is, any neuronal description adequate to the task might be true of some system that is not conscious.

17. See also Bigelow and Pargetter (199), Foss (1989), Kitcher (1979), Levin (1986), Lewis (1973, 1990), Loar (1985), Nemirow (1980, 1990), and Papineau (1993); though see Horgan (1984), Lycan (1993), Pereboom (1994), Schick (1992), Tye (1986), and Van Gulick (1990, 1993) in rebuttal.

18. This follows Churchland (1989, pp. 62-66).

19. Flanagan suggests that really what this point turns on are different notions of description and that the skeptics' conditions for an adequate description are unfounded and too strong (Flanagan, personal communication). He may be correct.

20. In what follows, I shall adopt the semantic view of theories to discuss the connection because I believe that the notion of theories as models best captures the structure of modern computational theories in the cognitive sciences. However, I have no doubt that the same arguments could be translated into other views of theory structure.

21. See Suppe (1989) for discussion of these points.

22. See Wilkes (1988) for an in-depth discussion of this point.

23. I should point out that conceptions of the fundamental properties of consciousness are not uniform even across our linguistic community. More particular notions of consciousness are influenced in part by the particular community in which one's discussion of consciousness is embedded and what one takes the purpose of the conversation to be. One of my goals in these first few chapters is to delimit the central properties of consciousness as understood by a large number of scientists and philosophers (though certainly not all; see especially chapter 8).

24. See also Churchland (1979) and Maxwell (1962) for additional arguments.

25. See also Hardcastle (1992), van Fraassen (1980) for discussion.

26. I take some of the following examples from Suppe (1989).

27. See also Bogen and Woodward (1988) for a point similar to mine.

28. As far as I know, this thought experiment appeared in the philosophical literature first with Locke, when he examined the possibility that "*the same Object should produce in several Men's Minds different* Ideas at the same time; e.g., the *Idea*, that a *Violet* produces in one Man's Mind by his Eyes, were the same that a *Marigold* produced in another Man's, and *vice versa*" (1689/1975: 389). This idea reappeared in the early years of this century during the logical positivist's movement as an attack on the verificationist's theory of meaning. Classic formulations appear in Black (1949), Lewis (1929), Reichenbach (1938), Schlick (1959), Smart (1963), Wisdom (1952), and Wittgenstein (1968). For more contemporary discussions, see Block (1980b), Dennett (1988), Hardin (1988), and Shoemaker (1975a, b, 1982).

29. See also Shoemaker (1982) for a similar idea.

30. For a good, recent account of this theory, see Hurvitch (1981).

31. Though see Lycan (1973).

32. See also Harrison (1973) for a similar point.

33. I get this point from van Brakel (1992); see also Churchland and Churchland (1981).

34. See above, Churchland (1979), Sellars (1956).

35. These examples come from van Brakel (1992); see also van Brakel (forthcoming) for an extensive list of references.

36. One might respond that we do seem to find universal primacy of focal colors (Berlin and Kay 1969). That is, for each color category people across cultures pick the same hue as its best exemplar. However, this sort of evidence just shows that the most saturated

exemplar within a category is primary. It says nothing about the existence of the categories themselves.

37. The speculation is that Newton was influenced by the Pythagorean harmonic series in music; see Campbell (1983), Helmholtz (1911), van Brakel (1992).

38. See discussion in van Brakel (1992).

39. Indeed, Lehky and Sejnowski (1988) argue that to determine the processing task of any cell properly, one has to look at where the information the cell processed goes and what it does there. If this be the case, then we know even less about how visual perception works since we have not yet mapped our entire visual system.

40. See also Shoemaker (1982).

41. See discussion in Kandel and Schwartz (1985).

42. See also discussion in Flanagan (1985, 1992), Hardcastle (1992).

43. This sort of perspective is examined more carefully in chapter 6.

44. See also McCulloch (1988).

45. Though see Newton (1986). Chapter 7 discusses this notion of meaning in greater detail and whether it is a way around the problem of absent qualia.

46. Akins (1993) advocates a similar moral.

47. Chalmers (forthcoming) makes this point.

48. Chapter 7 discusses this point in more detail.

49. See Churchland (1979), Hardcastle (1992) for related discussion.

50. Though see Nelkin (1993) for a different conclusion.

51. I get this example from Wilkes (1988).

52. Cf., Mandler and Kessen (1959), Wilkes (1988).

53. See Churchland (1988) for discussion.

54. P.S. Churchland (1983) and Nisbett and Ross (1980) argue for the same point.

55. See also Mandler (1984).

56. This effect is most prominent in children (Lepper *et al.* 1973).

57. Though see Otta (1983).

58. Seminal work in echolocation is due to Supa, Cotzin, and Dallenbach (1944); see also Arias *et al.* (1993), Boehm (1986), Schenkman and Jansson (1986).

59. See also Humphreys *et al.* (1992)

60. This syndrome was first documented in Anton (1899).

61. See also Joseph *et al.* (1984), Marks (1981), Natsoulas (1987), Sperry (1965, 1977, 1985) for related discussion.

62. See, e.g., Kelley and Jacoby (1993).

63. See Wilkes (1988: 35-37).

64. Flanagan (1992) makes a similar point concerning Wilkes's argument. However, he is less sanguine that this will be enough of a unifying feature to support a *single* theory of consciousness (Flanagan 1992, personal communication).

65. Daniel Dennett (1988) takes this question seriously and argues that our folk understanding of qualia as something intrinsic, ineffable, and immediately and infallibly known is not helpful. For example, he points out that our own judgments about our own qualia are little better than those made by an outside observer. When we judge our qualia to be the same as or different from another experience, we compare our present conscious state with a memory of some prior state. If we had immediate access to our conscious states, as our folk intuitions about consciousness would lead us to believe, we would be able to make these judgments infallibly. But there are at least two ways in which we could err in our judgments; we could misremember our previous states, or the internal standard which we make the judgments by could be askew. So, Dennett concludes, we might as well as rely on more respectable methods of gathering information objectively.

　　However, Dennett assumes that our judgments about qualia are part of the qualitative experiences themselves. He does so because he believes we have no reason to accept any (other) "intrinsic" property of our subjective experiences except our own reactions to them. For evidence, he again points to the possibility of mistaken judgments. Since nothing about our qualitative experience, including our judgments about that experience, would indicate where any breakdown in veridical reporting had occurred, he concludes that nothing interesting can come of out alleged qualitative experience. Since we cannot distinguish our qualia any more finely than noting a particular disposition or a behavioral reaction, there is no reason to assume anything in addition to these reactions — nothing would come of such a hypothesis. (Kitcher 1979 draws a similar conclusion; see also Dennett 1981.) All that we really can discuss cogently are our abilities to perceive and judge, not how we make those discriminations, nor how the states seem to us with respect to other states, our only meter stick. Therefore, it would be best to discuss only the objective properties of objects, overlaid with idiosyncratic subjective interpretations. Unlike using memories, the objective properties would remain constant as a standard for measure against our continually evolving subjective experiences. If all we have access to are the verbal reports of our perceptions, why should we posit a conscious quale separate from our judgments about our experiences? Dennett (and Kitcher) find no good reasons.

66. I should emphasize that while I believe that converging intuitions prevent my conception and eventual identification from being idiosyncratic — indeed, I believe that it should be widely applicable — other investigators belonging to different scientific communities may take other characteristics to be fundamental and hence may devise substantially different physical systems.

67. See also Fowler *et al.* (1981), Kemp-Wheeler and Hill (1988), Tipper (1985).

68. See also Fowler *et al.* (1981), Kemp-Wheeler and Hill (1988), Mandler (forthcoming), Marcel (1983a).

69. Moreover, we know from other experiments in psychology that changing the type of encoding an input receives influences tasks involving conscious memory, while it has little or the opposite influence on tests of "unconscious" memory, such as those relying on masked priming (Graf *et al.* 1982, Graf and Mandler 1984, Jacoby 1983, Jacoby and Dallas 1981, Schacter 1990, Schacter and Graf 1986a, Winnick and Daniel 1970). We also know that changing the modality between study and test has no effect on conscious memory, while it impairs unconscious memory results (Graf *et al.* 1985, Jacoby and Dallas 1981, Kirshner *et al.* 1983, Kirshner and Smith 1974, Roediger and Blaxton 1987, Schacter and Graf 1986a); that unconscious memory primes last substantially longer (on the order of weeks) than do primes for conscious recall or recognition (Jacoby and Dallas 1981, Komatsu and Ohta 1984, Tulving *et al.* 1982); that proactive and retroactive interference affect unconscious and conscious memory tasks differently (Graf and Schacter 1987, Sloman *et al.* 1988); and that success on an unconscious memory task is stochastically independent of success on a conscious task (Eich 1984, Graf and Mandler 1984, Jacoby and Witherspoon 1982, Schacter *et al.* 1988, Tulving *et al.* 1982; see also Musen and Treisman 1990, although see Mandler 1990 and Ostergaard 1992 in rebuttal).

70. See also Mandler (1975), Tyler (1992) for similar arguments.

71. McGinn (1982) argues that even though consciousness is a purely natural phenomena, we will never be able to develop a theory of it because the problem is too hard. Developing a theory of consciousness would, of course, refute his claim.

72. This term is due to Flanagan (1992).

73. See Derruchet and Baveux (1989), Gordon (1988), Mandler (1984), Schacter (1985a), Schacter and Moscovitch (1984), Squire (1987).

74. Originally, psychologists assumed that the controlled processing picked out the contents in short term store (STS) (for discussion, see Forster and Grovier 1978). Nowadays, although most expect to find some sort of connection, exactly what the relationship is between controlled processing and STS is not clear.

75. Please refer to footnote 69 for a quick list of the relevant evidence.

76. Priming studies, however, like the one touched upon in chapter 3, do not fit neatly into the hypothesized dichotomy; rather, they appear to reflect the *interaction* of our memory systems. See below.

77. See also Squire (1987) for discussion.

78. The following discussion is based on Squire and Zola-Morgan (1991).

79. Delayed nonmatching-to-sample is a task in which subjects are briefly presented with a single object. Then after a delay ranging up to 10 minutes, they are shown the original object plus a novel one and are rewarded if they pick the new object from the old-new pair. See Alvarez-Royo (1992), Malamut *et al.* (1984), Zola-Morgan and Squire (1984).

80. See also Desimone (1992).

81. See McNaughton and Wilson (1994).

82. Though we can only speculate on the mechanisms involved in our mnemonic changes, "long-term potentiation" (LTP) in the hippocampus may be the mechanism responsible for first forming the episodic memories. "LTP" refers to long-lasting increases in the strength of a synaptic response caused by the activation of the neuronal pathway and triggered by changes in the response components mediated by the NMDA or AMPA synaptic receptors (Bliss and Lomo 1973, Doyere *et al.* 1993, Lynch and Baudry 1984, Lynch and Granger 1992, Swanson *et al.* 1982). For example, we know that when rats learn new smells, LTP lays down the neuronal circuits involving the hippocampus and the sensory cortices, creating (perhaps) their equivalent of a "controlled access" memory. Most importantly, the magnitude of LTP is correlated with speed of learning in rats (Barnes 1979, Squire 1987). Presumably, the more rats learn about a smell, the more the synaptic response is potentiated. We can tentatively conclude that, in adult mammals at least, when the environment activates certain neuronal circuits in the medial temporal lobe system, LTP, in virtue of this activation, reinforces the circuits such that the organism learns and can later recall it explicitly.

83. See Schacter and Moscovith (1984) for a summary.

84. Much of the following research is reported and discussed in Schacter and Moscovitch (1984).

85. See also Cohen *et al.* (1977), Mandler (1984), and McCall *et al.* (1977).

86.   See also Reber (1992) for more discussion.

87.   See above and O'Keefe and Nadel (1978).

88.   For review, see Fagen and Rovee-Collier (1982).

89.   See discussion in Kimble (1969), Schacter and Moscovitch (1984).

90.   *Cf.*, Fox *et al.* (1979), Gratch *et al.* (1974), Harris (1973), Luria (1959).

91.   See also McKee and Squire (1992).

92.   See also Kinsbourne and Wood (1975).

93.   Though see Squire and McKee (1993), who suggest that implicit priming is stronger is amnesics than normals.

94.   See also Gardner *et al.* (1973), Graf *et al.* (1985), Schacter (1985b), Schacter *et al.* (1991), Shimamura and Squire (1984).

95.   Though see Diamond and Rozin (1984), Graf *et al.* (1984).

96.   Other pathologies which reveal clear dissociations between implicit and explicit memory include patients under anesthesia (Jelicic and Bonke 1993, Jelicic *et al.* 1992, Kihlstrom *et al.* 1990), subjects with word-meaning deafness (Schacter *et al.* 1993), and some frontal lobe lesions (Shimamura *et al.* 1992).

97.   We should pause for a moment and consider the sort of theory being developed here. We can understand the moves made in this section as an instance of the various domains working to extend one another in the cognitive sciences. We have been able to enlarge our theory of automatic and explicit memory with respect to properties that can be investigated by developmental psychology and clinical neurology, but which, because of inherent limits on experimental methodology, are beyond the testing capabilities of neurophysiology. Mutually reinforcing theoretical models come out of the different experimental paradigms to refine the definitions and descriptions contained in the general theory. Even though the individual models are of different organisms (e.g., the theory of the medial temporal lobe circuit outlined above), we should be able to combine these different models into one general account of automatic and explicit memory (in certain organisms).
      Methodologically, the various individual models and explanations suggest variations on the psychological tests to give the different subjects. For example, the clinical neurology data suggest that one should try to develop an abstract version of a nonmatching-to-sample task for lesioned monkeys to determine how "cognitive" their deficits are. A second advantage to using data from different disciplines is that we uncover different avenues of investigation and confirmation for analogous phenomena.

98. See especially Winograd (1975).

99. E.g., Cohen (1984), Squire (1986), Squire and Cohen (1984).

100. See also Hardcastle (forthcoming), Kitcher (1992) for discussion.

101. See Cohen (1984), Squire and Cohen (1984), Squire (1987).

102. See also Keane *et al.* (1992) for a different type of dissociation.

103. See also Jurnigen and Ostergaard (1993) for collaborating neurophysiological evidence.

104. *Cf.*, Schacter *et al.* (1988).

105. Though this section discusses only visually presented stimuli, similar results have been found in the auditory domain. See Schacter and Church (1992) as well as the discussion in chapter 9.

106. Jacoby and Dallas (1981) report that the number and spacing of repetitions affect the perceptual identification task and the recognition task in a similar fashion (though the priming effect on lexical decision tasks does not decrease with increasing time lags between the first and second presentation of the word in normal subjects (Scarborough *et al.* 1977, Scarborough *et al.* 1979)). Subjects are better at both tasks when exposed to multiple instances of the stimuli.

107. See also Hinzman *et al.* (1972), Morton (1979).

108. See also Schacter and Graf (1989).

109. See also Graf and Schacter (1989), Schacter and McGlynn (1992).

110. Unlike the skill systems, which are probably located throughout the corticostriatal areas (Wang, Aigner, and Mishkin 1992), Schacter hypothesizes that the perceptual memory systems are found in the posterior cortical areas, such as inferior temporal cortex and the extra-striate occipital areas (Polster *et al.* 1991, Schacter 1990, Schacter *et al.* 1990, 1991, Tulving and Schacter 1990).

111. Jacobson (1973) suggests that the greater the economy of description available for a stimuli, the greater its power to mask previous stimuli. Likewise, Taylor and Chabot (1978) show that backward masking is enhanced to a greater degree when the target is followed by a stimulus meaningful at a "same" level of analysis as the target than when the stimulus is meaningful only at a "lower" level (e.g. a word followed by another word versus a pseudo-word). Masking is even more pronounced when the second stimulus is understandable at a "higher" level than the target (a pseudo-word followed by a word versus another pseudo-word).

112. In dissent, Marcel concludes that any unconscious "perceptual" analysis must code multiple aspects of the incoming information — his memory system must rely on more than a purely "structural" analysis since it appears to segment incoming information into all possible descriptions of events, objects, meanings, etc. However, the data are also consistent with the output of an early nonsemantic perceptual system priming more than one item in explicit memory. In fact, because unconscious priming data are so closely tied to the modality and graphemes of the stimuli, it would be surprising if the semantic aspects of the words did play any large role in determining the output of the system.

113. See Mandler (1984), Minsky (1981, 1986), Rumelhart (1980), Schank and Abelson (1977) for classic discussions of schemas (also known as frames or scripts).

114. This division is somewhat artificial, since the memory systems do interact with one another regularly and extensively (Jacoby and Kelley 1992).

115. See also Bachevalier and Mishkin (1984).

116. See LeDoux et al. (1989), Shimamura and Squire (1988).

117. See also Mayes (1992).

118. Although I shall discuss the ST system as though it were a single unit, it is entirely likely that the ST "system" is actually several systems lumped together. (For example, in chapter 9 I outline evidence that suggests that there are distinct, specialized systems for at least words and faces.)

119. See also Metcalfe et al. (1992).

120. See also Lynch and Granger (1992) for a different version of serial mnemonic processes.

121. See also Roediger et al. (1992).

122. "Chain of processing" is a bit vague and metaphorical. However, at this point in the discussion I can do no better. I refer the reader to chapter 6, section 4, in which what I mean by "processing chain" is cashed out in terms of attractors in phase space.

123. See also Bachevalier and Mishkin (1984), Garbiel et al. (1986), Goldman-Rakic (1987).

124. See also Squire (1987).

125. See also Squire (1992).

126. See also Reber (1992).

127. Cf., Derruchet and Bareux (1989).

128. Though I believe we have several independent mnemonic processors, I think only two are important in understanding consciousness, the ST and the SE. Hence, I shall focus on only these two for the remainder of the text.

129. Contemporary philosophers who explicitly assume this perspective include Dennett (1991), Fodor (1987), Stich (1984), and Van Gulick (1981).

130. See Farah (1990), especially chapter 4, for discussion.

131. Chapter 6 contains a discussion of how agnosia is related to consciousness.

132. See Farah (1990: 97-99).

133. See also Farah (1990, 1994) for more arguments to this conclusion.

134. See McClelland and Rumelhart (1986), Rumelhart and McClelland (1986) for details on this type of architecture.

135. See Farah (1990: 100-104) for discussion.

136. See Hinton (1981) for an example of this type of device, as reported in Farah (1990: 102).

137. Notice that this framework too is congenial to the framework I outlined in chapter 4. Indeed, if we wish to make a neurally plausible story, then something like this will probably be the most accurate.

138. Gary Cottrell has suggested that my version of SE memory fits well with a recurrent, "winner-take-all" connectionist network (personal communication).

139. I owe Harlan Miller for this information.

140. See also Forrest (1974).

141. See Morgan (1977) for details.

142. Gregory goes on to argue that a Wittgensteinian sort of perceptual ambiguity is very important for deciding when some entity exhibits true understanding. If a computer is fed or discovers parameters in the world, why should it not interpret these much as we do? If it does, then Gregory suggests that it should also suffer from perceptual ambiguities similar to ours as alternative interpretations of the data are made available. If this were to happen, then we could argue that the machine understands its sensory inputs similar to the way we understand ours.

143. Though see Fendrich et al. (1992) in rebuttal.

144. This point is discussed in greater detail in the next chapter; see also Hardcastle (1992, forthcoming).

145. It is tempting to conclude that infants are not conscious like we are, but it is unclear what we could mean by such a claim. If we have delimited the phenomena of consciousness in terms of SE memory and interpretive perceptions, then if anything lacks those attributes, then it is not conscious, by (our bounded) definition.

146. In particular, delayed-response function in pre-frontal cortex has been precisely localized to the principal sulcus (also known as Walker's area 46, and Brodman's area 9) (Goldman 1971, Goldman and Rosvold 1970, Goldman et al. 1971, Gross and Weiskrantz 1964, Mishkin 1957).

147. See also Kubota and Niki (1971).

148. Older human infants are able to perform delayed-response tasks before their frontal lobes are mature, and infant monkeys can perform the task even with their prefrontal cortex oblated (Goldman-Rakic et al. 1983). Goldman-Rakic argues that these results indicate that the prefrontal cortex does not assume its functional role in the cognitive system until relatively late in development and, prior to the frontal lobe taking over controlled memory functions, cortico-striatal connections allow the recall needed for delayed-response tasks to take place. Exactly how this structure operates is not known, but neuroscientists suspect that it is linked to operant and classical conditioning in young primates and humans (Bachevalier and Mishkin 1984).

149. See, e.g., Changeux and Danchin (1976), Changeux et al. (1973), Changeux et al. (1984).

150. Dan Lloyd suggested that infants then have a diminished form of consciousness (personal communications). However, I do not know what to make of that suggestion. I know what my consciousness is like; I know what it is like to aware of faint stimuli; I know what it is like to have only a few semantic connections for a given stimuli. But I do not know what a *diminished* consciousness would be. That, to me, is the same as saying that there is no consciousness (that I can understand) and to speak otherwise is only to obfuscate the issue.

151. This case is recorded in "Search for Mind," the first show in PBS series "The Mind" (WNET/New York in association with BBS, 1988).

152. George Mandler points out that 9 month old infants can do deferred imitation, and anterograde amnesics cannot (personal communication), which again suggests different mechanisms at work between young infants and amnesics. See also Mandler (1988, 1992) for more details on the development and competence of infants.

153. Notice that this understanding of what is required for an SE system means that severe agnosics may not be conscious in the same way we are. If patients are unable to

categorize any object or event along any dimension, then they would be more like the pigeons than the chimpanzees and so how to understand their experiences remains open. Although it may at first seem to be a little strange to hold that alert and responsive humans may not be conscious (in the ways we are), upon reconsideration, I don't believe that this position is so counter-intuitive. Can you imagine what it would be like to experience an array of visual input without understanding any of that input along any lines? Would we want to maintain that such a person is conscious in the same ways we are (in the visual domain)? Certainly the answers are far from clear. What their experiences are like does seem to be a nontrivial question for those on the outside looking in.

154. See also Akins (forthcoming).

155. Michael Tye (1991) argues that a tarted up version of the 2.5 D sketch corresponds to our phenomenology. Akins (forthcoming) though argues convincingly that revising the third level does not overcome the paradox.

156. This is Akins's analysis of Dennett, at any rate.

157. As do Ramachandran and Churchland (1993).

158. The following discussion is based on Kitcher (1990), as well as personal conversation with Patricia Churchland and Alex Levine; though see also Bird (1973) and Stroud (1979).

159. See Fodor (1975) for a classic example.

160. See Gibson (1959), Shaw and Bransford (1977). I should note that Gibson's ecological understanding of perception is still alive and well today. Marjorie Grene, for example, continually hurrumphs at my attempts to discuss mental representation, since, as she loudly and often proclaims, she is "a Gibsonian."

161. See, e.g., Treisman (1986).

162. See, e.g., Hubel and Livingstone (1987), Livingstone and Hubel (1987).

163. See Kandel and Schwartz (1987) for relevant neurophysiology; see also Damasio (1989), Goldman and Rosvold (1972), Goldman-Rakic (1987), Goldman-Rakic et al. (1983), Sereno (1990).

164. See, e.g., Blakeslee (1992), Bressler et al. (1993), Crick and Koch (1990), Flanagan (1992), Horgan (1994), Joliot et al., Koch (1992), Neuenschwander and Varela (1993), Stryker (1989, 1991).

165. Notice, however, that Treisman's hypothesis is at odds with how I believe perception and memory interact.

166. See also Coltheart (1980), Mewhort et al.(1981).

167. See also Hilz and Cavius (1970), Hochberg (1971), Morgan and Alba (1985), Van Der Horst et al. (1967).

168. See Prinzmetal and Keysar (1989).

169. See also Legéndy (1970) for discussion.

170. More sophisticated versions of this problem exist in which a few symbols can be active at a time in some system without collapse.

171. Cf., von der Malsburg (1987: 424).

172. See also König et al., (1992), Legéndy (1970), Sejnowski (1981).

173. Cf., von der Malsburg (1982, 1987).

174. Cf., Eckhorn and Reitbock (1988).

175. See also Engel et al. (1992), Schwartz et al. (1991), Young et al. (1992).

176. See also Engel et al. (1991).

177. See also Kretier et al. (1992).

178. See also Engel et al., (1991a, b), von der Malsburg and Buhman (1992). These results have now been extended to include interareal synchronization of area 17 and the posteromedial lateral supraslyvian area (PMLS), which is a visual association area specialized for motion.

179. There is some concern that stimulus-induced non-oscillatory synchronizations may be more fundamental for feature binding (Kruse et al. 1992).

180. See also Bressler et al. (1993), König et al. (1992), Neuenschwander and Varela (1993) for additional evidence.

181. E.g., Cotterill and Nielsen (1991), Desmond and Moore (1991), Finkel and Edelman (1989), Humel and Biederman (1992), Sporns et al. (1989, 1991, 1992); Tonomi et al. (1992), Wilson and Bower (1991).

182. See also Lumer and Huberman (1991).

183. These are the same confusions that I believe plague Kant (cf., section 6.2 above).

184. See also Horn et al. (1991), Baird (1991b) for discussion.

185. An apparent exception to this finding is Engel *et al.* (1991b). They found synchronization between areas specialized for spatial continuity (area 17) and coherence of motion (PMLS area). Area 17 engages in a high resolution, fine-grained analysis of local features, while PMLS has large receptive fields, is strongly directionally selective, but poorly-trained for orientation. This interareal synchronization serves to bind local with global features. However, from a higher level psychological perspective, it is not clear that these two areas do in fact code different *psychologically* defined features. Taken together, both areas could still be concerned with shape alone in that they (possibly) differentiate among objects by uniting different orientation of outlines with coherent motion. There is still no evidence that 40 Hz oscillations or other synchronous firing patterns tie radically different features domain together.

186. Until recently, about the only place where phase-locked 40 Hz oscillations were reliably found in unanesthetized animals was motor cortex (see Flament *et al.* 1992, Gaal *et al.* 1992, Murthy and Fetz 1992, Murthy *et al.* 1992, Smith and Fetz 1989). However, even though the oscillation results remain difficult to reproduce (though see Engel *et al.* 1992, Kreiter *et al.* 1992, Schwartz *et al.* 1992), they have now been found in areas 17 and 18 of alert cats. Unfortunately, the discharges were also found in a wide range of states not connected to stimulus interpretation, including saccadic eye movements and slow wave sleep (Lee *et al.* 1992). Hence, synchronous oscillations cannot be *sufficient* for feature binding (though they may still be necessary).

187. See also Edelman (1992), Kanedo and Tsuda (1994), Tsuda (1991, 1992, 1994, 1995), Tsuda and Barna (1994) for a similar perspective.

188. Tsuda's (1991, 1992, 1994, Tsuda and Barna 1994, Tsuda and Matsumoto 1984) notion of itinerant chaos is particularly important here.

189. See also Nicolis (1987).

190. Here, a non-linear dynamical system attractor is manifested as a coherent oscillation pattern on an EEG.

191. See also Baird (1986a, b), Freeman (1979a-c, 1983b), Freeman and Baird (1987), Freeman and Schneider (1982), Freeman and Skarda (1985a), Freeman *et al.* (1988).

192. *Cf.*, Freeman (1983), Basar (1988), Basar *et al.* (1989), Basar-Eroglu (1990), Basar-Eroglu and Basar (1991).

193. They call this process a form of "pattern recognition."

194. See also Baird (1991a-d), Baird *et al.* (1991).

195. See Baird (1991a-d), Baird *et al.* (1991), Freeman and Baird (1987).

196. See also Steinbüchel *et al.* (1992) for a slightly different perspective.

197. See also Basar (1980, 1988), Pfurtscheller *et al.* (1988).

198. This view of binding differs from both Mort Mishkin's and Antonio Damasio's (Damasio 1989, Mishkin 1982; see also Newman 1995 for review). Mishkin holds that the thalamus is crucial in the binding process. At the moment, there little evidence to warrant any definitive conclusions concerning the role of thalamus in binding (see Jones 1985, Steriade and Llinas 1988). However, I should note that persons who suffer from thalamic infarcts to do not seem to display binding problems; instead (aside from amnesia and characteristic frontal lobe disorders), the *rate* of information processing is slowed (Stuss *et al.* 1988). (These data might mean that insofar as binding is concerned, the thalamus plays only a modulatory role, similar to the monoamine systems (Foote 1985, Foote *et al.* 1983, Foote and Morrison 1987, Sapir 1987).) Other projection systems appear to relate to the level of arousal in an organism. It is really only when the so-called "association" cortices are damaged that we find binding disrupted, e.g. the various agnosias, Balint's syndrome, optic ataxia (Damasio 1985, 1987, Damasio and Benton 1979, Damasio *et al.* 1990).

This model of binding also makes Damasio's "convergence zones" unnecessary (although *exactly* what Damasio means by a "convergence zone" is not clear). If Damasio believes that our brains require localized combinatorial codes for proper feature binding in individual objects and for the spatial and temporal relationships of objects in events, then these codes would be unnecessary, if connectivity and the response properties of cortical neurons can completely determine what gets bound to what. No extra codes would be needed. Although there is very little data to support any speculations, I suspect that the sensory pathways themselves, plus the various feedback connections, determine what to bind together; at least, there does not seem to be any neuronal processor external to the cortex that selects which cortical cells should be linked together via some firing pattern. (My interpretation of the data is not without difficulties, however. Some of the more difficult binding problems, for example those involved in analyzing faces, appear to require activation by sub-cortical structures (Damasio 1985).)

199. See also Nunez (1981, 1989, 1993) and Kinsbourne (1988) for a different theory of the same type.

200. *Cf.*, Ermentrout (1979).

201. See Horwitz *et al.* (1967), Krill (1963), Penfield and Perot (1963), Siegel (1977) for relevant experiments.

202. Though see Winters and Wallach (1970).

203. Ermentrout (1979) details the mathematics.

204. Though see Charpak *et al.* (1992), Buzsaki (1989), Buzsaki *et al.* (1983), Nakamura *et al.* (1992), Schwender *et al.* (1991) for corroborating evidence.

205. Horgan (1987: 497-498). Though Horgan is concerned with the inverted spectrum and I with absent qualia, I believe his argument works for both. I follow this analysis in detail because the thought experiment he argues against still flourishes (*cf.*, Chalmers forthcoming).

206. See also Levin (1986).

207. Since (I suspect) few of us have solid intuitions about what is really imaginable, we also need to consider Horgan's second question: Even if we could successfully imagine some situation, does that mean that imagined situation is really physically possible? We could conceivably decide that our imagination need not be subservient to our prior assumption of mechanism, and so it is possible to fuse the two imaginings into a single complex situation. But if our notion of what counts as successful imagining is that weak, we could then argue that the third condition is modally unrealizable; it asserts something which has no place in the range of genuinely possible worlds. As Horgan suggests, we can compare imagining the absent qualia world with imagining that the moon is made of green cheese and that it persists in its present size, shape, and motion without any violations of (real) physical law (1987: 499).

208. Exactly what qualia supervene upon though is controversial (see Lycan 1993).

209. Dan Lloyd has raised the question of whether "knowability" can be cashed out as a true psychological property (Lloyd, personal communication). I suggest that it can be insofar as one can define it in terms of belief states (or potential belief states) and the relation those states have to the world. At least, I see no obvious barriers to thinking of knowability in those terms and I believe this is the sort of picture that Block and Shoemaker have as well.

210. This is a version of Shoemaker's original argument against the possibility of absent qualia. He gives a different argument in his reply to Block. That argument is considered in section 7.5 below.

211. Some pains might not be consciously felt, *cf.*, chapter 3.

212. Though see Dennett (1978a) for an opposing view.

213. I use the caveat "tendency" deliberately as a way of skirting the argument in chapter 1 that we do not have transparent introspective awareness of our conscious mental states. Even though we can separate the feeling of pain from our higher-order judgment that we are in pain, the conscious sensation of pain presumably causes this judgment regularly.

214. This is Block's phrase.

215. If we believe that psychological definitions cannot capture all the relevant aspects of mental states, then we could easily make such an assumption.

216. Larry Davis (unpublished) first formulated this term (*cf.*, Block 1980a).

217. We should briefly consider a second sort of creature, those who lack the capacity to have any sort of qualitative state whatsoever (see Davis 1982: 239-241). Since none of their states are qualia states, it is trivially true that the qualitative character of their mental states are inaccessible to introspection. Nevertheless, these creatures, if they ever had an ersatz pain, would deny that the state is inaccessible to introspection. They would deny that they are nonconscious. By hypothesis, these creatures feel nothing, but their denials of this fact would be sincere. As guaranteed by the functional identity of ersatz pain to real pain, they have every reason to believe that their pains are just as genuine as everyone else's. Moreover, we could not judge them unreasonable for denying that their states are merely ersatz.

218. This is Block's (1980a) way of phrasing the first premise.

219. Dan Lloyd suggests that one might be a "parochial functionalist" (Lloyd, personal communication). We could maintain that qualia were constituted by causal properties, but these causal defined properties might not be available to introspection. This sort of position might circumvent Shoemaker's argument without being chauvinistic. Ultimately, I shall agree with this sort of approach; however, the trick is to make this sort of causal definition intuitively plausible. That is, since whether we are having a qualitative experience is tied so closely to our introspective abilities, one needs to be clear on how to dissociate the psychological definition from the experience itself without having the theory entail the awkward conclusion that we do not know when we are conscious. I believe that my solution overcomes this potential difficulty.

220. See also Conee (1985: 364).

221. *Cf.*, chapter 3.

222. *Cf.*, Churchland (1986: 361); see also Hardcastle (1992, forthcoming).

223. This is a type of epiphenomenalism that is not metaphysical at all (Godfrey-Smith 1988; Horgan 1987). It holds that mentality, though it is completely physical, is not doing anything interesting in the brain. No psychological or neuroscientific theory would refer to it in its explanations of cognition or brain function. We could compare this position with the attitude that evolutionary biologists take toward the chin. (I owe this example to Godfrey-Smith.) This process of natural selection gave us the chin all right, but in this instance there was selection *of* something without selection *for* that thing (Sober 1984). The pattern of bone growth that produces the skull gives us the chin as a byproduct of bipedal gait. The muscles in the head and neck are shifted relative to four-footed creatures. Since our heads have to "balance" on the spinal column, our neck muscles are smaller and the jaw muscles are placed at a different angle, which puts greater force on the jaw bone. Greater force means more bone; hence, chins. (Ed Gruberg told me this story.) Consciousness might also be such a phenotypic freerider. We could also take Stich's argument that intentionality is not a proper psychological *explanans* as an

example of this sort of functionalist epiphenomenalism (Stich 1983). A similar position with respect to consciousness would be that consciousness results from some brain process, but that it does is not theoretically very interesting. (This last point is discussed in chapter 2.)

224. Shoemaker though does has a ready response to Block (Shoemaker 1981). Remember the crux of Shoemaker's argument is that if absent qualia were possible, then not only would we have no way of telling whether others experienced merely ersatz pain, but we would not be able to tell about *ourselves* whether we experience genuine pains. For my grounds for thinking that my pains are real are just the same as an "imitation" person whose pains are ersatz. He argues that the first premise of his argument should be amended to read: "If absent qualia are possible, then the presence or absence of the qualitative character of pain would make no difference to its causal consequences *that would make it possible for anyone to distinguish cases of genuine pain from cases of ersatz pain"* (1981, p. 588, italics his). So to refute this amended premise, then, it is not enough to simply point out, as Block does, that friends of absent qualia need not be committed to epiphenomenalism, nor it is enough to point out that having the same causal etiology as defined in a physical system does not entail having the same total causal role.

225. The claim that we must *accept* that absent qualia are not possible is a weaker claim than we must *believe* that absent qualia are not possible since it is possible to accept and use a scientific theory without believing it (*cf.*, van Fraassen 1980).

226. See also Block (1980a).

227. See also Lycan (1981).

228. See also Horgan (1984).

229. We might think of the hypothesized relationship on analogy with regulators in cars. Regulators take in electrical energy and then redistribute it according to need. I would argue that conscious mental states resemble the electrical energy the regulator "computes" over and the executive processors are similar to regulators (or perhaps regulators and alternators taken together).

230. *Cf.*, Norman and Shallice (1988).

231. See, e.g., Allport (1988), Baars (1985, 1988a, 1989a, b), Johnson-Laird (1983, 1988), Karmiloff-Smith (1988), Lahav (1993), Mandler (1975, 1984, 1985, 1988, 1989), Norman and Shallice (1988), Oatley (1988), Shallice (1988a, b), Umita (1988). However, Shallice (1988a) expresses some reservations about this model, and Posner and Klein (1973) and Johnson-Laird (1983) seem to identify the executive system with a higher level serial schema.

232. This hypothesized connection between executive processors and behavior is essentially the same as the one envisioned in the multiple memory framework. The major difference

between the two approaches is that executive phenomena are *not* conscious in the multiple memory framework.

233. Even though it is traditionally assumed that the structure of some physical system is supposed to be irrelevant to its psychological description, interdisciplinary cognitive scientists rely on neurophysiological evidence to help support their functional analyses of cognitive processes nonetheless. They do so in roughly the following manner. They analyze some cognitive process or other as a psychologically described process and then compare it to some physiologically described neural process, which exists quite separate from any higher level functional descriptions. If they can draw parallels between the two levels of analysis and among the independently derived descriptions, they then use this parallelism to justify using evidence about underlying "structure" to support arguments about instantiated "function." They base these sorts of arguments on the belief that if two descriptions are over the same state space, then they may use data supporting one description as evidence for the other.

Psychologists assume that if the functional description of consciousness they give is the same as the functional description of some brain area neuroscientists give, then (because the functional descriptions are over the same state space) the structure of consciousness just is the structure of that brain area, and whatever we know about that brain area will thereby increase our knowledge of consciousness. For example, cognitive psychologists try to identify the theoretical psychological entity "consciousness" just as a neurophysiological structure in the hopes of explaining why their higher level information processing theories of consciousness are adequate.

In this way, theories in neuroscience should be able to support theories in psychology. Indeed, this position reflects a fairly traditional reductionist position in psychology: there is a law-like correspondence between psychological theories and neuroscience, and this correspondence helps explain the accuracy of the psychological theories (*cf.*, Fodor 1974, 1978; 1981; also see Bechtel 1982, 1983; Hardcastle 1992, forthcoming, Mayr 1982, Wimsatt 1976 for modern revisionist versions of the "pseudo-reductive" relationship between neuroscience and psychology).

234. In contrast, the multiple memory framework postulates two types of *memories*, one of which is semantically schematic.

235. See also discussion in chapter 5 above.

236. I should point out that adults with lesioned or oblated prefrontal cortices still show evidence of SE memories, even if they cannot act upon them appropriately. This contrasts with young infants who, quite apart from their inability to seek complex goals, show *no* evidence of SE memory.

237. Though these are the two most plausible and widely accepted interpretations, others also abound. Some stress mnemonic processes; others emphasize spatial perception, attentional functions, motor control, kinesthesis or proprioception as the primary disrupted function.

238. I should point out, though, that the two main interpretations are not antithetical; one needs to be able to synthesize schemas to be able to use "representational memory" in order to respond to novel stimuli, just as one needs to be able to access and pick schemas from memory in order to temporally integrate them. However, no one involved in these debates seems interested in developing this sort of synthetic account.

239. Norman and Shallice appear to be guilty of the latter.

240. In both cases, the neuropsychological description of the processing attributes of the frontal lobe specify a possible decomposition of the psychological description of conscious processing. So, in either case, the more specific description of some neuropsychological interpretation refines the information processing description of conscious processing, and psychology could use the structural properties of the frontal lobes to fix the referents of consciousness.

241. This discussion is based on Goldman-Rakic (1987).

242. See chapter 4 for discussion of the hippocampal formation's relation to LTS episodic memories.

243. See Fuster (1980) for discussion.

244. See Goldman-Rakic (1987) for specific references.

245. See also Baars (1993).

246. In separate work, Baars concurs that these neural structures are not necessary (Baars 1993).

247. See also Foote and Morrison (1987), Sapir (1987) for a good review of the literature.

248. This discussion is based on Steriade and Llinas (1988). See their review article for specific references.

249. *Cf.*, Damasio (1985).

250. And these effects are not limited to visual deficits either. Complete bilateral lesions of primary auditory cortex chronically impairs tonal consonance perception, even though the cognitive functions which hierarchically structure pitch information and generate harmonic expectancies during music perception are spared. These functions, incidentally, have been tied to the thalamocortical auditory system (Tramo *et al.* 1990).

251. Moreover, at least agnosics show implicit priming effects (Humphreys *et al.* 1992), which is consistent with what one would expect if the multiple memory system framework for explaining consciousness were correct.

252. Jackendoff (1987) does advocate this methodological approach, but only insofar as it would further develop a strict information-processing theory of consciousness.

253. If my hunches are correct, then the property of being a qualitative experience would actually exist at the level of networks or below, so that it would be a property of the structures that instantiate our actual mental states and our psychological information processing.

254. See also Dennett (1992).

255. See also Kutas and Van Petten (1988).

256. This anterior negative effect can also be elicited along with the N400 when the prime is 100 msec long (Neville et al. 1989). (In these cases, subjects are conscious of the primes.) This fact corroborates my hypothesis that the early negative component is independent of consciousness.

257. Average response time to identity primed shapes (532.54 msec; s.e. = 27.09 msec), mirror priming (reaction time: 493.44 msec; s.e. = 29.87 msec), and category priming (reaction time: 562.52; s.e. = 26.49) was significantly faster than the unprimed targets (mean reaction time: 581.59 msec; s.e. = 22.42 msec) ($t(9) = -5.6$; $p < .001$, $t(9) = -7.3$; $p < .001$; $t(9) = -1.8$; $p < .001$, respectively). Though the mean reaction time for mirror priming is less than the reaction time for identity priming, the difference was not significant ($t(9) = 1.6$).

258. These results call into question previous suggestions that the general N400 effect is specific to linguistic or semantic events (e.g., Kutas and Van Petten 1988, Holcomb and Neville 1991, Rugg and Doyle 1992).

259. However, these P3 effects were not the same across the various priming variables. As can be seen in Figure 9.6A, there is a main effect for latency in the identity primed condition (main effect of priming condition: $F(1, 9) = 13.67, p < .005$), with the primed peak occurring on the order of 120 msec earlier. In addition, the amplitude of the identity primed P3 waveform was larger frontally and smaller posteriorly than the amplitude of the unprimed waveform (priming condition x electrode site effect: $F(4, 36) = 4.76, p < .04$).

The P3 component in the mirror primed condition was also significantly different from the unprimed component. Here, however, the amplitude of the mirror primed P3 was less than the amplitude of the unprimed component at all electrode sites (main effect of priming condition: $F(1, 9) = 10.42, p < .01$). Surprisingly, there were no latency effects in the unmasked mirror priming condition.

As is clear in Figure 9.7C, there is a significant main effect for amplitude in the category priming condition (main effect for priming condition: $F(1, 9) = 11.69, p < .008$). Indeed, the mean amplitude for the analyzed epoch was significantly less with category priming than with no priming (main effect for priming condition: $F(1, 9) = 6.63, p < .03$). There was also a significant effect for latency (main effect of category priming x electrode site: $F(4, 36) = 4.62$, $p < .006$), with the primed P3 peaking earlier than the unprimed one in the bilateral posterior regions.

260. The most prominent feature in the identity priming difference wave, and a component also found in the right hemisphere of the mirror priming difference wave (though absent in the category priming difference wave), is a large negativity peaking at about 375 msec, with a duration ranging from 100-300 msec. This "N375" is followed by a longer positivity, onsetting at approximately 450 msec and continuing for several hundred msec. (This positivity is present in the difference waves for all priming conditions.)

The N375 effect has significantly greater amplitude under the identity priming condition than with mirror priming (main effect of amplitude: $F(1, 9) = 12.55$, $p < .006$; main effect for mean amplitude: $F(1, 9) = 4.78$, $p < .06$). In the mirror priming difference waves, the peak amplitude of the N375 is greater over the right hemisphere and absent at the occipital sites (effect of priming condition x electrode sites: $F(4, 36) = 7.32$, $p < 006$).

In contrast to the N375, there were no significant differences in the size between the identity priming difference wave and the mirror priming difference wave for the positivity reflecting latency or amplitude shifts in the P3. The positive effect in the category priming difference wave has a different morphology. It onsets earlier and lasting longer, reflecting the different sort of P3 attenuation seen with category priming. Nonetheless, the general distribution of the P3 effect is the same.

261. Helen Neville has suggested that there might only be a shift in latency in the P3, which would account for the N400-like effects (Neville, personal communication).

262. Average response time to identity primed targets (543.6 msec; s.e. = 22.19 msec), mirror primed targets (532.3; s.e = 25.29), and category primed targets (554.27 msec; s.e. = 21.54) were not significantly faster than the unprimed targets (538.89 msec; s.e. = 18.64 msec).

263. An enhanced positivity began bilaterally over the N1 waveform in both the identity and mirror primed conditions (mean amplitude main effect of identity priming condition: $F(1, 9) = 7.60$, $p < .02$; of mirror priming condition: $F(1, 9) = 6.14$, $p < .04$). This effect induced a longer latency in both the priming conditions (peak latency main effect for identity priming condition: $F(1, 9) = 12.77$, $p < .005$; of mirror priming condition: $F(1, 9) = 23.24$, $p < .0009$) and a greater peak amplitude in the identity priming condition (mean effect of condition: $F(1, 9) = 12.52$, $p < .006$). There were no significant effects with category priming other than an increase in latency in the primed condition (main effect of condition: $F(1, 9) = 18.18$, $p < .002$).

The bilateral positivity continues through the P2 in both the identity and mirror priming conditions (main effect for mean amplitude for identity priming condition: $F(1, 9) = 9.62$, $p < .01$; for mirror priming condition: $F(1, 9) = 47.03$, $p < .0001$). The amplitude of the P2 is less in the identity primed condition over both hemispheres (main effect for peak amplitude: $F(1, 9) = 6.76$, $p < .03$) and over the right hemisphere in the mirror priming condition (peak amplitude condition x hemisphere effect: $F(1, 9) = 5.31$, $p < .05$).

264. Masked identity priming effects begin between 50 and 100 msec and continued to remain significantly different from the unprimed condition until 150 to 200 msec (amplitude main effect for 50-100 msec: $F(1, 9) = 11.99$, $p < .007$; for 100-150 msec: $F(1, 9) = 5.48$, $p < .04$; for 150-200 msec: $F(1, 9) = 6.18$, $p < .03$). A significant difference in amplitude again returned between 250 and 300 msec ($F(1, 9) = 6.37$, $p < .03$).

Amplitude differences began in the masked mirror priming condition between 100 and 150 msec and continued through 250 to 300 msec (100-150 msec: $F(1, 9) = 8.79$, $p < .02$; 150-200 msec: $F(1, 9) = 9.59$, $p < .01$; 200-250 msec: $F(1, 9) = 22.85$, $p < .001$; 250-300 msec = 10.68, $p < .01$).

There were no significant differences in amplitude sustained over 100 msec with masked category priming.

265. These data from using completely novel, nonverbal stimuli also suggest that priming is not a phenomenon which requires previously established memories.

266. Dretske (1995) disagrees with the claim, arguing that the mind — though clearly physical — should be understood apart from its biology. However, I think that ultimately we belong on the same side of the fence.

References

Adey, W.R., F.R. Bell, & B.H. Dennis. 1962. "Effects of LSD-25, Psilocybin, and Psilocin on Temporal Lobe EEG Patterns and Learned Behavior in the Cat". *Neurology* 12.591-602.

Adrian, E.D. 1942. "Olfactory Reactions in the Brain of the Hedgehog". *Journal of Physiology* 100.459-473.

Akins, K. 1993. "A Bat Without Qualities?" *Consciousness: Philosophical and Psychological Essays* ed. by M. Davies & G. Humphreys. New York: Blackwell.

Akins, K. Forthcoming. Review of Michael Tye's *The Imagery Debate*. To appear in *Philosophical Review*.

Akins, K. & S. Winger. Forthcoming. "Ships in the Night: Churchland and Ramachandran on Dennett's Theory of Consciousness."

Alexander, S. 1920. *Space, Time, and Deity*. 2 Vols. London: Macmillan.

Allport, D. 1988. "What Concept Consciousness?" *Consciousness in Contemporary Science* ed. by A. Marcel & E. Bisiach, 159-182. Oxford: Clarendon Press.

Alvarez-Royo, P., S. Zola-Morgan, & L.R. Squire. 1992. "Impairment of Long-Term Memory and Sparing of Short-Term Memory in Monkeys with Lesions of the Hippocampal Formation". *Society of Neuroscience Abstract* 18.387.

Anderson, J., & G. Bower. 1973. *Human Associative Memory*. Washington, D.C.: Winston.

Angeli, S.J., E.A. Murray, & M. Mishkin. 1993. "Hippocampectomized Monkeys Can Remember One Place But Not Two". *Neuropsychologia* 31.1021-1030.

Anton, G. 1899. "Über die Selbstwahrnehmung der Herderkrankungen des Gehirns durch den Kranken bei Rindendblindheit and Rindentaubheit". *Archiv für Psychatrie and Nervenkrankheiten* 32.86-127.

Arias, C., C.A. Curet, H.F. Moyano,& S. Joekes. 1993. "Echolocation: A Study of Auditory Functioning in Blind and Sighted Subjects". *Journal of Visual Impairment and Blindness* 8773-77.

Atkinson, R.C., & R.M. Shiffrin. 1968. "Human Memory: A Proposed System and Its Control Processes". *The Psychology of Learning Motivation: Advances in Research and Theory, Volume 2* ed. by K.W. Spence & J.T. Spence. New York: Academic Press.

Baars, B.J. 1985. "Conscious Contents Provide the Nervous System with Coherent, Global Information". *Consciousness and Self-Regulation: Advances in Research and Theory, Volume 3* ed. by R.J. Davidson, G.E. Schwartz, & D. Shapiro. New York: Plenum Press.

Baars, B.J. 1988. "Momentary Forgetting as a 'Resetting' of a Conscious Global Workspace Due to Competition Between Incompatible Contexts". *Psychodynamics and Cognition* ed. by M.J. Horowitz, 269-293. Chicago: Chicago University Press.

Baars, B.J. 1989. *A Cognitive Theory of Consciousness*. New York: Cambridge University Press.

Baars, B.J. 1993. "How Does a Serial, Integrated and Very Limited Stream of Consciousness Emerge from a Nervous System That is Mostly Unconscious, Distributed, Parallel and of Enormous Capacity?" *Experimental and Theoretical Studies of Consciousness*. *Ciba Foundation Symposium 174*, 282-303, Chichester: Wiley.

Baars, B.J., & G. Newman. 1988. "Convergent Cognitive and Neurophysiological Evidence for a Global Workspace Theory of Consciousness". ms.

Baars, B.J., & G. Newman. 1994. "A Neurobiological Interpretation of Global Workspace Theory". *Consciousenss in Philosophy and Cognitive Neuroscience* ed. by A. Revonsuo & M. Kampinen, 211-226, Hillsdale, New Jersey: Lawrence Erlbaum.

Bachevalier, J., & M. Mishkin. 1984. "An Early and a Late Developing Memory System for Learning and Retention in Infant Monkeys". *Behavioral Neuroscience* 98.770-778.

Badalyan, L.O., P.A. Temin, S.A. Groppa, & M.Y. Nikanorova. 1991. "Neuropsychic Disorders in Vitamin B12 Deficiency". *Zhurnal Navopalologii i Psikhiatrii imeni S.S. Korsakova* 91.89-90.

Baddeley, A.D., & R.H. Logie. Forthcoming. "Auditory Imagery and Working Memory". To appear in *Auditory Imagery* ed. by D. Reisberg. Hillsdale, New Jersey: Erlbaum.

Baddeley, A.D., & B. Wilson. 1988. "Frontal Amnesia and the Dysexutive Syndrome. Special Issue: Single-Case Studics in Amnesia: Theoretical Advances". *Brain Dynamics*, 43-71, New York: Springer.

Baird, B. 1986a. "Bifurcation Analysis of Oscillating Network Model of Pattern Recognition in the Rabbit Olfactory Bulb". *Neural Networks for Computing, AIP Conference Proceedings* ed. by J. Denker. Snobird, Utah.

Baird, B. 1986b. "Nonlinear Dynamics of Pattern Formation and Pattern Recognition in the Rabbit Olfactory Bulb". *Physica* 22D.150-175.

Baird, B. 1991a. "A Bifurcation Theory Approach to the Programming of Periodic Attractors in Network Models of Olfactory Cortex". *Advances in Neural Information Processing Systems 1* ed. by D.S. Touretzky, 459-468, San Mateo, California: Morgan Kaufman.

Baird, B. 1991b. "Associative Memory in a Simple Model of Oscillating Cortex". *Advances in Neural Processing Systems 2* ed. by D.S. Touretzky, 68-75, San Mateo, California: Morgan Kaufman.

Baird, B. 1991c. "Hierarchical Sensory-Motor Architecture of Oscillating Cortical Area Subnetworks". *IJCCN Proceedings*. Seattle, Washington.

Baird, B. 1991d. "Learning with Synpatic Nonlinearities in a Coupled Oscillator Model of Olfactory Cortex". *Analysis and Modeling of Neural Systems*. ed. by F.H. Eeckman.

Baird, B., W.J. Freeman, F.H. Eeckman, & Y. Yao. 1991. "Applications of Chaotic Neurodymanics in Pattern Recognition". *SPIE Proceedings, Volume 1469*.

Barinaga, M. 1992. "Unraveling the Dark Paradox of Blind Sight". *Science* 258.1438-1439.

Barnes, C.A. 1979. "Memory Deficits Associated with Senescence: A Behavioral and Neurophysiological Study in the Rat". *Journal of Comparative Physiological Psychology* 93.74-104.

Barrett, S.E., & M.D. Rugg. 1989. "Event-Related Potentials and the Semantic Matching of Faces". *Electroencephalography and Clinical Neurophysiology* 60.343-355.

Barrett, S.E., M.D. Rugg, & D.I. Perrett. 1988. "Event-Related Potentials and the Matching of Familiar and Unfamiliar Faces". *Neuropsychologia* 26.105-117.

Bartus, R.T., & T.E. Levere. 1977. "Frontal Decortication in Rhesus Monkeys: A Test of the Interference Hypothesis". *Brain Research*,119.233-248.

Basar, E. 1972. "A Study of the Time and Frequency Characteristics of the Potentials Evoked in the Acoustical Cortex". *Kybernetik* 10.61-64.

Basar, E. 1980. *EEG-Brain Dynamics: Relations Between EEG and Brain Evoked Potentials.* Amsterdam: Elsevier.

Basar, E. 1983. "Synergetics of Neural Populations: A Survey on Experiments". *Synergetics of the Brain* ed. by E. Basar, H. Flohr, H. Haken, & A.J. Mandell, 183-200, New York: Springer-Verlag.

Basar, E. 1988. "EEG-Dynamics and Evoked Potentials in Sensory and Cognitive Processing By the Brain". *Dynamics of Sensory and Cognitive Processing By the Brain* ed. by E. Basar, 30-55, New York: Springer-Verlag.

Basar, E., & C. Ozesmi. 1972. "The Hippocampal EEG Activity and a Systems Analytical Interpretation of Averaged Evoked Potentials in the Brain". *Kybernetik* 12.45-54.

Basar, E., & P. Ungan. 1973. "A Component Analysis and Principles Derived for the Understanding of Evoked Potentials in the Brain: Studies in the Hippocampus". *Kybernetik* 12.133-140.

Basar, E., C. Basar-Eroglu, J. Röschke & A. Shütt, A. 1989. "The EEG Is a Quasi-Deterministic Signal Anticipating Sensory Cognitive Tasks". *Biological Cybernetics* 25.41-48.

Basar, E., A. Gönder, & P. Ungan. 1976. "Important Relation Between EEG and Brain Evoked Potentials: II. A System Analysis of Electrical Signals from the Human Brain". *Biological Cybernetics* 25.41-48.

Basar, E., B. Rosen, C. Basar-Eroglu, & F. Greitshus. 1987. "The Associations Between 40 Hz-EEG and the Middle Latency Response of the Auditory Evoked Potential". *International Journal of Neuroscience* 33.103-117.

Basar-Eroglu, C. 1990. *Eine Vergleichende Studie Corticaler und Subcorticaler Ereigniskrelierter Potentiale des Katzengehirns.* Habilitationsschrift. Medizinische Universität zu Lübeck.

Basar-Eroglu, C., & E. Basar. 1985. "An Analysis of Field Potentials of the Cat Cerebellum". *Pflügers Archiv* 403.R55.

Basar-Eroglu, C., & E. Basar. 1991. "A Compound P300-40 Hz Response of the Cat Hippocampus". *International Journal of Neuroscience* 60.227-237.

Bechtel, W. 1982. "Two Common Errors in Explaining Biological and Psychological Phenomena". *Philosophy of Science* 49.549-574.

Bechtel, W. 1983. "A Bridge Between Cognitive Science and Neuroscience: The Functional Architecture of the Mind". *Philosophical Studies* 44.319-330.

Bechtel, W., & R.C. Richardson. 1993. *Discovering Complexity: Decomposition and Localization as Strategies in Scientific Research.* Princeton, New Jersey: Princeton University Press.

Bem, D.J. 1972. "Self-Perception Theory". *Advances in Experimental Social Psychology, Volume 6* ed. by L. Berkowitz. New York: Academic Press.

Benson, D.F., & D.T. Stuss. 1990. "Frontal Lobe Influences on Delusions: A Clinical Perspective". *Schizophrenia Bulletin* 16.403-411.

Bentin, S., G. McCarthy, & C.C. Wood. 1985. "Event-Related Potentials Associated with Semantic Processing". *Electroencephalography and Linear Neurophysiology* 60.343-355.

Berglund, M., L. Gustafson, & B. Hagberg. 1979. "Amnestic-Confabulatory Syndrome in Hydrocephalic Dementia and Korsakoff's Psychosis in Alcoholism". *Acta Psychiatrica Scandanavia* 60.323-333.

Bergson, H. 1913/1962. *Matter and Memory*. London: G. Allen and Unwin.

Berlin, B., & P. Kay. 1969. *Basic Color Terms: Their Universality and Evolution*. Berkeley: University of California Press.

Bigelow, J. & R. Pargetter. 1990. "Acquaintance with Qualia". *Theoria*.

Bird, G. 1973. *Kant's Theory of Knowledge: An Outline of One Central Argument in the Critique of Pure Reason*. New York: Humanities Press.

Bishop, D.V.M. 1983. "Linguistic Impairment After Left Hemidecortication for Infantile Hemiplegia? A Reappraisal". *Quarterly Journal of Experimental Psychology* 35A.199-207.

Bishop, D.V.M. 1988. "Can The Right Hemisphere Mediate Language As Well as The Left? A Critical Review of Recent Research". *Cognitive Neuropsychology* 5.353-367.

Black, M. 1949. *Language and Philosophy*. Ithaca, New York: Cornell.

Blakeslee, S. 1992. "Nerve Cell Rhythm May Be Key to Consciousness". *The New York Times* October 27. C1.

Bliss, T.V.P., & T. Lomo. 1973. "Long-Lasting Potentiation of Synaptic Transmission in the Dentate Area of the Anesthetized Rabbit Following Stimulation for the Perforant Path". *Journal of Physiology* 232.331-356.

Block, N. 1980a. "Are Absent Qualia Impossible?" *Philosophical Review* LXXXIX.257-274.

Block, N. 1980b. "What is Functionalism?" *Readings in the Philosophy of Psychology, Volume 1* ed. by N. Block, 171-184, Cambridge, Massachusetts: Harvard University Press.

Block, N. 1992. "Begging the Question Against Phenomenal Consciousness". *Behavioral and Brain Sciences* 15.205-206.

Block, N. Forthcoming. "On a Confusion about a Function of Consciousness". To appear in *Behavioral and Brain Sciences*.

Block, N., & J.A. Fodor. 1972. "What Psychological States Are Not". *Philosophical Review* LXXXI.159-181.

Boehm, R. 1986. "The Use of Echolocation as a Mobility Aid for Blind Persons". *Journal of Visual Impairment and Blindness* 80.953-954.

Bogen, J., & J. Woodward. 1988. "Saving the Phenomena". *Philosophical Review* XCVII.303-352.

Bregman, A., & A. Rudnicky. 1975. "Auditory Segregation: Stream or Streams?" *Journal of Experimental Psychology: Human Perception and Peformance* 1.263-267.

Brentano, F. 1874. *Psychology from an Empirical Standpoint*. Leipzig: Duncker and Humbolt.

Bressler, S.L. 1984. "Spatial Organization of EEGs from Olfactory Bulb and Cortex". *Electroencephalography and Clinical Neurophysiology* 57.270-276.

Bressler, S.L. 1994. "Dynamic Self-Organization in the Brain as Observed by Transcient Cortical Coherence". *Origins: Brain and Self Organization* ed. by K. Pribram, 536-545, New York: Lawrence Erlbaum Associates.

Bressler, S.L., & W.J. Freeman. 1980. "Frequency Analysis of Olfactory System EEG in Cat, Rabbit, and Rat". *Electroencephalography and Clinical Neurophysiology* 5.19-24.

Bressler, S.L., R. Coppola, & R. Nakamura. 1993. "Episodic Multiregional Cortical Coherence at Multiple Frequencies During Visual Task Performance". *Nature* 366.153-156.

Brody, L.R. 1981. "Visual Short-Term Cued Recall Memory in Infancy". *Child Development* 52.242-250.

Brooks, D.N., & D. Baddeley. 1976. "What Can Amnesics Learn?" *Neuropsychologia* 14.111-122.

Brown, A.S. & D.B. Mitchell. 1994. "A Reevaluation of Semantic Versus Nonsemantic Processing in Implicit Memory". *Memory and Cognition* 22.533-541.

Burns, B., & B.E. Shepp. 1988. "Dimensional Interactions and the Structure of Psychological Space: The Representation of Hue, Saturation, and Brightness". *Perception and Psychophysics* 43.494-507.

Butters, N., W.C. Heindel, & D.P. Salmon. 1990. "Dissociation of Implicit Memory in Dementia: Neurological Implications". *Bulletin of the Psychonomic Society* 28.359-366.

Buzsaki, G. 1989. "Two-Stage Model of Memory Trace Formation: A Role for 'Noisy' Brain States". *Neuroscience* 31.551-570.

Buzsaki, G., L.S. Leung, & C.H. Vanderwolf. 1983. "Cellular Bases of Hippocampal EEG in the Behaving Rat". *Brain Research Review* 6.139-171.

Campbell, F.W. 1983. "Prologue". *Color Vision: Physiology and Psychophysics* ed. by J.D. Mollon & L.T. Sharpe. London: Academic Press.

Cantor, J.R., D. Zillman, & J.. Bryant. 1975. "Enhancement of Experienced Arousal in Response to Erotic Stimuli Through Misattribution of Unrelated Residual Arousal". *Journal of Personality and Social Psychology* 32.69-75.

Cartwright, N. 1983. *How the Laws of Physics Lie.* Oxford: Clarendon Press.

Castelucci, V., & E.R. Kandell. 1976. "An Invertebrate System for the Cellular Study of Habituation and Sensitization". *Habituation* ed. by T.J. Tighe & R.N. Leaton. Hillsdale, New Jersey: Erlbaum.

Chalmers, D.J. Forthcoming. *Toward a Theory of Consciousness.* Cambridge, Massachusetts: The MIT Press.

Changeux, J-P. 1984. *The Neuronal Man: The Biology of Man,* translated by L. Garey. New York: Pantheon Books.

Changeux, J-P., & A. Danchin. 1976. "Selective Stabilization of Developing Synapses as a Mechanism for the Specification of Neuronal Networks". *Nature* 264.705-712.

Changeux, J-P., Ph. Courrege, & A. Danchin. 1973. "A Theory of Epigenesis of Neural Networks by Selective Stabilization of Synapses". *Proceedings of the National Academy of Science USA* 70.2974-2978.

Changeux, J-P., T. Heidman, & P. Patte. 1984. "Learning By Selection". *The Biology of Learning* ed. by P. Marler & H.S. Terrance, 115-133, Berlin: Springer-Verlag.

Charpak, S., D. Pare, & R. Llinas. 1992. "Entorhinal Cortex E. Generates 40 Hz Hippocampal Oscillations". *Society for Neuroscience Abstracts* 18.917.

Churchland, P.M. 1979. *Scientific Realism and the Plasticity of Mind.* New York: Cambridge University Press.

Churchland, P.M. 1983. "Reduction, Qualia, and the Direct Introspection of Brain States". *Journal of Philosophy* 82.8-28.

Churchland, P.M. 1984. *Matter and Consciousness*. Cambridge, Massachusetts: The MIT Press.

Churchland, P.M. 1989. *A Neurocomputational Perspective: The Nature of Mind and the Structure of Science*. Cambridge, Massachusetts: The MIT Press.

Churchland, P.M., & P.S. Churchland. 1981. "Functionalism, Qualia, and Intentionality". *Philosophical Topics* 1.

Churchland, P.S. 1983. "Consciousness: The Transmutation of a Concept". *Pacific Philosophical Quarterly* 64.80-95.

Churchland, P.S. 1986. *Neurophilosophy: Toward a Unified Science of the Mind-Brain.* Cambridge, Massachusetts: The MIT Press.

Cohen, L.B., J.S. DeLoache, & R. Pearl. 1977. "An Examination of Interference Effects in Infants' Memory for Faces". *Child Development* 48.88-96.

Cohen, N.J. 1984. "Preserved Learning Capacity in Amnesia: Evidence for Multiple Memory Systems". *Neuropsychology of Memory* ed. by L.R. Squire & N. Butters, 83-103, New York: Gulford Press.

Cohen, N.J., & L. Squire. 1980. "Preserved Learning and Retention Pattern-Analyzing Skill in Amnesia: Dissociation of 'Knowing How' and 'Knowing That'". *Science* 210.207-209.

Collins, A., & E. Loftus. 1975. "A Spreading-Activation Theory of Semantic Processing". *Psychological Review* 82.407-428.

Coltheart, M. 1980. "Iconic Memory and Visible Persistence". *Perception and Psychophysics* 27.183-228.

Conee, E. 1985. "The Possibility of Absent Qualia". *The Philosophical Review* XCIV.345-366.

Corkin, S. 1965. "Tactually-Guided Maze Learning in Man: Effects of Unilateral Cortical Excisions and Bilateral Hippocampal Lesions". *Neuropsychologia* 3.339-351.

Corkin, S. 1968. "Acquisition of Motor Skill After Bilateral Medial Temporal-Lobe Damage". *Neuropsychologia* 6.255-265.

Corkin, S. 1984. "Lasting Consequences of Bilateral Medial Temporal Lobectomy: Clinical Course and Experimental Findings in H.M.". *Seminars in Neurology* 4.249-259.

Cornell, E.H. 1975. "Infants' Visual Attention to Pattern Arrangement and Orientation". *Child Development* 46.229-232.

Corter, C.M., K.J. Zucker, & R.F. Galligan. 1980. "Patterns in the Infants' Search for Mother During Brief Separation". *Devleopmental Psychology* 16.62-69.

Cotterill, R.M., & C. Nielsen. 1991. "A Model for Cortical 40 Hz Oscillations Invokes Inter-Area Interactions". *Neuroreport* 2.289-292.

Cowey, A., & P. Stoerig. 1991. "The Neurobiology of Blindsight". *Trends in Neuroscience* 14.140.

Cowey, A., & P. Stoerig. 1992. "Reflections on Blindsight". *The Neuropsychology of Consciousness* ed. by A.D. Milner & M.D. Rugg, 11-37, New York: Academic Press.

Crick, F.H.C. 1993. *The Astonishing Hypothesis*. New York: Basic Books.

Crick, F.H.C., & C. Koch. 1990. "Towards a Neurobiological Theory of Consciousness". *Seminars in Neuroscience* 2.263-275.

Critchley, M. 1979. *The Divine Banquet of the Brain*. New York: Raven Press.

Cyander, M., N. Berman, & A. Hein. 1976. "Recovery of Function in Cat Visual Cortex Following Prolonged Deprivation". *Experimental Brain Research* 25.139-156.

Cytowic, R.E. 1993. *The Man Who Tasted Shapes A Bizarre Medical Mystery Offers Revolutionary Insights into Emotions, Reasoning, and Consciousness.* New York: Jeremy Tarcher/Putnam.

D'Amato, M.R., D.P. Salmon, & M. Colombo. 1985. "Extent and Limits of the Matching Concept in Monkeys (*Cebus apella*)". *Journal of Experimental Psychology: Animal Behavior Processes* 11.35-51.

Dalla-Barba, G., L. Cipolotti, & G. Denes. 1990. "Autobiographical Memory Loss and Confabulation in Korsakoff's Syndrome: A Case Report". *Cortex* 26.525-534.

Damasio, A.R. 1985. "Disorders of Complex Visual Processing: Agnosias, Achromatopsia, Balint's Syndrome, and Related Difficulties of Orientation and Construction". *Principles of Behavioral Neurology* ed. by M.M. Mesulam, 259-288, Philadelphia: F.A. David.

Damasio, A.R. 1989. "The Brain Binds Entities and Events by Multiregional Activation from Convergence Zones". *Neural Computation* 1.123-132.

Damasio, A.R., & A.L. Benton. 1979. "Impairment of Hand Movements under Visual Guidance". *Neurology* 29.170-178.

Damasio, A.R., D. Tranel, & J. Damasio. 1990. "Face Agnosia and the Neural Substrates of Memory". *Annual Review of Neuroscience* 13.89-109.

Davidson, D. 1970. "Mental Events". *Essays on Actions and Events.* New York: Clarendon Press.

Davis, L. 1982. "Functionalism and Absent Qualia". *Philosophical Studies* 41.231-251.

Davis, M., D.S. Gendelman, M.D. Tischler, & J.H. Kehne. 1982. "A Primary Acoustic Startle Circuit: Lesion and Stimulation Studies". *Journal of Neuroscience* 2.791-805.

Dember, W., & D. Purcell. 1967. "Recovery of Masked Visual Targets by Inhibition of the Masking Stimulus". *Science* 157.1335-1336.

Dennett, D.C. 1978a. "Toward a Cognitive Theory of Consciousness". *Minnesota Studies in the Philosophy of Science, Volume 9: Perception and Cognition, Issues in the Foundation of Psychology* ed. by C.W. Savage, 201-228, Minneapolis: University of Minnesota Press.

Dennett, D.C. 1978b. "Why a Computer Can't Feel Pain". *Synthese* 38.3.

Dennett, D.C. 1981. "Wondering Where the Yellow Went". *Monist* 64.102-108.

Dennett, D.C. 1982. "How to Study Consciousness Empirically or Nothing Comes to Mind". *Synthese* 53.158-180.

Dennett, D.C. 1988. "Quining Qualia". *Consciousness in Contemporary Science* ed. by A. Marcel & E. Bisiach, 42-77, Oxford: Clarendon Press.

Dennett, D.C. 1991. *Consciousness Explained.* Cambridge, Massachusetts: The MIT Press.

Dennett, D.C., & M. Kinsbourne, M. 1992. "Time and the Observer: The Where and When of Consciousness in the Brain". *Brain and Behavioral Sciences* 15.183-200.

Derruchet, P., & D. Baveux. 1989. "Correlational Analysis of Explicit and Implicit Memory Performance". *Memory and Cognition* 17.77-86.

Desimone, R. 1992. "The Physiology of Memory: Recordings of Things Past". *Science* 258.245-247.

Desmond, J.E., & J.W. Moore. 1991. "Altering the Synchrony of Stimulus Trace Processes: Tests of a Neural-Network Model". *Biological Cybernetics* 65.161-169.

Dirks, J., & E.J. Gibson. 1977. "Infants' Perception of Similarity Between Live People and Their Photographs". *Child Development* 48.124-130.

Doyere, V., F. Burette, C.R. Negro, & S. Laroche. 1993. "Long-Term Potentiation of Hippocampal Afferents and Efferents to Prefrontal Cortex: Implications for Associative Learning". *Neuropsychologia* 31.1031-1053.

Dretske, F.I. 1981. *Knowledge and the Flow of Information.* Cambridge, Massachusetts: The MIT Press.

Dretske, F.I. 1989. *Explaining Behavior: Reasons in a World of Causes.* Cambridge, Massachusetts: The MIT Press.

Dretske, F.I. 1995. *Naturalizing the Mind.* Cambridge, Massachusetts: The MIT Press.

Dynes, S.B., & B. Delautte. 1992. "Phase-Locking of Auditory-Nerve Discharges to Sinusoidal Electric Stimulation of the Cochlea". *Hearing Research* 58.79-90.

Ebbinghaus, H. 1902. *The Principles of Psychology.* Leibzig: Veit.

Eckhorn, R., & H.J. Reitbock. 1988. "Assessment of Cooperative Firing in Groups of Neurons: Special Concepts for Multiunit Recordings from the Visual System". *Brain Dynamics* ed. by E. Basar, 219-227, Berlin: Springer-Verlag.

Eckhorn, R., R. Bauer, & H.J. Reitbock. 1988. "Discontinuities in Visual Cortex and Possible Functional Implications". *Dynamics of Sensory and Cognitive Processing by the Brain* ed. by E. Basar & T.H. Bullock. New York: Springer. Springer Series in Brain Dynamics, Volume 2.

Eckhorn, R., R. Bauer, W. Jordan, M. Brosch, W. Kruse, & M. Munk. 1988. "Functionally Related Modules of Cat Visual Cortex Show Stimulus-Evoked Coherent Oscillations: A Multiple Electrode Study". *Investigations in Opthamological Visual Science* 28.12.

Eckhorn, R., R. Bauer, W. Jordan, M. Brosch, W. Kruse, M. Munk, & H.J. Reitbock. 1988. "Coherent Oscillations: A Mechanism of Feature Linking in the Visual Cortex". *Biological Cybernetics* 60.121-130.

Eckhorn, R., H.J. Reitbock, M. Arndt, & P. Dicke. 1989. "A Neural Network for Feature Linking Via Synchronous Activity: Results from Cat Visual Cortex and from Simulations". *Models of Brain Function* ed. by R.M.J. Cotteril. Cambridge, England: Cambridge University Press.

Eggemont, J.J 1991. "Rate and Synchroniztion Measure of Periodicity Coding in Cat Primary Auditory Cortex". *Hearing Research* 56.153-167.

Eich, J.E. 1984. "Memory for Unattended Events: Remembering With and Without Awareness". *Memory and Cognition* 12.105-111.

Engel, A.K., A.K. Kreiter, & W. Singer. 1992. "Oscillatory Responses in the Superior Temporal Sulcus of Anaesthetized Macaque Monkeys". *Society for Neuroscience Abstracts* 18.12.

Engel, A.K., A.K. Kreiter, P. Konig, & W. Singer. 1991. "Synchronization of Oscillatory Neuronal Responses between Striate and Extrastriate Cortical Areas of the Cat". *Proceedings of the National Academy of Sciences of the United States of America* 88.6048-6052.

Engel, A.K., P. Konig, & W. Singer. 1991. "Direct Physiological Evidence for Scene Segmentation by Temporal Coding". *Proceedings of the National Academy of Sciences of the United States of America* 88.9136-1940.

Engel, A.K., P. Konig, A.K. Kreiter, & W. Singer. 1991. "Interhemispheric Synchronization of Oscillatory Neuronal Responses in Cat Visual Cortex". *Science* 252.1177-1179.

Ermentrout, R. 1979. "A Mathematical Theory of Visual Hallucination Patterns". *Biological Cybernetics* 34.137-150.

Eslinger, P., & A. Damasio. 1985. "Severe Disturbance of Higher Cognition After Bilateral Frontal Ablation". *Neurology* 35.1731-1741.

Everatt, J., & G. Underwood. 1992. "Parafoveal Guidance and Priming Effects During Reading: A Special Case of the Mind Being Ahead of the Eyes". *Consciousness and Cognition* 1.186-197.

Fagan, J.F. 1971. "Infants' Recognition Memory for a Series of Visual Stimuli". *Journal of Experimental Child Psychology* 11.244-250.

Fagan, J.F. 1973. "Infants' Delayed Recognition Memory and Forgetting". *Journal of Experimental Child Psychology* 16.424-450.

Fagan, J.F. 1979. "The Origins of Facial Pattern Recognition". *Psychological Development From Infancy* ed. by M. Bornstein & W. Kessen . Hillsdale, Ner Jersey: Erlbaum.

Fagan, J.F., & C.K. Rovee-Collier. 1982. "A Conditioning Analysis of Infant Memory". *The Expression of Knowledge* ed. by R.L. Issacson and N. Spear . New York: Plenum Press.

Farah, M. 1990. *Visual Agnosia: Disorders of Object Recognition and What They Tell Us About Normal Vision.* Cambridge, Massachusetts: The MIT Press.

Farah, M. 1994. "Neuropsychological Inference with an Interactive Brain: A Critique of the Locality Assumption". *Behavioral and Brain Sciences* 17.43-61.

Fendrich, R., C.M. Wessinger, & M.S. Gazzaniga. 1992. "Residual Vision in a Scotoma: Implication for Blindsight". *Science* 258.1489-1491.

Ferraro, G.R., D.A. Balota, & L.T. Connor. 1993. "Implicit Memory and the Formation of New Associations in Nondemented Parkinson's Disease Individuals and Individuals with Senile Dementia of the Alzheimer Type: A Serial Reaction Time SRT. Investigation". *Brain and Cognition* 21.163-180.

Ferrier, D. 1886. *Functions of the Brain 2nd Edition.* . New York: Plenum Press.

Feustal, T.C., R.M. Shiffrin, & A. Salasoo. 1983. "Episodic and Lexical Contributions to the Repetition Effect in Word Identification". *Journal of Experimental Psychology: General* 112.309-346.

Finkel, L.H., & G.M. Edelman. 1989. "Integration of Distributed Cortical Systems by Reentry: A Computer Simulation of Interactive Functionally Segregated Visual Areas". *Journal of Neuroscience* 9.3188-3208.

Finkelstein, J.C., & L.A. Walker. 1976. "Evaluation Apprehension as a Mediator of Responses to Pupil-Size Cues". *Personality and Social Psychology Bulletin* 2.474-477.

Flade, A., & G. Linder. 1979. "Pupillary Size and Its Role in the Perception of Persons". *Zeitschrift fur Experimentelleund Angewandte Psychologie* 26.436-447.

Flament, D., P.A. Fortier, & E.E. Fetz. 1992. "Coherent 25- to 35-Hz Oscillations in the Sensorimotor Cortex of Awake Behaving Monkeys". *Proceedings of the National Academy of Sciences of the United States of America* 89.5670-5674.

Flanagan, O. 1985. "Consciousness, Naturalism, and Nagel". *The Journal of Mind and Behavior* 6.373-390.

Flanagan, O. 1992. *Consciousness Reconsidered.* Cambridge, Massachusetts: The MIT Press.

Fodor, J.A. 1974. "Special Sciences". *Synthese* 28.77-115.

Fodor, J.A. 1975. *The Language of Thought.* New York: Thomas Y. Crowell, Company.

Fodor, J.A. 1978. "Computation and Reduction". *Minnesota Studies in the Philosophy of Science: Perception and Cognition, Volume 9* ed. by W. Savage. Minneapolis: The University of Minnesota Press.

Fodor, J.A. 1981. *RePresentations: Philosophical Essays on the Foundations of Cognitive Science*. Cambridge, Massachusetts: The MIT Press.

Fodor, J.A. 1987. *Psychosemantics*. Cambridge, Massachusetts: The MIT Press.

Fodor, J.A. & Z. Pylyshyn. 1988. "Connectionism and Cognitive Architecture: A Critical Analysis". *Cognition* 28.3-71.

Foote, S.L. 1985. "Anatomy and Physiology of Brain Monoamine Systems". *Psychiatry, Volume 3*. New York: J.B. Lippencott Company, chapter 44.

Foote, S.L., & J.H. Morrison. 1987. "Extrathalamic Modulation of Cortical Function". *Annual Review of Neuroscience* 10.67-105.

Foote, S.L., F.E. Bloom, & G. Aston-Jones. 1983. "Nucleus Locus Ceruleus: New Evidence of Anatomical and Physiological Specificity". *Physiological Reviews* 63.844-899.

Forrest, D.W. 1974. "Von Senden, Mesmer, and the Recovery of Sight in the Blind". *American Journal of Psychology* 87.719-722.

Forster, K.I. 1981. "Priming and the Effects of Sentence and Lexical Contexts on Naming Time: Evidence for Autonomous Lexical Processing". *The Quarterly Journal of Experimental Psychology* 33A.465-495.

Forster, K.I., & C. Davis. 1984. "Repetition Priming and Frequency Attenuation in Lexical Access". *Journal of Experimental Psychology: Learning, Memory, and Cognition* 10.680-698.

Forster, K.I., C. Davis, C. Schoknech, & R. Carter. 1987. "Masked Priming with Graphemically Related Forms: Repetition or Partial Activation?" *The Quarterly Journal of Experimental Psychology* 39A.211-251.

Forster, P.M., & E. Grovier. 1978. "Discrimination Without Awareness?" *The Quarterly Journal of Experimental Psychology* 30.289-295.

Foss, J. 1989. "On the Logic of What It Is Like to Be a Conscious Subject". *Australasian Journal of Philosophy* 67.305-320.

Fowler, C.A., G. Wolford, & R. Slade. 1981. "Lexical Access With and Without Awareness". *Journal of Experimental Psychology: General* 110.341-362.

Fox, N., J. Kagan, & S. Weiskopf. 1979. "The Growth of Memory During Infancy". *Genetic Psychology Monographs* 99.91-130.

Freeman, W.J. 1975. *Mass Action in the Nervous System*. New York: Academic Press.

Freeman, W.J. 1978. "Spatial Properties of an EEG Event in the Olfactory Bulb and Cortex". *Electroencephography and Clinical Neurophysiology* 44.586-605.

Freeman, W.J. 1979a. "Nonlinear Gain Mediating Cortical Stimulus-Response Relations". *Biological Cybernetics* 33.237.

Freeman, W.J. 1979b. "Nonlinear Dynamics of Paleocortex Manifested in the Olfactory EEG". *Biological Cybernetics* 35.21.

Freeman, W.J. 1979c. "EEG Analysis Gives Model of Neuronal Template Matching Mechanism for Sensory Search witih Olfactory Bulb". *Biological Cybernetics* 35.221.

Freeman, W.J. 1983a. "Dynamics of Image Formation by Nerve Cell Assemblies". *Synergetics of the Brain* ed. by E. Basar, H. Flohr, H. Haken, & A.J. Mandell, 102-121, Berlin: Springer-Verlag.

Freeman, W.J. 1983b. "The Physiological Basis of Mental Images". *Biological Psychiatry* 18.1107-1123.

Freeman, W.J. 1987. "Simulation of Chaotic EEG Patterns with a Dynamical Model of the Olfactory System". *Biological Cybernetics* 56.139.

Freeman, W.J. 1994a. "Role of Chaotic Dynamics in Neural Plasticity". *Progress in Brain Research, Volume 102* ed. by J. van Pelt, M.A. Corner, H.M.B,. Uylings, & F.H. Lopes de Silva, 319-333, Amsterdam: Elsevier Science B.V.

Freeman, W.J. 1994b. "Chaos in the CNS: Theory and Practice". *Flexibility and Constraint in Behavioral Systems* ed. by R.J. Greenspan & C.P. Kyriacou, 177-184, New York: John Wiley & Sons Limited.

Freeman, W.J. 1994c. "Neural Networks and Chaos". *Journal of Theoretical Biology* 171.13-18.

Freeman, W.J. 1995a. "Chaos in the Brain: Possible Roles in Biological Intelligence". *International Journal of Intelligence Systems* 10.71-88.

Freeman, W.J. 1995b. *Societies of Mind: A Study in the Neurosicence of Love and Hate.* Hillsdale, New Jersey: Lawrence Erlbaum Associates.

Freeman, W.J., & B. Baird. 1987. "Relation of Olfactory EEG to Behavior: Spatial Analysis". *Behavioral Neuroscience* 101.393.

Freeman, W.J. & J.M. Barrie. 1994. "Chaotic Oscillations and the Genesis of Meaning in Cerebral Cortex". *Temporal Coding in the Brain* ed. by G. Buzáki et al., 13-37, Berlin: Springer-Verlag.

Freeman, W.J., & W. Schneider. 1982. "Changes in Spatial Patterns of Rabbit Olfactory EEG with Conditioning to Odors". *Psychophysiology* 19.44-56.

Freeman, W.J., & C.A. Skarda. 1985a. "Spatial EEG Patterns, Nonlinear Dynamics, and Perception: The Neo-Sherrington View". *Brain Research Review* 10.147-175.

Freeman, W.J., & C.A. Skarda. 1985b. "A Perspective on Brain Theory: Nonlinear Dynamics of Neural Masses". xerox.

Freeman, W.J., & C.A. Skarda. 1990. "Representations: Who Needs Them?" *Brain Organization and Memory: Cells, Systems, and Circuits* ed. by J.L. McGaugh, N. Weinberger, & G. Lynch, 375-380, New York: Oxford.

Freeman, W.J., & C.A. Skarda. 1991. "Mind/Brain Science: Neuroscience on Philosophy of Mind". *John Searle and HIs Critics* ed. by E. Lepore & R. van Gulick, 115-127, Oxford: Blackwell.

Freeman, W.J., & B.W. van Dijk. 1987. "Spatial Patterns of Visual Cortical EEG During Conditioned Reflex in a Rhesus Monkey". *Brain Research* 422.267.

Freeman, W.J., & G. Viana Di Prosco. 1985. "EEG Spatial Pattern Differences with Discriminated Odors Manifest Chaotic and Limit Cycle Attractors in Olfactory Bulb of Rabbits". *Brain Theory* ed. by G. Palm & A. Aertson, 97-119, Berlin: Springer-Verlag.

Freeman, W.J., Y. Yao, & B. Burke. 1988. "Central Pattern Generating and Recognizing in Olfactory Bulb: A Correlation Learning Rule". *Neural Networks* 1.277.

Freud, S. 1895. *On the Origins of Psychoanalysis*, ed. by J. Strachey in *The Standard Edition of the Complete Psychological Works of Sigmund Freud, Volume 1.* London: Hogarth Press.

Freud, S. 1900. *The Interpretation of Dreams*, ed. by J. Strachey in *The Standard Edition of the Complete Psychological Works of Sigmund Freud, Volumes 4-5.* London: Hogarth Press.

Freud, S. 1910. *Five Lecture on Psychoanalysis*, ed. by J. Strachey in *The Standard Edition of the Complete Psychological Works of Sigmund Freud, Volume 11.* London: Hogarth Press.

Freud, S. 1933. *New Introductory Lecture on Psychoanalysis*, ed. by J. Strachey in *The Standard Edition of the Complete Psychological Works of Sigmund Freud, Volume 22.* London: Hogarth Press.

Freud, S. 1938. *Outline of Psycho-Analysis*, ed. by J. Strachey in *The Standard Edition of the Complete Psychological Works of Sigmund Freud, Volume 23.* London: Hogarth Press.

Fuster, G.M., & G.E. Alexander. 1971. "Neuron Activity Related to Short Term Memory". *Science* 173.652-694.

Fuster, J.M. 1973. "Unit Activity in Prefrontal Cortex During Delayed-Response Performance: Neuronal Correlates of Transient Memory". *Journal of Neurophysiology* 36.61-78.

Fuster, J.M. 1980. *The Prefrontal Cortex: Anatomy, Physiology, and Neuropsychology of the Frontal Lobe.* New York: Raven Press.

Gaal, G., J.N. Sanes, & J.P. Donoghue. 1992. "Motor Cortex Oscillatory Neural Activity During Voluntary Movement in *Macaca fasicularis*". *Society for Neuroscience Abstracts* 18.848.

Gabrielli, J.D.E., W. Milberg, M.M. Keane, & S. Corkin. 1990. "Intact Priming of Patterns Despite Impaired Memory". *Neuropsychologia* 28.417-427.

Garbiel, M., *et al.* 1986. "An Executive Function of the Hippocampus: Pathway Selection for Thalamic Neuronal Significance Code". *The Hippocampus, Volume 4* ed. by R.L. Isaacson & R.A. Pribham. New York: Raven Press.

Garnder, H., F. Boller, J. Moreines, & L. Butters. 1973. "Retrieving Information from Korsakoff Patients: Effects of Categorical Cues and Reference to the Task". *Cortex* 9.165-175.

Gardner, L.E. 1968. "Retention and Overhabituation of a Dual-Component Response in *Lubricus Terrestris*". *Journal of Comparative and Physiological Psychology* 66.315-318.

Gault, F.P., & R.N. Leaton. 1963. "Electrical Activity of the Olfactory System". *Electroencephalography and Clinical Neurophysiology* 15.299-304.

Gazzaniga, M.S. 1985. *The Social Brain.* New York: Basic Books.

Gazzaniga, M.S. 1988. "Brain Modularity: Towards a Philosophy of Conscious Experience". *Consciousnes in Contemporary Science* ed. by A.J. Marcel & E. Bisiach, 218-238, Oxford: Clarendon Press.

Gazzaniga, M.S. & J.E. LeDoux. 1978. *The Integrated Mind.* New York: Plenum Press.

Gazzaniga, M.S., J.D. Holtzman, & C.S. Smylie. 1987. "Speech Without Conscious Awareness". *Neurology* 37.682-685.

Gazzaniga, M.S., J.E. LeDoux, V.T. Volpe, & C.S. Smylie. 1979. "Plasticity in Speech Organization Following Commissurotomy". *Brain* 102.805-815.

Gellman, R.S., & F.A. Miles. 1985. "A New Role for the Cerebellum in Conditioning?" *Trends in Neuroscience* 8.181-182.

Ghose, G.M., & R.D. Freeman. 1990. *Society of Neuroscience Abstract* 16.523.

Gianotti, G. 1975. "Confabulation of Denial in Senile Dementia: An Experimental Design". *Psychiatria Clinica* 8.99-108.

Gillan, D.J., D. Premack, & G. Woodruff. 1981. "Reasoning in the Chimpanzee: I, Analogical Reasoning". *Journal of Experimental Psychology: Animal Behavioral Processes* 7.1-17.

Gluck, MA., & C.E. Myers. 1993. "Hippocampal Mediation of Stimulus Representation: A Computational Theory". *Hippocampus* 3.491-516.

Godfrey-Smith, P. 1988. "Jackendoff's Epiphenomenal Consciousness". Unpublished manuscript.

Goldman, P.S. 1971. "Functional Development of the Prefrontal Cortex in Early Life and the Problem of Neuronal Plasticity". *Experimental Neurology* 32.366-387.

Goldman, P.S., & H.E. Rosvold. 1970. "Localization of Function within the Dorsolateral Prefrontal Cortex of the Rhesus Monkey". *Experimental Neurology* 30.290-304.

Goldman, P.S., H.E. Rosvold, B. Vest, & T.W. Galkin. 1971. "Analysis of the Delayed Alternation Deficit Produced by Dorsolateral Prefrontal Lesions in the Rhesus Monkeys". *Journal of Comparative Physiological Psychology* 77.212-220.

Goldman-Rakic, P.S. 1987. "Circuitry of Primate Prefrontal Cortex and Regulation of Behavior by Representational Memory". *Handbook of Physiology — The Nervous System V*, 373-417, Bethesda, Maryland: American Physiological Society.

Goldman-Rakic, P.S., I. Isseroff, M. Schwartz, & N. Bugbee. 1983. "The Neurobiology of Cognitive Development". *The Handbook of Child Development* ed. by F. Plum & V. Mountcastle, 282-331, Bethesda, Maryland: American Physiological Society.

Gordon, B. 1988. "Preserved Learning of Novel Information in Amnesia: Evidence for Multiple Memory Systems". *Brain and Cognition* 7.257-282.

Gottfried, A.W., S.A. Rose, & W.H. Bridger. 1977. "Cross-Modal Transfer in Human Infants". *Child Development* 48.118-123.

Gottfried, A.W., S.A. Rose, & W.H. Bridger. 1979. "Effects of Visual, Haptic, and Manipulatory Experiences on Infants' Visual Recognition Memory of Objects". *Developmental Psychology* 14.305-312.

Graf, P., & G. Mandler. 1984. "Implicit and Explicit Memory for New Associations in Normal and Amnesic Subjects". *Journal of Experimental Psychology: Learning, Memory, and Cognition* 11.501-518.

Graf, P., & D. Schacter. 1987. "Selective Effects of Interference on Implicit and Explicit Memory for New Associations". *Journal of Experimental Psychology: Learning, Memory, and Cognition* 12.45-53.

Graf, P., & D. Schacter. 1989. "Unitization and Grouping Mediate Dissociations in Memory for New Associations". *Journal of Experimental Psychology: Learning, Memory, and Cognition* 15.930-940.

Graf, P., G. Mander, & P. Haden. 1982. "Simulating Amnesic Symptoms in Normal Subjects". *Science*, 218: 1243-1244.

Graf, P., A.P. Shimamura, & L.R. Squire. 1985. "Priming Across Modalities and Priming Across Category Levels: Extending the Domain of Preserved Function in Amnesia". *Journal of Experimental Psychology: Learning, Memory, and Cognition* 11.385-395.

Graf, P., L.R. Squire,& G. Mandler. 1984. "The Information That Amnesic Patients Do Not Forget". *Journal of Experimental Psychology: Learning, Memory, and Cognition* 10.164-178.

Grafman, J., H.J. Weingartner, P.A. Newhouse, K. Thompson, K., *et al.* 1990. "Implicit Learning in Patients with Alzheimer's Disease". *Pharmacopsychiatry* 23.94-101.

Grajski, K.A., & W.J. Freeman. 1989. "EEG Correlates of Nonassociative and Associative Olfactory Learning in Rabbits". *Behavioral Neuroscience* 103.790-804.

Gratch, G. 1976. "On Levels of Awareness of Objects in Infants and Students Thereof". *Merrill-Palmer Quarterly* 22.157-176.

Gratch, G., K.J. Appel, W.F. Evans, G.K. LeCompte, & N.A. Wright. 1974. "Piaget's Stage IV Object Concept Error: Evidence of Forgetting or Object Conception?" *Child Development* 45.71-77.

Gray, C.M. & W. Singer. 1987. "Stimulus Dependent Neuronal Oscillations in the Cat Visual Cortex Area 17". *Neuroscience [Suppl]* 22.1301P.

Gray, C.M., & W. Singer. 1989. "Stimulus-Specific Neuronal Oscillations in Orientation Columns of Cat Visual Cortex". *Proceedings of the National Academy of Sciences of the United States of America* 86.1698-1702.

Gray, C.M., A.K. Engel, P. Konig, & W. Singer. 1992. "Synchronization of Oscillatory Neuronal Responses in Cat Striate Cortex: Temporal Properties". *Visual Neuroscience* 8.337-347.

Gray, C.M., P. Konig, A.K. Engel, & W. Singer. 1989. "Oscillatory Responses in Cat Visual Cortex Exhibit Inter-Columnar Synchronization which Reflects Global Stimulus Properties". *Nature* 338.334-337

Green, M.L., S.K. Kraus, & R.G. Green. 1979. "Pupillary Responses to Pictures and Descriptions of Sex-Stereotyped Stimuli". *Perceptual and Motor Skills* 49.759-764.

Gregory, R.L. 1966. *Eye and Brain: The Psychology of Seeing*. New York: McGraw-Hill.

Gregory, R.L. 1981. *Mind in Science*. London: Weidenfeld and Nicolson.

Gregory, R.L. 1990. "In Defense of Artificial Intelligence — A Reply to Searle". *Mindwaves: Thoughts on Intelligence, Identity, and Consciousness* ed. by C. Blakemore & S. Greenfield, 235-246, Cambridge, Massachusetts: Basil Blackwell.

Gregory, R.L., & J. Wallace. 1963. *Recovery from Infant Blindness: A Case Study.* Experimental Psychology Society Monographs II. Cambridge, England: Heffer.

Gross, C.G., & L. Weiskrantz. 1964. "Some Changes in Behavior Produced by Lateral Frontal Lesions in the Macaque". *The Frontal Granular Cortex and Behavior* ed. by J.M. Warren & K. Akert , 74-101, New York: McGraw-Hill.

Groves, P.M., & R.F. Thompson. 1970. "Habituation: A Dual Process Theory". *Psychology Review* 77.419-450.

Hacaen, H. 1976. "Acquired Aphasia in Children and the Ontogenesis of Hemispheric Functional Specialization". *Brain and Language* 3.114-134.

Haist, F., G. Musen, & L.R. Squire. 1991. "Intanct Priming of Words and Nonwords in Amnesia". *Psychobiology* 19.275-285.

Hameroff, S. 1994. "Quantum Coherence in Microtubules: A Neural Basis for Emergent Consciousness?". *Journal of Consciousness Studies* 1.91-118.

Hannay, A. 1987. "The Claims of Consciousness: A Critical Survey". *Inquiry* 30.395-434.

Hardcastle, V.G. 1992. "Reduction, Explanatory Extension, and the Mind/Brain Sciences". *Philosophy of Science* 59.408-428.

Hardcastle, V.G. 1993a. "The Naturalists versus the Skeptics: The Debate Over a Scientific Understanding of Consciousness". *The Journal of Mind and Behavior* 14.27-50.

Hardcastle, V.G. 1993b. "An ERP Analysis of Priming Using Novel Visual Stimuli". Paper presented at the Southern Society for Philosophy and Psychology, New Orleans.

Hardcastle, V.G. 1994. "Psychology's Binding Problem and Possible Neurobiological Solutions". *Journal of Consciousness Studies* 1.66-90.

Hardcastle, V.G. Forthcoming. *How to Build a Theory in Cognitive Science.* Albany, New York: State University of New York Press.

Hardin, C.L. 1988. *Color for Philosophers: Unweaving the Rainbow.* Hackett: Indianapolis.

Hardin, C.L. 1990. "Color and Illusion". *Mind and Cognition* ed. by W. Lycan, 555-567, Cambridge, Massachusetts: Blackwell.

Harnad, S. 1989. "Editorial Commentary". *Brain and Behavioral Sciences* 12: 183.

Harris, P.L. 1973. "Perserverative Errors in Search by Young Infants". *Child Development* 44.28-33.

Harrison, B. 1973. *Form and Content.* Oxford: Blackwell.

Harth, E., & G. Wong. 1973. "Stationary States and Transcients in Neural Populations". *Journal of Theoretical Biology* 40.77.

Hashtroudi, S., L.D. Chrosmiak, & B.L. Schwartz. 1991. "Effects of Aging on Priming and Skill Learning". *Psychology and Aging* 6.605-615.

Hatfield, G. 1988. "Neuro-Philosophy Meets Psychology: Reduction, Autonomy, and Physiological Constraints". *Cognitive Neuropsychology* 5.723-746.

Heindel, W.C., M.N. Butters, & D.P. Salmon. 1988. "Impaired Learning of a Motor Skill in Patients with Huntington's Disease". *Behavioral Neuroscience* 102.141-147.

Helmholtz, H. 1911. *Handbuch der Physiologischen Optik, Band II.* Hamburg: Voss.

Hernandez-Peion, R., A. Lavin, C. Acocer-Cuaron, & J.R. Marcelin. 1960. "Electrical Activity of the Olfactory Bulb During Wakefulness and Sleep". *Electroencephalography and Clinical Neurophysiology* 12.41-58.

Hess, R. 1975. "The Role of Pupil Size in Communication". *Scientific American* 233.110-119.

Hicks, R.A., R.J. Perregrini, & N. Tomlinson. 1978. "Attributions of Female College Students to Male Photographs as a Function of Attractiveness and Pupil Size". *Perceptual and Motor Skills* 47.1265-1266.

Hicks, R.A., S.L. Williams, & F. Ferrante. 1979. "Eye Color and the Pupillary Attributions of College Students to Happy and Angry Students". *Bulletin of the Psychonomic Society*, 13.55-56.

Hilz, R. & C.R. Cavius. 1970. "Wavelength Discrimination Measured with Square-Wave Gratings". *Journal of the Optical Society of America* 60.273-277.

Hinton, G.E. 1981. "A Parallel Computation That Assigns Canonical Object-Based Frames of Refernce". *Proceedings of the International Joint Conference on Artificial Intelligence.* Vancouver, Canada.

Hintzman, D.L., R.A. Block, & N.R. Inskeep. 1972. "Memory for Mode of Input". *Journal of Verbal Learning and Verbal Behavior* 11.741-749.

Hitzig, E. 1874. *Untersuchen über dass Gehirn.* Berlin Hirschwald.

Hochberg, J. 1971. "Perception I: Color and Shape". *Woodworth and Schlosberg's Experimental Psychology* ed. by J.W. Kling & L.A. Riggs, 396-550, New York: Holt, Rinehart, and Winston.

Holcomb, P.J. 1988. "Automatic and Attentional Processing: An Event-Related Brain Potential Analysis of Semantic Priming". *Brain and Langauge* 35.66-85.

Holcomb, P.J. & W.B. McPherson. 1994. "Event-Related Brain Potentials Reflect Semantic Priming in an Object Decision Task". *Brain and Cognition* 24.259-276.

Holcomb, P.J., and Neville, H.J. 1990. "Auditory and Visual Semantic Priming in Lexical Decision: A Comparison Using Event-Related Potentials". *Language and Cognitive Processes* 5.281-312.

Holden, A.V. 1976. "Models of the Stochastic Activity of Neurons". *Lecture Notes in Biomathematics, 12.* New York: Springer.

Horel, J.A. 1992. "Recall of Unexpected Stimuli while Temporal Cortex Is Suppressed with Cold". *Society for Neuroscience Abstracts* 18.387.

Horgan, T. 1984. "Functionalism, Qualia, and the Inverted Spectrum". *Philosophy and Phenomenological Research* 44.453-469.

Horgan, T. 1986. "Jackson on Physical Information and Qualia". *Philosophical Quarterly* 32.147-152.

Horgan, T. 1987. "Supervenient Qualia". *The Philosophical Review* XCVI.491-520.

Horn, D., D. Sagi, & M. Usher. 1991. "Segmentation, Binding, and Illusory Conjunctions". Technical Report CS91-07, Weismann Institute of Science.

Horwitz, M.J., J.E. Adams, & B.B. Rutkin. 1967. "Evoked Hallucinations in Epilepsy". *Psychiatry Speculator* 11.4.

Hubel, D.H. 1988. *Eye, Brain, and Vision.* New York: Scientific American Library.

Hubel, D.H. & M.S. Livingstone. 1987. "Segregation of Form, Color, and Stereopsis in Primate Area 18". *The Journal of Neuroscience* 7.3378-3415.

Hume, D. 1735/1958. *A Treatise of Human Nature.* New York: Oxford University Press.

Hume, D. 1777/1975. *Enquiries Concerning Human Understanding and Concerning the Principles of Morals.* London: Oxford.

Humel, J.E., & I. Biederman. 1992. "Dynamic Binding in a Neural Network for Shape Recognition". *Psychological Review* 99.480-517.

Humphreys, G.W., & M.J. Riddoch. 1987. *To See But Not To See: A Case Study of Visual Agnosia.* Hillsdale, New Jersey: Erlbaum.

Humphreys, G.W., T. Troscianko, M.J. Riddoch, M. Boucart, N. Donnelly, & G.F.A. 1992. "Covert Processing in Different Visual Recognition Systems". *The Neuropsychology of Consciousness* ed. by A.D. Milner & M.D. Rugg, 36-68, New York: Academic Press.

Hurvitch, L.M. 1981. *Color Vision.* Sunderland: Sinauer.

Huxley, T. 1874. "On the Hypothesis That Animals Are Automata". Reprinted in T. Huxley 1898. *Methods and Results: Essays.* New York: Appleton.

Hyarinin, J., A. Poranen, & Y. Jokinen. 1980. "Influence of Attentive Behavior on Neuronal Responses to Vibration in Primary Somatosensory Cortex of the Monkey". *Journal of Neurophysiology* 43.870-882.

Jackendoff, R. 1987. *Consciousness and the Computational Mind.* Cambridge, Massachusetts: The MIT Press.

Jackson, F. 1982. "Epiphenomenal Qualia". *Philosophical Quarterly* 32.127-136.

Jackson, F. 1986. "What Mary Didn't Know". *Journal of Philosophy* 83.291-295.

Jacobson, J. 1973. "Effects of Association upon Masking and Reading Latency". *Canadian Journal of Psychology* 27.58-69.

Jacoby, L.L. 1983. "Remembering the Data: Analyzing Interactive Processes in Reading". *Journal of Verbal Learning and Verbal Behavior* 22.485-506.

Jacoby, L.L., & C. Kelley. 1992. "Unconscious Influences of Memory: Dissociations and Automaticity". *The Neuropsychology of Consciousness* ed. by A.D. Milner & M.D. Rugg, 201-233, New York: Academic Press.

Jacoby, L.L., & D. Witherspoon. 1982. "Remembering Without Awareness". *Canadian Journal of Psychology* 36.300-324.

Jacoby, L.L., & M. Dallas. 1981. "On the Relationship Between Autobiographical Memory and Perceptual Learning". *Journal of Experimental Psychology: General* 13.456-463.

Jagadeesh, B., C.M. Gray, & D. Ferster. 1992. "Visually Evoked Oscillations of Membrane Potential in Cells of Cat Visual Cortex". *Science* 257.552-554.

Jelicic, M., & B. Bonke. 1993. "Implicit Memory for Stimuli Presented During Anaesthesia: Role of Anaesthetic Cocktail and Memory Test". *Medical Hypotheses* 41.353-354.

Jelicic, M., B. Bonke, G. Walters, & H. Phaf. 1992. "Implicit Memory for Words Presented During Anaesthesia". *European Journal of Cognitive Psychology* 4.71-80.

Jernigan, T.L.,& A.L. Ostergaard. 1993. "Word Priming and Recognition Memory Are Both Affected by Mesial Temporal Lobe Damage". *Neuropsychology* 714-26.

Johnson-Laird, P. 1983. *Mental Models*. Cambridge, England: Cambridge University Press.

Johnson-Laird, P. 1988. "A Computational Analysis of Consciousness". *Consciousness in Contemporary Science* ed. by A. Marcel & E. Bisiach, 357-368, Oxford: Clarendon Press.

Joliot, M., U. Ribary, & R. Llinas. 1994. "Human Oscillatory Brain Activity Near 40 Hz Coexists with Cognitive Temporal Binding". *Proceedings from the National Academy of Sciences, U.S.A.* 91.1178.

Jones, E.G. 1985. *The Thalamus*. New York: Plenum Press.

Joseph, R. 1986. "Confabulation and Delusional Denial: Frontal Lobe and Lateralized Influences". *Journal of Clinical Psychology* 42.507-520.

Joseph, R., R.E. Gallagher, W. Holloway, & J. Kahn. 1984. "Two Brains, One Child: Interhemispheric Information Transfer Deficits and Confabulatory Responding in Children Aged 4, 7, 10". *Cortex* 20.317-331.

Kammen, D., C. Koch, & P.J. Holmes. 1991. "Collective Oscillations in the Visual Cortex". *Advances in Neural Information Processing Systems 2* ed. by D. S. Touretzky, 76-83, San Mateo, California: Morgan Kaufman.

Kandel, E.R., & J.H. Schwartz. 1985. *Principles of Neural Science, Second Edition*. New York: Elsevier.

Kaneko, K. & Tsuda, I. 1994. "Constructive Complexity and Artificial Reality: An Introduction". *Physica D* 75: 1-10.

Karmiloff-Smith, A. 1988. "The Child is a Theoretician, Not an Inductivist". *Mind and Language* 3.183-195.

Keane, M.M., H. Clarke, & S. Corkin. 1992. "Impaired Perceptual Priming and Intact Conceptual Priming in a Patient with Bilateral Posterior Cerebral Lesions". *Society for Neuroscience Abstracts* 18.386.

Keele, S. 1973. *Attention and Human Performance*. Pacific Palisades, California: Goodyear.

Kelley, C.M., & L.L. Jacoby. 1993. "The Construction of Subjective Experience: Memory Attributions". *Consciousness* ed. by M. Davies & G.W. Humphreys, 75-89, Cambridge, Massachusetts: Basil Blackwell.

Kemp-Wheeler, S.M., & A.B. Hill. 1988. "Semantic Priming Without Awareness: Some Methodological Considerations and Replications". *The Quarterly Journal of Experimental Psychology* 40A.671-692.

Kersteen-Tucker, Z.A., & R.T. Knight. 1989. "Cortical Lesions Dissociate Short and Long Term Components of Repetition Priming". *Society of Neuroscience Abstracts* 15.245.

Kihlstrom, J.F., D.L. Schacter, R.C. Cork, C.A. Hurt, *et al.* 1990. "Implicit and Explicit Memory Following Surgical Anesthesia". *Psychological Science* 1.303-306.

Kimble, D.P. 1969. "Possible Inhibitory Functions of the Hippocampus". *Neuropsychologia* 7.235-244.

Kinsbourne, M. 1988. "Integrated Field Theory of Consciousness". *Consciousness in Contemporary Science* ed. by A.J. Marcel & E. Bisiach, 239-256, Oxford: Clarendon Press.

Kinsbourne, M., & F. Wood. 1975. "Short-Term Memory and the Amnesic Syndrome". *Short-Term Memory* ed. by D.D. Deutsch & J.A. Deutsch, 258-291, New York: Academic Press.

Kinsbourne, M., & F. Wood. 1982. ."Theoretical Considerations Regarding the Episodic-Semantic Memory Distinction". *Human Memory and Amnesia* ed. by L.S. Cermak, 195-217, Hillsdale, New Jersey: Lawrence Erlbaum Associates.

Kinsbourne, M., & G. Winocur. 1980. "Response Competition and Interference Effects in Paired-Associate Learning by Korsakoff Amnesics". *Neuropsychologia* 18.541-548.

Kirkland, J., & J. Smith. 1978. "Preferences for Infant Pictures with Modified Eye-Pupils". *Journal of Biological Psychology* 20.33-34.

Kirshner, K., & M.C. Smith. 1974. "Modality Effects in Word Identification". *Memory and Cognition* 2.637-640.

Kirshner, K., D. Milech, & P. Standon. 1983. "Common and Modality-Specific Processes in the Mental Lexicon". *Memory and Cognition* 11.621-630.

Kitcher, P.W. 1979. "Phenomenal Qualities". *American Philosophical Quarterly* 16.123-129.

Kitcher, P.W. 1990. *Kant's Transcendental Psychology*. New York: Oxford University Press.

Kitcher, P.W. 1992. *Freud's Metapsychology*. New York: Oxford University Press.

Kluft, R.P. 1984. "An Introduction to Multiple Personality Disorder". *Psychiatric Annals* 14.19-24.

Klüver, H. 1967. *Mescal and the Mechanisms of Hallucinations*. Chicago: University of Chicago Press.

Knaudt, P. 1990. "ERPs Elicited by Upright and Inverted Faces Presented in Primed and Unprimed Conditions". Unpublished manuscript.

Koch, C. 1992. "The Connected Brain". *Discover* 12.96-98.

Koffka, D. 1922. "Perception: An Introduction to Gestalt-theorie". *Psychology Bulletin* 19.531-585.

Koffka, D. 1935. *Principles of Gestalt Psychology*. New York: Harcourt.

Kohler, W. 1920. *Static and Stationary Physical Gestalts*. Braunschweig: Vieweg.

Kohler, W. 1929. *Gestalt Psychology*. New York: Liveright.

Kohler, W. 1947. *Gestalt Psychology: An Introduction to New Concepts in Modern Psychology*. New York: Liveright.

Kojima, S., & P.S. Goldman-Rakic. 1982. "Delayed-Related Activity of Prefrontal Cortical Neurons in Rhesus Monkeys Performing Delayed Response". *Brain Research* 248.43-49.

Kojima, S., & P.S. Goldman-Rakic. 1984. "Functional Analysis of Spatially Discriminitive Neurons in Prefrontal Cortex of Rhesus Monkey". *Brain Research* 291.229-240.

Kolb, B. 1992. "Brain Development, Plasticity, and Behavior". *Brain Development and Cognition* ed. by M. Johnson, 338-356, Cambridge, Massachusetts: Blackwell.

Komatsu, S.I., & N. Ohta. 1984. "Priming Effects in Word-Fragment Completion for Short- and Long-Term Retention Intervals". *Japanese Psychological Research* 26.194-200.

König, P, A.E. Engel, & W. Singer. 1992. "Gamma-Oscillations as a Vehicle for Synchronization". *Society for Neuroscience Abstracts* 18.12.

Kopelman, M.D. 1987a. "Two Types of Confabulation". *Journal of Neurology, Neurosurgery and Psychiatry* 50.1482-1487.

Kopelman, M.D. 1987b. "Amnesia: Organic and Psychogenic". *British Journal of Psychiatry* 150.428-442.

Kreiter, A.K., A.K. Engel, & W. Singer. 1992. "Stimulus Dependent Synchronization in the Caudal Superior Temporal Sulcus of Macaque Monkeys". *Society for Neuroscience Abstracts* 18.12.

Krieger, D., & M. Dillbeck. 1987. "High Frequency Scalp Potentials Evoked by a Reaction Time Task". *Electroencephalography and Clinical Neurophysiology* 67.222-230.

Krill, A.E., H.J. Alpert, & A.M. Ostfield. 1963. "Effects of a Hallucinogenic Agent in Titally Blind Subjects". *Archive Ophthalmology* 69.180-185.

Kripke, S. 1980. *Naming and Necessity*. Cambridge, Massachusetts: Harvard University Press.

Kristofferson, A., J. Galloway, & R. Hanson. 1975. "Complete Recovery of a Masked Visual Target". *Bulletin of the Psychonomic Society* 13.5-6.

Kruger, J., & M. Mayer. 1990. "Two Types of Neuronal Synchrony in Monkey Striate Cortex". *Biological Cybernetics* 64.135-140.

Kruse, W., R. Eckhorn, T. Schanze, & H.J. Reitboeck. 1992. "Stimulus-Induced Oscillatory Sychronization is Inhibited by Stimulus-Locked Non-Oscillatory Synchronization in Cat Visual Cortex: Two Modes that Might Support Feature Linking". *Society for Neuroscience Abstracts* 18.292.

Kubota, K., & Niki. 1971. "Prefrontal Cortical Unit Activity and Delayed Alternation Performance in Monkeys". *Journal of Neurophysiology* 34.337-347.

Kulpe, O. 1893. *Outline of Psychology*. Leipzig: Englemann.

Kutas, M., & C. Van Petten. 1988. "Event-Related Potential Studies of Language". *Advances in Physiology 3* ed. by P.K. Ackles, J.R. Jennings, & M.G.H. Coles. Greenwich, Connecticut: JAI Press.

Kutas, M., T. Lindamood, & S.A. Hillyard. 1984. "Word Expectancy and Event-Related Brain Potentials During Sentence Processing". *Preparatory States and Processes* ed. by S. Kornblum & J. Requin. Hillsdale, New Jersey: Lawrence Erlbaum Associates.

Kutas, M., C. Van Petten, & M. Besson. 1988. "Event-Related Potential Asymmetries During Reading of Sentences". *Electroencephalography and Clinical Neurophysiology* 69.218-233.

LaBerge, D. 1973a. "Attention and the Measurement of Perceptual Learning". *Memory and Cognition* 1.268-276.

LaBerge, D. 1973b. "Identification of the Time to Switch Attention: A Test of a Serial and Parallel Model of Attention". *Attention and Performance IV* ed. by S. Kownblum. New York: Academic Press.

LaBerge, D. 1975. "Acquisition of Automatic Processing in Perceptual and Associative Learning". *Attention and Performance V* ed. by P.M.A. Rabbitt & S. Dornic. New York: Academic Press.

LaBerge, D., & S. Samuals. 1974. "Toward a Theory of Automatic Information Processing Reading". *Cognitive Psychology* 6.293-323.

Lahav, R. 1993. "What Neuropsychology Tells Us about Consciousness". *Philosophy of Science* 60.67-85.

Langacker, R.W. 1987. *Foundations of Cognitive Grammar.* Stanford, California: Stanford University Press.

Lavin, A., C. Alcocer-Cuaron,& R. Hernandez-Peion. 1959. "Centrifugal Arousal in the Olfactory Bulb". *Science* 129.332-333.

Leaton, R.N. 1974. "Long-Term Retention of the Habituation of Lick Suppression in Rats". *Journal of Comparative and Physiological Psychology* 87.1157-1164..

LeDoux, J.E., L. Romanski, & A. Zagoraris. 1989. "Indelibility of Subcortical Emotional Memories". *Journal of Cognitive Neuroscience* 1.238-243.

Lee, C., J. Kim, J. Park,& S. Chung. 1992. "Oscillatory Discharges of the Visual Cortex in the Behaving Cats". *Society for Neuroscience Abstracts* 18.292.

Legéndy, C.R. 1970. "The Brain and Its Information Trapping Device". *Progress in Cybernetics, Volume 1* ed. by J. Rose, 309-338, New York: Gordon and Beach.

Lehky, S.R., & T.J. Sejnowsk. 1988. "Network Model of Shape-from-Shading: Neural Function Arises from Both Receptive and Projective Fields". *Nature* 333.452-454.

Leiphart, J., J.P. Rosenfeld, & J.D. Gabrieli. 1993. "ERP Correlates of Implicit Priming and Explicit Memory Tasks". *International Journal of Psychophysiology* 15.197-206.

Lennie, P., & M. D'Zmura. 1988. "Mechanisms of Color Vision". *Critical Reviews in Neurobiology* 3.333-400.

Lepper, M.R., D. Greene, & R. Nisbett. 1973. "Undermining Children's Intrinsic Interest with Extrinsic Reward: A Test of the Overjustification Hypothesis". *Journal of Personality and Social Psychology* 28.129-137.

Levin, J. 1985. "Functionalism and the Argument from Conceivability". *Canadian Journal of Philosophy Supplement* 11.85-104.

Levin, J. 1986. "Could Love Be Like a Heat Wave? Physicalism and the Subjective Character of Experience". *Philosophical Studies* 49.245-261.

Levine, J. 1983. "Materialism and Qualia: The Explanatory Gap". *Pacific Philosophical Quarterly* 64.354-361.

Levine, J. 1987. *"The Nature of Psychological Explanation* by Robert Cummins, a Critical Notice". *The Philosophical Review* 96.249-274.

Levine, J. 1993. "On Leaving Out What It Is Like". *Consciousness: Psychological and Philosophical Essays* ed. by M. Davies & G. Humphreys. Oxford: Blackwell.

Lewis, C.I. 1929. *Mind and the World Order.* New York: Scribner's.

Lewis, D. 1973. "Postscript to 'Mad Pain and Martian Pain'". *Philosophical Papers, Volume 1.* New York: Oxford.

Lewis, D. 1990. "What Experience Teaches". *Mind and Cognition* ed. by W. Lycan, 499-519, Oxford: Blackwell.

Linsker, L., & A. Abramson. 1970. "The Voicing Dimension: Some Experiments in Comparative Phonetics". *Proceedings of the Sixth International Congress of Phonetic Sciences*, Prague, 1967. Prague: Academia.

Livingstone, M.S. & D.H. Hubel. 1987. "Psychophysical Evidence for Separate Channels for the Perception of Form, Color, Movement, and Depth". *The Journal of Neuroscience* 7.3416-3468.

Llado, F., U. Ribrary, A. Ioannides, J. Volkman, M. Joliot, A. Mogilner,& R. Llinas. 1992. "Coherent Oscillations in Primary Motor and Sensory Cortices Detected Using MEG and MFT". *Society for Neuroscience Abstracts* 18.848.

Llinas, R.R., A.A. Grace, & Y. Yarom. 1991. "In Vitro Neurons in Mammalian Cortical Layer 4 Exhibit Intrinsic Oscillatory Activity in the 10- to 50-Hz Frequency Range". *Proceedings of the National Academy of Sciences of the United States of America* 88.897-901.

Loar, B. 1985. "Phenomenal States". *Philosophical Perspectives 4: Action Theory and Philosophy of Mind* ed. by J. Tomberlin, 81-108, Atascadero, California: Ridgeview Publishing Company.

Locke, J. 1689/1975. *An Essay Concerning Human Understanding* ed. by P. Nidditch. New York: Oxford.

Lumer, E. & B.A. Huberman. 1991. "Binding Hierarchies: A Basis for Dynamic Perceptual Grouping". Unpublished manuscript.

Luria, A.R. 1959. "The Directive Function of Speech in Development and Dissolution". *Word* 15.341-352.

Lycan, W.G. 1973. "Inverted Spectrum". *Ratio* 15.315-319.

Lycan, W.G. 1981. "Form, Function, and Feel". *Journal of Philosophy* 78.

Lycan, W.G. 1985. "What is the 'Subjectivity' of the Mental?" *Philosophical Perspectives 4: Action Theory and Philosophy of Mind* ed. by J. Tomberlin, 109-130, Atascadero, California: Ridgeview Publishing Company.

Lycan, W.G. 1987. *Consciousness*. Cambridge, Massachusetts: The MIT Press.

Lycan, W.G. 1993. "Functionalism and Recent Spectrum Inversions". Paper presented at American Philosophical Association — Eastern Division, Atlanta.

Lynch, G., & M. Baudry. 1984. "The Biochemistry of Memory: A New and Specific Hypothesis". *Science* 224.1057-1063.

Lynch, G., & R. Granger. 1992. "Variations in Synaptic Plasticity and Types of Memory in Corticohippocampal Networks". *Journal of Cognitive Neuroscience* 4.189-199.

Mackay-Soroka, S., S.E. Trehub, D.H. Bull, & C.M. Corter. 1982. "Effects of Encoding and Retrieval Conditions on Infants' Recognition Memory". *Child Development* 53.815-818.

Mackintosh, N.J. 1987. "Animal Minds". *Mindwaves: Thoughts on Intelligence, Identity, and Consciousness* ed. by C. Blakemore & S. Greenfield, 111-122, Cambridge, Massachusetts: Basil Blackwell.

Mackintosh, N.J., B. Wilson, & R.A. Boakes. 1985. "Differences in Mechanisms of Intelligence Among Vertebrates". *Philosophical Transactions of the Royal Society of London*.

Mahut, J., & M. Moss. 1984. *Neuropsychology of Memory* ed. by L.R. Squire & N. Butters, 297-315, New York: Guilford Press.

Malamut, B.L., R.C. Saunders, & M. Mishkin. 1984. "Monkeys with Combined Amygdalo-Hippocampal Lesions Succeed in Object Discrimination Learning Despite 24-Hour Intertrial Intervals". *Behavioral Neuroscience* 98.759-769.

Malloy, P., A. Bihrle, J. Duffy, & C. Cimino. 1993. "The Orbitomedial Frontal Syndrome". *Archives of Clinical Neuropsychology* 8.185-201.

Mandler, G. 1975. "Consciousness: Respectable, Useful, and Probably Necessary". *Information Processing and Cognition: The Loyola Symposium* ed. by R. Solso, 229-254, Hillsdale, New Jersey: Lawrence Erlbaum Associates.

Mandler, G. 1984. *Mind and Body: Psychology of Emotion and Stress.* New York: W.W. Norton and Company.

Mandler, G. 1985. *Cognitive Psychology: An Essay in Cognitive Science.* Hillsdale, New Jersey: Lawrence Erlbaum Associates.

Mandler, G. 1988. "Problems and Direction in the Study of Consciousness". *Psychodynamics and Cognition* ed. by M.J. Horowitz, 21-45, Chicago: University of Chicago Press.

Mandler, G. 1989. "Toward a Cognitive Theory of Consciousness". Unpublished manuscript.

Mandler, G. 1990. "Your Face Looks Familiar but I Can't Remember Your Name: A Review of Dual Process Theory". *Relating Theory and Data: Essays on Human Memory in Honor of Bennett B. Murdock* ed. by W.E. Hockley & S. Lewandowsky. Hillsdale, New Jersey: Lawrence Erlbaum Associates.

Mandler, G. Forthcoming. "Memory: Conscious and Unconscious". To appear in *Memory— An Interdisciplinary Approach* ed. by P.R. Solomon, G.R. Goethals, C.M. Kelley, & R.B. Stephens. New York: Springer.

Mandler, G. & B.J. Shebo. 1982. "Subitizing: An Analysis of Its Component Processes". *Journal of Experimental Psychology: General* 111.1-22.

Mandler, G., & W. Kesson. 1959. *The Language of Psychology.* New York: Springer.

Mandler, J.M. 1984. "Representation and Recall in Infancy". *Infant Memory: Its Relation to Normal and Pathological Memory in Humans and Other Animals* ed. by M. Moscovitch, 75-101, New York: Plenum Press.

Mandler, J.M. 1988. "How to Make a Baby I". *Cognitive Development.*

Mandler, J.M. 1992. "How to Make a Baby II: Conceptual Primitives". *Psychological Review* 99.87-604.

Mangone, C.A., D.B. Hier, P.B. Gorelick, & R.J. Ganellen. 1991. "Impaired Insight in Alzheimer's Disease". *Journal of Geriatric Psychiatry and Neurology* 4.189-193.

Marcel, A.J. 1980. "Conscious and Preconscious Recognition of Polysemous Words: Locating the Selective Effects of Prior Verbal Context". *Attention and Performance, VIII* ed. by R. Nickerson. Hillsdale, New Jersey: Lawrence Erlbaum Associates.

Marcel, A.J. 1983a. "Consciousness, Masking, and Word Recognition". *Cognitive Psychology* 15.198-237.

Marcel, A.J. 1983b. "Conscious and Unconscious Perception: An Approach to the Relations Between Phenomenal Experience and Perceptual Processes". *Cognitive Psychology* 15.238-300.

Marks, C.E. 1981. *Commissurotomy, Consciousness, and Unity of Mind.* Montgomery, Vermont: Bradford Books.

Marr, D.C. 1982. *Vision: A Computational Investigation into the Human Representation and Processing of Visual Information.* San Francisco: Freeman.

Maxwell, G. 1962. "On the Ontological Status of Theoretical Entities". *Minnesota Studies in the Philosophy of Science, Volume III* ed. by H. Fiegl & G. Maxwell. Minneapolis: University of Minnesota Press.

Mayes, A.R. 1992. "Automatic Memory Processes in Amnesia: How Are They Mediated?" *The Neuropsychology of Consciousness* ed. by A.D. Milner & M.D. Rugg, 235-261, New York: Academic Press.

Mayr, E. 1982. *The Growth of Biological Thought: Evolution, Diversity, and Inheritance.* Cambridge, Massachusetts: Harvard University Press.

McAffee, L.J., A. Robert, & R.A. Hicks. 1982. "Attributions of male College Students to Variations in Facial Features in the Line Drawing of a Woman's Face". *Bulletin of the Psychonomic Society* 19.143-144.

McAndrews, M.P., E.L. Glisky, & D.L. Schacter. 1987. "When Priming Persists: Long-Lasting Implicit Memory for a Single Episode in Amnesic Patients". *Neuropsychologia* 25.497-506.

McCall, R.B., C.B. Dennedy, & C. Dodds. 1977. "The Interfering Effect of Distracting Stimuli on the Infant's Memory". *Child Development* 48.79-87.

McCallum, W.C., S.F. Farmer, & P.K. Pocock. 1984. "The Effects of Physical and Semantic Incongruities on Auditory Event-Related Potentials". *Electroencephalography and Clinical Neurophysiology* 62.203-208.

McClelland, J.L, D.E. Rumelhart, & G.E. Hinton. 1986. "The Appeal of Parallel Distributed Processing". Rumelhart, McClelland, & the PDP Research Group 1986.

McClelland, J.L., D.E. Rumelhart, & the PDP Research Group. 1986. *Parallel Distributed Processing: Explorations in Microcognition, Vol. 2.* Cambridge, Massachusetts: The MIT Press.

McCulloch, R. 1988. "What It Is Like". *Philosophical Quarterly* 38.1-19.

McDaniel, K.D., & L.D. McDaniel. 1991. "Anton's Syndrome in a Patient with Posttraumatic Optic Neuropathy and Bifrontal Contusions". *Archives of Neurology* 48.101-105.

McGinn, C. 1982. *The Subjective View.* Oxford: Clarendon Press.

McGinn, C. 1989. "Can We Solve the Mind-Body Probelm?". *Mind* 48.349-366.

McGinn, C. 1991. *The Problem of Consciousness.* Oxford: Blackwell.

McKee, R., & L.R. Squire. 1992. "On the Devleopment of Declarative Memory". *Society for Neuroscience Abstracts* 18.386.

McNaughton, B., & M. Wilson. 1994. "Ensemble Neural Codes for Spatial Experience and Their Reactivation During Sleep". Paper presented at Toward a Scientific Basis for Consciousness Conference, Tuscon, Arizona.

McTaggart, J.M.E. 1927. *The Nature of Existence.* Cambridge: Cambridge University Press.

Mellor, D.H. 1921. *Real Time.* Cambridge: Cambridge University Press.

Mesulam, M.M. 1985. "Visuperceptual Function in Visual Agnosia". *Neurology* 38.1754-1759.

Metcalfe, J., G.W. Cottrell& W.E. Mencl. 1992. "Cognitive Binding: A Computational-Modeling Analysis of a Distinction Between Implicit and Explicit Memory". *Journal of Cognitive Neuroscience* 4.289-298.

Mewhort, D.K., A.J. Campbell, F.M. Marchetti, & J.D. Campbell. 1981. "Identification, Localization, and 'Iconic Memory': An Evaluation of the Bar-Probe Task". *Memory and Cognition* 9.50-67.

Milner, B., S. Corkin, & H.L. Teuber. 1968. "Further Analysis of the Hippocampal Amnesic Syndrome: 14-Year Follow-Up Study of H.M." *Neurophysiologia* 6.215-234.

Minsky, M. 1981. "A Framework for Representing Knowledge". *Mind Design* ed. by J. Haugeland, 95-128, Cambridge, Massachusetts: The MIT Press.

Minsky, M. 1986. *The Society of Mind.* Cambridge, Massachusetts: The MIT Press.

Mishkin, M. 1957. "Effects of Small Frontal Lesions on Delayed Alternation in Monkeys". *Journal of Neurophysiology* 20.615-622.

Mishkin, M. 1982. "A Memory System in the Monkey". *Philosophical Royal Society of London Biology* 298.85-95.

Mollon, J.D. & E. Scharpe. 1983. *Color Vision: Physiology and Psychophysics.* London: Academic Press.

Morgan, C.L. 1923. *Emergent Evolution.* Ondon: Williams and Norgate.

Morgan, M.J. 1977. *Molyneux's Question: Vision, Touch, and the Philosophy of Perception.* New York: Cambridge University Press.

Morgan, M.J. & T.S. Alba. 1985. "Positional Acuity with Chromatic Stimuli". *Vision Research* 25.689-695.

Morton, J. 1979. "Facilitation in Word Recognition: Experiments in Causing Change in the Logogen Models". *Processing of Visible Language, Volume 1.* ed. by P.A. Kolers, M.E. Wrolstad, & H. Bouma, 259-268, New York: Plenum Press.

Moscovitch, M. 1982. "Multiple Dissociations of Function in Amnesia". *Human Memory and Amnesia* ed. by L.S. Cermak, 337-370, Hillsdale, New Jersey: Lawrence Erlbaum Associates.

Moscovitch, M. 1984. *Infant Memory: Its Relation to Normal and Pathological Memory in Humans and Other Animals.* New York: Plenum Press.

Muller, J. 1827/1840. *Grundriss der Vorlesungen uber die Physiologie.* Bonn: Bei T. Habicht.

Murthy, V.N., & E.E. Fetz. 1992. "Coherent 25- to 35-Hz Oscillations in the Sensorimotor Cortex of Awake Behaving Monkeys". *Proceedings of the National Academy of Sciences of the United States of America* 89.5670-5674.

Murthy, V.N., D.F. Chen, & E.E. Fetz. 1992. "Spatial Extent and Behavioral Dependence of Coherence of 25-35 Hz Oscillations in Primate Sensorimotor Cortex". *Society for Neuroscience Abstracts* 18.847.

Musen, G. 1989. "Implicit and Explicit Memory for Novel Visual Patterns". Unpublished manuscript.

Musen, G., & L.R. Squire. 1991. "Intact Text-Specific Reading Skill in Amnesia". *Journal of Experimental Psychology: Learning, Memory, and Cognition* 16.1068-1076.

Musen, G., & A. Treisman. 1990. "Implicit and Explicit Memory for Visual Patterns". *Journal of Experimental Psychology: Learning, Memory, and Cognition* 16.127-137.

Nagel, T. 1974. "What Is It Like To Be a Bat?" *Philosophical Review* LXXXIII.435-451; reprinted in T. Nagel. 1979. *Mortal Questions,* 165-180, New York: Cambridge.

Nakamura, K., A. Mikami, & K. Kubota. 1992. "Oscillatory Neuronal Activity Related to Visual Short-Term Memory in Monkey Temporal Pole". *Neuroreport* 3.117-120.

Natsoulas, T. 1987. "Consciousness and Commissurotomy: I. Spheres and Streams of Consciousness". *The Journal of Mind and Behavior* 8.435-468.

Neisser, U. 1982. *Memory Observed: Remembering in Natural Contexts.* New York: Freeman Press.

Nelkin, N. 1993. "What is Consciousness?" *Philosophy of Science* 60.419-434.

Nemirow, L. 1980. "Review of Thomas Nagel's *Mortal Questions*". *Philosophical Review* 89.473-477.

Nemirow, L. 1990. "Physicalism and the Cognitive Role of Acquaintance". *Mind and Cognition* ed. by W. Lycan, 490-499, Oxford: Blackwell.

Neuenschwander, S., & F.J. Varela. 1993. "Visually Triggered Neuronal Oscillations in the Pigeon: An Autocorrelation Study of Tectal Activity". *European Journal for Neuroscience* 5.870-881.

Neville, H.J., & D. Lawson. 1987. "Attention to Central and Peripheral Visual Space in a Movement Detection Task: III. Separate Effects of Auditory Deprivation and Acquisition of a Visual Language". *Brain Research* 405.284-294.

Neville, H.J. & C. Weber-Fox. 1994. "Cerebral Subsystems Within Language". *Structural and Functional Organization of the Neocortex: Proceedings of a Symposium in the Memory of Otto D. Creutzfeldt, May 1993* ed. by B. Albowitz, K. Albus, U. Kuhnt, H.-Ch. Nothdurft, & P. Wahle, 424-438, Berlin: Springer-Verlag.

Neville, H.J., M.E. Pratarelli, & K.I. Forster. 1989. "Distinct Neural Systems for Lexical and Episodic Representations of Words". *Society of Neuroscience Abstract* 15.

Newman, J. Forthcoming. "Review: Thalamic Contributions to Attention and Consciousness". To appear in *Consciousness and Cognition*.

Newton, I. 1952. *Opticks*. New York: Dover Publications.

Newton, N. 1986. "Churchland on Direct Introspection of Brain States". *Analysis* 46.97-102.

Nicolis, J.S. 1987. "Chaotic Dynamics in Biological Information Processing: A Heuristic Outline". Unpublished manuscript.

Nisbett, R.E., & L. Ross. 1980. *Human Inference: Strategies and Shortcomings of Social Judgment*. Englewood Cliffs, New Jersey: Prentice Hall.

Nisbett, R.E., & T.D. Wilson. 1977. "The Halo Effect: Evidence for Unconscious Alterations of Judgments". *Journal of Personality and Social Psychology* 35.250-256.

Nissen, M.J., & P. Bullemer. 1987. "Attentional Requirements of Learning: Evidence from Performance Measures". *Cognitive Psychology* 19.1-32.

Nonneman, A.J., J.V. Corwin, C.L. Sahley, & J.P. Vicedomini. 1984. "Functional Development of the Pre-Frontal System". *Early Brain Damage, Volume 2: Neurobiology and Behavior*, 139-153, New York: Academic Press.

Norman, D.A., & T. Shallice. 1988. "Attention to Action: Willed and Automatic Control of Behavior". *Consciousness and Self-Regulation: Adavnces in Research and Theory, Volume 4* ed. by R.J. Davidson, G.E. Schwartz, & D. Shapiro, 1-18, New York: Plenum Press.

Nunez, P.L. 1981. *Electric Fields of the Brain. The Neurophysics of EEG*. New York: Oxford University Press.

Nunez, P.L. 1989. "Generation of Human EEG by a Combination of Long and Short Range Neocortical Interactions". *Brain Topography* 1.199-215.

Nunez, P.L. 1993. *Neocortical Dynamics and Human EEG Rhythms*. New York: Oxford University Press.

O'Keefe, J., & L. Nadel. 1978. *The Hippocampus as a Cognitive Map*. Oxford: Clarendon Press.

Oatley, K. 1988. "On Changing One's Mind: A Possible Function of Consciousness". *Consciousness in Contemporary Science* ed. by A. Marcel & E. Bisiach, 369-390, Oxford: Clarendon Press.

Olton, D.S. 1978. "Characteristics of Spatial Memory". *Cognitive Processes in Animal Behavior* ed. by S.H. Hulse, J. Fowler, & W.K. Honig. Hillsdale, New Jersey: Lawrence Erlbaum Associates.

Olton, D.S. 1979. "Mazes, Maps, and Memory". *American Psychology* 34.588-596.

Olton, D.S., & R.J. Samuelson. 1976. "Remembrance of Places Past: Spatial Memory in Rats". *Journal of Experimental Psychology: Animal Behavior Processes* 2.97-116.

Ostergaard, A.L. 1992. "A Method for Judging Measures of Stochastic Dependence: Further Comments on the Current Controversy". *Journal of Experimental Psychology: Learning, Memory, and Cognition* 18.413-420.

Otta, E. 1983. "Facial Expression and Pupil Size". *Psychologia* 9.19-33.

Ottoson, T., & S. Zeki. 1985. *Central and Peripheral Mechanisms of Color Vision.* New York: Macmillan.

Paller, K.A. 1990. "Recall and Stem-Completion Priming Have Different Electrophysiological Correlates and Are Modified Differentially by Directed Forgetting". *Journal of Experimental Psychology: Learning, Memory, and Cognition* 16.1021-1032.

Paller, K.A., & M. Kutas. 1992. "Brain Potentials During Memory Retrieval: Neurophysiological Indications of the Distinction Between Conscious Recollection and Priming". *Journal of Cognitive Neuroscience* 4.375-391.

Papineau, D. 1993. "Physicalism, Consciousness, and the Antipathic Fallacy". *Australasian Journal of Philosophy* 71.169-183.

Papousek, H. 1969. "Experimental Studies of Appetitional Behavior in Human Newborns and Infants". *Early Behavior* ed. by H.W. Stevenson, E.H. Hess, & H.L. Rheingold. New York: John Wiley & Sons, Limited.

Paritsis, N.C., & D.J. Stewart. 1983. *A Cybernetic Approach to Color Perception.* New York: Gordon and Beach.

Parkin, A.J. 1982. "Residual Learning Capacity in Organic Amnesics". *Cortex* 18.417-440.

Parkin, A.J. 1984. "Amnesic Syndrome: A Lesion-Specific Disorder?" *Cortex* 20.479-508.

Penfield, W., & P. Perot. 1963. "The Brain's Record of Auditory and Visual Experience: A Final Summary and Discussion". *Brain* 86.595-696.

Pereboom, D. 1994. "Bats, Brain Scientists, and the Limitations of Introspection". *Philosophy and Phenomenological Research* 54.315-329.

Perfect, T.J., J.J. Downes, P. Davies, & K. Wilson. 1992. "Preserved Implicit Memory for Lexical Inofmration in Alzheimer's Disease". *Perceptual and Motor Skills* 74.747-754.

Pfurtscheller, G., J. Steffan, & H. Maresch. 1988. "ERP Mapping and Functional Topography: Temporal and Spatial Aspects". *Functional Brain Imaging* ed. by G. Pfurtscheller & F.H. Lopes de Silva, 117-130, Toronto: Huber.

Piaget, J. 1954. *The Construction of Reality in the Child.* New York: Basic Books.

Polster, M.R., L. Nadel, & D.L. Schacter. 1991. "Cognitive Neuroscience Analyses of Memory: A Historical Perspective". *Journal of Cognitive Neuroscience* 2.95-116.

Posner, M.I. 1993. "Seeing the Mind". *Science* 262.673-674.

Posner, M.I., & R.M. Klein. 1973. "On the Functions of Consciousness," *Attention and Performance IV* ed. by S. Kornblum, 21-35, New York: Academic Press.

Posner, M.I., & C. Snyder. 1975a. "Attention and Cognitive Control". *Information Processing and Cognition: The Loyola Symposium* ed. by R. Solso. Hillsdale, New Jersey: Lawrence Erlbaum Associates.

Posner, M.I., & C. Snyder. 1975b. "Facilitation and Inhibition in the Processing of Signals". *Attention and Performance V* ed. by P.M.A. Rabbitt & S. Dornic. New York: Academic Press.

Prinzmetal, W. 1981. "Principles of Feature Integration in Visual Perception". *Perception and Psychophysics* 30.330-340.

Prinzmetal, W., & B. Keysar, B. 1989. "Functional Theory of Illusory Conjunctions and Neon Colors". *Journal of Experimental Psychology: General* 118.165-190.

Prinzmetal, W., D.E. Presti, & M.I. Posner. 1986. "Does Attention Affect Visual Feature Integration?" *Journal of Experimental Psychology: Human Perception and Performance* 12.361-369.

Ptito, A., F. Lepore, M. Ptito, & M. Lassonde. 1991. "Target Detection and Movement Discrimination in the Blind Field of Hemispherectomized Patients". *Brain* 114.497.

Rakic, P., J-P. Bourgeois, M.E. Eckenhoff, N. Zeceric, & P.S. Goldman-Rakic. 1986. "Concurrent Overproduction of Synapses in Diverse Regions of the Primate Cerebral Cortex". *Science* 232.232-235.

Ramachandran, V.S. 1990. "Visual Perception in People and Machines". *AI and the Eye* ed. by A. Balke & T. Troscianko, 21-77, New York: John Wiley & Sons, Limited.

Ramachandran, V.S. & S.M. Anstis. 1986. "The Perception of Apparent Motion". *Scientific American* 254.101-109.

Ramachandran, V.S., & P.S. Churchland. 1993. "Filling In Versus Finding Out". *Dennett and His Critics* ed. by B. Dahlbom. New York: Blackwell.

Reber, A.S. 1992. "The Cognitive Unconscious: An Evolutionary Perspective". *Consciousness and Cognition* 1.93-133.

Reichenbach, H. 1938. *Experience and Prediction*. Chicago: University Press.

Restak, R.M. 1988. *The Mind*. New York: Bantam Books.

Rey, G. 1983. "A Reason for Doubting the Existence of Consciousness". *Consciousness and Self-Regulation* ". ed. by R.J. Davidson, G.E. Schwartz, & D. Shapiro. New York: Plenum Press.

Rey, G. 1988. "A Question About Consciousness". *Perspectives on Mind* ed. by H.R. Otto & J.A. Tuedio, 5-24, Dordrecht: Reidel.

Rhodes, P.A. 1992. "The Long Open Time of the NMDA Channel Facilitates the Self-Organization of Invariant Object Responses in Cortex". *Society for Neuroscience Abstracts* 18.740.

Ribot, T. 1890/1938. *Psychologie de l'Attention*. Paris: F. Alcan.

Ribrary, U., A.A. Ionnides, K.D. Singh, R. Hasson, J.P. Bolton, F. Lado, A. Mogilner, & R. Llinas. 1991. "Magnetic Field Tomography of Coherent Thalamocortical 40-Hz Oscillations in Humans". *Proceedings of the National Academy of Sciences of the United Sates of America* 88.11037-11041.

Roediger, H.L., & T.A. Blaxton. 1987. "Retrieval Modes Produce Dissociations in Memory for Surface Information". *Memory and Cognitive Processes: The Ebbinghaus Centennial Conference*. Hillsdale, New Jersey: Erlbaum.

Roediger, H.L., M.S. Weldon, L. Michael, & G.L. Riegler. 1992. "Direct Comparison of Two Implicit Memory Tests: Word Fragment and Word Stem Completion". *Journal of Experimental Psychology: Learning, Memory, Cognition* 18.1251-1269.

Rolfe, S.A., & R.H. Day. 1981. "Effects of the Similarity and Dissimilarity Between Familiarization and Test Objects on Recognition Memory in Infants Following Unimodal and Bimodal Familiarization". *Child Development* 52.1308-1312.

Rorty, R. 1982. "Comments on Dennett". *Synthese* 53.181-187.

Rose, S.A., A.W. Gottfried, & W.H. Bridger. 1978. "Cross-Modal Transfer in Infants: Relationship to Prematurity and Socioeconomic Background". *Developmental Psychology* 14.643-652.

Rose, S.A., A.W. Gottfried, & W.H. Bridger. 1979. "Effects of Haptic Cues on Visual Recognition Memory in Fullterm and Preterm Infants". *Infant Behavior and Development* 2.55-67.

Rugg, M.D. 1985. "The Effects of Semantic Priming and Word Repetition on Event-Related Potentials". *Psychopathology* 22.642-647.

Rugg, M.D. 1992. "Conscious and Unconscious Processes in Langauge and Memory— Commentary". *The Neuropsychology of Consciousness* ed. by A.D. Milner & M.D. Rugg, 263-278, New York: Academic Press.

Rugg, M.D., & M.C. Doyle. 1992. *Cognitive Electrophysiology* ed. by H. Heinze, T. Munte, & G.R. Mangun. Cambridge, Massachusetts: Mirkhauser Boston.

Rumelhart, D. 1980. "Schemata: The Building Blocks of Cognition". *Theoretical Issues in Reading Comprehension* ed. by R. Spire, B. Bruce, & W. Brewer. Hillsdale, New Jersey: Lawrence Erlbaum Associates.

Rumelhart, D., R. McClelland,& the PDP Research Group. 1986. *Parallel Distributed Processing: Explorations in the Microstructure of Cognition.* Cambridge, Massachusetts: The MIT Press.

Russell, B. 1912/1959. *The Problems of Philosophy.* Oxford: Oxford University Press.

Salasoo, A., R.M. Shiffrin, & T.C. Feustal. 1985. "Building Permanent Memory Codes: Codification and Repetition Effects in Word Identification". *Journal of Experimental Psychology: General* 114.50-77.

Salmon, W. 1984. *Scientific Explanation and the Causal Structure of the World.* Princeton: Princeton University Press.

Sandson, J., M..L. Albert, & M.P. Alexander. 1986. "Confabulation in Aphasia". *Cortex* 22.621-626.

Sapir, C.B. 1987. "Diffuse Cortical Projection Systems: Anatomical Organization and Role in Cortical Function". *Handbook of Physiology — The Nervous System V*, 169-210, Bethesda, Maryland: American Physiological Society.

Saunders, E.A. 1991. "Rorschach Indicators of Chronic Childhood Sexual Abuse in Female Borderline Inpatients". *Bulletin of the Menninger Clinic* 55.48-71.

Scarborough, D.L., C. Cortese, & H.S. Scarborough. 1977. "Frequency and Repetition Effects in Lexical Memory". *Journal of Experimental Psychology: Human Perception and Cognition* 3.1-17.

Scarborough, D.L., C. Cortese, & H.S. Scarborough. 1979. "Accessing Lexical Memory: The Transfer of the Word Repetition Effects in Lexical Memory". *Memory and Cognition* 7.1-12.

Schacter, D.L. 1985a. "Multiple Forms of Memory in Humans and Animals". *Memory Systems of the Brain* ed. by N.M. Weinberger, J.L. McGaugh, & G. Lynch, 351-379, New York: The Guilford Press.

Schacter, D.L. 1985b. "Priming of Old and New Knowledge in Amnesic Patients and Normal Subjects". *Annals of the New York Academy of Sciences* 444.41-53.

Schacter, D.L. 1987. "Implicit Expressions of Memory in Organic Amnesia: Learning of New Facts and Associations". *Human Neurobiology* 6.107-118.

Schacter, D.L. 1990. "Perceptual Representation Systems and Implicit Memory: Toward a Resolution of the Multiple Memory Systems Debate". *Annals of the New York Academy of Sciences* 608.435-571.

Schacter, D.L. 1992. "Consciousness and Awareness in Memory and Amnesia: Critical Issues". *The Neuropsychology of Consciousness* ed. by A.D. Milner & M.D. Rugg, 179-200, New York: Academic Press.

Schacter, D.L., & B.A. Church. 1992. "Auditory Priming: Implicit and Explicit Memory for Words and Voices". *Journal of Experimental Psychology: Learning, Memory, and Cognition* 18.915-930.

Schacter, D.L., & P. Graf. 1986a. "Effects of Elaborate Processing on Implicit and Explicit Memory for New Associations". *Journal of Experimental Psychology: Learning, Memory, and Cognition* 12.432-444.

Schacter, D.L., & P. Graf. 1986b. "Preserved Learning in Amnesic Patients: Perspectives from Research on Direct Priming". *Journal of Clinical and Experimental Neuropsychology* 8.727-743.

Schacter, D.L., & P. Graf. 1989. "Modality Specificity of Implicit Memory for New Associations". *Journal of Experimental Psychology: Learning, Memory, and Cognition* 15.3-12.

Schacter, D.L., & S.M. McGlynn. 1989. "Implicit Memory: Effects of Elaboration Depend on Unitization". *American Journal of Psychology* 102.151-181.

Schacter, D.L., & M. Moscovitch. 1984. "Infants, Amnesics, and Dissociable Memory Systems". *Infant Memory: Its Relation to Normal and Pathological Memory in Humans and Other Animals* ed. by M. Moscovitch, 173-216, New York: Plenum Press.

Schacter, D.L., & E. Tulving. 1982. "Anmesia and Memory Research". *Human Memory and Amnesia* ed. by L.S. Cernak, 1-32, Hillsdale, New Jersey: Lawrence Erlbaum Associates.

Schacter, D.L., L.A. Cooper, & S. Delaney. 1990. "Implicit Memory for Unfamiliar Objects Depends on Access to Structural Descriptions". *Journal of Experimental Psychology: General* 119.5-24.

Schacter, D.L., L.A. Cooper, M. Tharan, & A.B. Rubens. 1991. "Preserved Priming of Novel Objects in Patients with Memory Disorders". *Journal of Cognitive Neuroscience* 3.117-130.

Schacter, D.L., M.P. McAndrews, & M. Moscovitch. 1988. "Access to Consciousness: Dissociations between Implicit and Explicit Knowledge in Neuropsychological Syndromes". *Thought Without Language* ed. by L. Weiskrantz. Oxford: Oxford University Press.

Schacter, D.L., S.M. McGlynn,W.P. Milberg, & B.A. Church. 1993. "Spared Priming Despite Impaired Comprehension: Implicit Memory in a Case of Word-Deafness". *Neuropsychology* 7.107-118.

Schacter, S., & J.E. Singer. 1962. "Cognitive, Social, and Physiological Determinants of Emotional State". *Psychological Review* 69.379-399.

Schank, R., & Abelson. 1977. *Scripts, Plans, Goals, and Understanding: An Inquiry into Human Knowledge Structures*. Hillsdale, New Jersey: Lawrence Erlbaum Associates.

Scheibel, A.B. 1980. "Anatomical and Physiological Substrates of Arousal". *The Reticular Formation Revisited* ed. by J.A. Hobson & M.A. Brazier. New York: Raven Press.

Scheibel, M.C., & A.B. Scheibel. 1967. "Anatomical Basis of Attentional Mechanisms in Vertebrate Brains". *The Neurosciences: A Study Program* ed. by G.C. Quarton, T. Melnechuck, & F.O. Schmitt. New York: Raven Press.

Schenkman, B.N., & G. Jansson. 1986. "The Detection and Localization of Objects by the Blind with the Aid of Long-Cane Tapping Sounds". *Human Factors* 28.607-628.

Schick, T.W. 1992. "The Epistemic Role of Qualititative Content". *Philosophy and Phenomenological Research* 52.383-393.

Schlick, M. 1959. "Positivism and Realism". *Logical Positivism* ed. by A.J. Ayer, 92-95, New York: Free Press.

Schneider, W., & R.M. Shiffrin. 1977. "Controlled and Automatic Human Information Processing: I. Detection, Search, and Attention". *Psychological Review* 84.1-66.

Schwartz, B.L., & S. Hashtroudi. 1991. "Priming Is Independent of Skill Learning". *Journal of Experimental Psychology: Learning, Memory, and Cognition* 17.1177-1187.

Schwartz, C., A. Aertsen,& J. Bolz. 1992. "Dynamics of Coherent Firing in Cat Visual Cortex". *Society for Neuroscience Abstracts* 18.292.

Schwender, D., I. Keller, B. Daschner, & C. Madler. 1991. "Sensory Information Processing During General Anesthesia — Acoustic-Evoked 30-40 Hz Oscillations and Intraoperative Wakefulness During Cesarean Section". *Anasthesiologie, Intensivmedizin, Notfallmedizin, Schmerztherapie* 26.17-24.

Searle, J. 1980. "Minds, Brains, and Programs". *Behavioral and Brain Sciences* 3.417-458.

Searle, J. 1984. *Minds, Brains, and Science*. London: BBC Publications.

Searle, J. 1987. "Mind and Brains Without Programs". *Mindwaves: Thoughts on Intelligence, Identity, and Consciousness* ed. by C. Blakemore & S. Greenfield, 209-234, Cambridge, Massachusetts: Basil Blackwell.

Searle, J. 1990a. "Is the Brain's Mind a Computer Program?" *Scientific American* 264.26-31.

Searle, J. 1990b. "Consciousness, Explanatory Inversion, and Cognitive Science". *Behavioral and Brain Sciences* 13.

Searle, J. 1992. *The Rediscovery of Mind*. Cambridge, Massachusetts: The MIT Press.

Segal, L.A. 1965. "The Nonlinear Interaction of a Finite Number of Disturbances to a Layer of Fluid Heated from Below". *Journal of Field Mechanics* 21.359.

Sejnowski, T. 1981. "Skeleton Fibers in the Brain". *Parallel Models of Associative Memory* ed. by G.E. Hinton & J.A. Anderson, 189-212, Hillsdale, New Jersey: Lawrence Erlbaum Associates.

Selfrige, O.G. 1955. "Pattern Recognition in Modern Computers". *Proceedings of the Western Joint Comptuer Conference*.

Sellars, W. 1956. "Empiricism and the Philosophy of Mind". *The Foundations of Science and the Concepts of Psychology and Psychoanalysis. Minnesota Studies in the Philosophy of Science, Volume 1* ed. by H. Feigl & M. Scriven. Minneapolis: University of Minnesota Press.

Sereno, M.I. 1990. "Language and the Primate Brain, " *CRL Newletter* 4.1-12.

Shallice, T. 1988a. "Information-Processing Models of Consciousness: Possibilities and Problems". *Consciousness in Contemporary Science* ed. by A.J. Marcel & E. Bisiach, 305-333, Oxford: Clarendon Press.

Shallice, T. 1988b. *From Neuropsychology to Mental Structure*. New York: Cambridge University Press.

Sherman, S.M. 1973. "Visual Field Deficits in Monocularly and Binocularly Deprived Cats". *Brain Research* 49.25-45.

Sherman, S.M. 1977. "The Effect of Cortical and Tactal Lesions on the Visual Field of Binocularly Deprived Cats". *Journal of Comparative Neurology* 172.231-246.

Shiffrin, R.M. 1975. "The Locus and Role of Attention in Memory". *Attention and Performance V* ed. by P.M.A. Rabbitt & S. Dornic. New York: Academic Press.

Shiffrin, R.M., & W. Geisler. 1973. "Visual Recognition in a Theory of Information Processing". *Contemporary Issues in Cognitive Psychology: The Loyola Symposium* ed. by R. Solso. Washington, D.C.: Winston.

Shiffrin, R.M., & W. Schneider. 1977. "Controlled and Automatic Human Information Processing: II. Perceptual Learning, Automatic Attending, and General Theory". *Psychological Review* 84.127-190.

Shimamura, A.P. 1986. "Priming Effects in Amnesia: Evidence for a Dissociable Function". *Quarterly Journal of Experimental Psychology* 38A.619-315.

Shimamura, A.P., & L.R. Squire. 1984. "Paired-Associated Learning and Priming Effects in Amnesia: A Neuropsychological Study". *Journal of Experimental Psychology: General* 113.556-570.

Shimamura, A.P., & L.R. Squire. 1988. "Long Term Memory in Amnesia: Cued Recall, Recognition Memory, and Confidence Ratings". *Journal of Experimental Psychology: Learning, Memory, and Cognition* 14.763-771.

Shimamura, A.P., F.B. Gershberg, P.J. Jurica, J.A. Mangels, *et al.* 1992. "Intact Implicit Memory in Patients with Frontal Lobe Lesions". *Neuropsychologia* 31.931-937.

Shoemaker, S. 1975a. "Functionalism and Qualia". *Philosophical Studies* 27.291-315.

Shoemaker, S. 1975b. "Phenomenal Similarity". *Critica* 7.3-37.

Shoemaker, S. 1981. "Absent Qualia are Possible — A Reply to Block". *Philosophical Review* 90.581-599.

Shoemaker, S. 1982. "The Inverted Spectrum". *Journal of Philosophy* 79.357-381.

Siegel, R.K. 1977. "Hallucinations". *Scientific American* 237.132-140.

Silva, L.R., Y. Amitai, & B.W. Conners. 1991. *Science* 251.432.

Simon, H.A. 1969. *The Sciences of the Artificial.* Cambridge, Massachusetts: The MIT Press.

Simpson, C. 1991. "Color Perception: Cross-Cultural Linguistic Translation and Relativism". *The Journal for the Theory of Social Behavior* 21.409-430.

Skarda, C.A., & W.J. Freeman. 1990. "Chaos and the New Science of the Brain". *Concepts in Neuroscience* 1.275-285.

Skinner, J.E., & C.D. Yingling. 1972. "Reconsideration of the Cerebral Mechanisms Underlying Selective Attention and Slow Potential Shifts: Central Gating Mechanisms That Regulate Event-Related Potentials and Behavior". *Attention, Voluntary Contraction, and Event-Related Cerebral Potentials: Progress in Clinical Neurophysiology, Volume 1* ed. by J.E. Desmedt, 30-69, Hillsdale, New Jersey: Lawrence Erlbaum Associates.

Sloman, S.A., C.A.G. Hayman, N. Ohta, & E. Tulving. 1988. "Forgetting and Interference in Fragment Completion". *Journal of Experimental Psychology: Learning, Memory, and Cognition* 14.223-239.

Smart, J.J.C. 1963. *Philosophy and Scientific Realism.* New York: Humanities.

Smith, W.S., & E.E. Fetz. 1989. "Effects of Synchrony Between Primate Corticomotoneuronal Cells on Post-Spike Facilitation of Muscles and Motor Units". *Neuroscience Letters* 96.76-81.

Sober, E. 1984. *The Nature of Selection: Evolutionary Theory in Philosophical Focus.* Cambridge, Massachusetts: The MIT Press.

Sperry, R.W. 1965. "Brain Bisection and Mechanisms of Consciousness". *Brain and Conscious Experience* ed. by J.C. Eccles, 298-313, New York: Springer-Verlag.

Sperry, R.W. 1969. "A Modified Concept of Consciousness". *Psychological Review* 76.532-536.

Sperry, R.W. 1977. "Fore-Brain Commissurotomy and Conscious Awareness". *Journal of Medicine and Philosophy* 2.101-126.

Sperry, R.W. 1985. "Consciousnes, Personal Identity, and The Divided Brain". *The Dual Brain*. ed. by D.F. Benson & E. Zaidel, 11-26, York: Guilford.

Sperry, R.W. 1987. "Structure and Significance of the Consciousness Revolution". *The Journal of Mind and Behavior* 8.37-65.

Sperry, R.W. 1991. "In Defense of Mentalism and Emergent Interactionism". *The Journal of Mind and Behavior* 12221-245.

Sporns, O., J.A. Gally, G.N. Reeke, Jr., & G.M. Edelman. 1989. "Reentrant Signalling Among Simulated Neuronal Groups Leads to Coherency in Their Oscillatory Activity". *Proceedings of the National Academy of Sciences of the United States of America* 86.7265-7269.

Sporns, O., G. Toponi, & G.M. Edelman. 1991. "Modeling Perceptual Groupings and Figure-Ground Segregation by Means of Active Reentrant Connections". *Proceedings of the National Academy o Sciences of the United States of America* 88.129-133.

Sporns, O., G. Toponi, & G.M. Edelman. 1992. "Constructive and Correlative Reentry in the Visual System: Computer Simulations and Psychophysics". *Society for Neuroscience Abstracts* 18.741.

Squire, L.R. 1986. "The Neuropsychology of Memory". *The Biology of Learning* ed. by P. Marler & H.S. Terrance, 667-695, New York: Springer-Verlag.

Squire, L.R. 1987. *Memory and the Brain.* New York: Oxford University Press.

Squire, L.R. 1992. "Declarative and Nondeclarative Memory: Multiple Brain Systems Supporting Learning and Memory". *Journal of Cognitive Neuroscience* 4.232-243.

Squire, L.R., & N.J. Cohen. 1984. "Human Memory and Amnesia". *Proceedings of the Conference on the Neurobiology of Learning and Memory* ed. by J. McGaugh, G. Lynch, & N. Weinberger, 3-64, New York: Guilford Press.

Squire, L.R., & R.D. McKee. 1992. "Influence of Prior Events on Cognitive Judgments". *Journal of Experimental Psychology: Learning, Memory, and Cognition* 18.106-115.

Squire, L.R., & R.D. McKee. 1993. "Declarative and Nondeclarative Memory in Opposition: When Prior Events Influence Amnesic Patients More Than Normals". *Memory and Cognition* 21.424-430.

Squire, L.R., & S. Zola-Morgan. 1991. "The Medial Temporal Lobe Memory System". *Science* 253.1380-1386.

Squire, L.R., J.G. Ojemann, F.M. Miezen, S.E. Peterson, T.O. Videen, *et al.* 1992. "Activation of the Hippocampus in Normal Humans: A Functional Anatomical Study of Memory". *Proceedings of the National Academy of Sciences U.S.A.* 89.1837-1841.

St. James-Roberts, I. 1981. "A Reinterpretation of Hemispherectomy Without Functional Plasticity of the Brain". *Brain and Language* 13.31-53.

Steinbüchel, N.v., E. Pöppel, & B. Hiltbrunner. 1992. "Independent Temporal Factors Underlying Cognitive Processes". *Society for Neuroscience Abstracts* 18.745.

Steriade, M., & R.R. Llinas. 1988. "The Functional States of the Thalamus and the Associated Neuronal Interplay". *Physiological Reviews* 68.649-725.

Steriade, M., R.C. Dossi, D. Pare, G. Oakson. 1991. "Fast Oscillations 20-40 (Hz) in Thalamocortical Systems and Their Potentiation By Mesopontine Cholinergic Nuclei in the Cat". *Proceedings of the National Academy of Sciences of the United States of America* 88.4396-4400.

Stich, S. 1983. *From Folk Psychology to Cognitive Science: The Case Against Belief.* Cambridge, Massachusetts: The MIT Press.

Straub, R.O., M.S. Seidenberg, H.S. Terrace, & T.G. Bever. 1979. "Serial Learning in the Pigeon". *Journal of the Experimental Analysis of Behavior* 32.137-148.

Stroud, B. 1977. *Hume.* Boston: Routledge and Keagan Paul.

Stryker, M. 1989. "Is Grandmother an Oscillation?" *Nature* 338.297-298.

Stryker, M.P. 1991. "Seeing the Whole Picture". *Current Biology* 1.252-253.

Stumpf, C. 1883. *Psychology of Tone.* Leipzig: Hirzel.

Stuss, D.T., M.P. Alexander, A. Lieberman, & H. Levine. 1978. "An Extraordinary Form of Confabulation". *Neurology* 28.1166-1172.

Stuss, P.T., A. Guberman, R. Nelson, & S. Larochelle. 1988. "The Neuropsychology of Paramedian Thalamic Infarcts". *Brain and Cognition* 8.348-278.

Supa, M., M. Cotzin, & K.M. Dallenbach, K.M. 1944. "'Facial Vision': The Perception of Obstacles by the Blind". *American Journal of Psychology* 57.133-183.

Suppe, F. 1989. *The Semantic Conception of Theories and Scientific Realism.* Chicago: University of Illinois Press.

Swanson, L.W., T.J. Teyler, & R.F. Thompson. 1982. "Hippocampal Long-Term Potentiation: Mechanisms and Implications for Memory". *Neuroscience Research Program Bulletin* 20.613-675.

Tanaka, K. 1993. "Neuronal Mechanisms of Object Recognition". *Science* 262.685-688.

Tarrahian, G.A., & R.A. Hicks. 1979. "Attribution of Pupil Size as a Function of Facial Valence and Age in American and Persian Children". *Journal of Cross Cultural Psychology* 10.243-250.

Taylor, G., & R. Chabot. 1978. "Differential Backward Masking of Words and Letters by Masks of Varying Orthographic Structure". *Memory and Cognition* 6.629-635.

Terrace, H.S. 1984. "Simultaneous Chaining: The Problem It Poses for Traditional Chaining Theory". *Quantitative Analyses of Behavior* ed. by R.J. Herrnstein & A. Wagner. Cambridge, Massachusetts: Ballinger.

Tipper, S.P. 1985. "The Negative Priming Effect: Inhibitory Priming By Ignored Objects". *Quarterly Journal of Experimental Psychology* 37A.571-590.

Tipper, S.P., & J. Driver. 1988. "Negative Priming Between Pictures and Words in a Selective Attention Task: Evidence for Semantic Processing of Ignored Stimuli". *Memory and Cognition* 16.64-70.

Tischler, M.D., & M. Davis. 1983. "A Visual Pathway That Mediates Fear-Conditioned Enhancement of Acoustic Startle". *Brain Research* 276.55-71.

Titchener, E.B. 1896. *An Outline of Psychology.* New York: Macmillan.

Titchener, E.B. 1898a. "The Postulates of a Structural Psychology". *Philosophical Review* 7.449-465.

Titchener, E.B. 1898b. *A Primer of Psychology.* New York: Macmillan.

Tomlinson, N., R.A. Hicks, & R.J. Pellegrini. 1978. "Attributions of Female College Students to Variations in Pupil Size". *Bulletin of the Psychonomic Society* 12.477-478.

Tononi, G., O. Sporns, & G.M. Edelman. 1992. "Reentry and the Problem of Integrating Multiple Cortical Areas: Simulation of Dynamic Integration in the Visual System". *Cerebral Cortex* 2.310-335.

Tramo, M.J., J.J. Bharucha, & F.E. Musiek. 1990. "Music Perception and Cognition Following Bilateral Lesions of Auditory Cortex". *Journal of Cognitive Neuroscience* 2.195-212.

Treisman, A. 1986. "Features and Objects in Visual Processing". *Scientific American* 254.114b-125.

Treisman, A. & G. Gelade. 1980. "A Feature Integration Theory of Attention". *Cognitive Psychology*, 12: 97-136.

Treisman, A. & H. Schmidt. 1982. "Illusory Conjunctions in the Perception of Objects". *Cognitive Psychology* 14.107-141.

Tsuda, I. 1991. "Chaotic Iternerancy as a Dynamical Basis of Mermeneutics in Brain and Mind". *World Futures* 32.167-184.

Tsuda, I. 1992. "Dynamic Link of Memory — Chaotic Memeory Map in Nonequilibrium Neural Networks". *Neural Networks* 5.313-326.

Tsuda, I. 1994. "Can Stochastic Renewal of Maps Be a Model for Cerebral Cortex?" *Physica D* 75. 165-178.

Tsuda, I. Forthcoming. "Chaotic Hermeneutics for Understanding the Brain". To appear in *Proceedings of the International Symposium on Endsphysics*, Santa Cruz: Aerial Press.

Tsuda, I. & G. Barna. 1994. "How Can Chaos Be a Cognitive Processor?" *Towards the Harnessing of Chaos* ed. by M. Yamaguti, 47-61, Amsterdam: Elsevier Science B.V.

Tsuda, I. & K. Matsumoto. 1983. "Noise-Induced Order — Complexity Theoretical Digression". *Chaos and Statistical Method: Proceedings of the Sixth Kyoto Summer Institute* ed. by Y. Kuramoto, 102-108, Berlin: Springer-Verlag.

Tulving, E., & D.L. Schacter. 1990. "Priming and Human Memory Systems". *Science* 247.301-306.

Tulving, E., D.L. Schacter,& H.A. Stark. 1982. "Priming Effects in Word-Fragment Completion Are Independent of Recognition Memory". *Journal of Experimental Psychology: Learning, Memory, and Cognition* 8.336-342.

Turbes, C.C. 1992. "Brain State Matrix: Computational Approaches to Neocortical Limbic Rythyms". *Society for Neuroscience Abstracts* 18.848.

Turvey, M. 1974. "Constructive Theory, Perceptual Systems, and Tacit Knowledge". *Cognition and Symbolic Processes* ed. by W. Weld & D. Palermo. Hillsdale, New Jersey: Lawrence Erlbaum Associates.

Tye, M. 1986. "The Subjective Qualities of Experience". *Mind* 95.1-17.

Tye, M. 1991. *The Imagery Debate*. Cambridge, Massachusetts: The MIT Press.

Tyler, L.K. 1993. "The Distinction Between Implicit and Explicit Language Function: Evidence from Aphasia". *The Neuropsychology of Consciousness* ed. by A.D. Milner & M.D. Rugg, 159-178, New York: Academic Press.

Umita, C. 1988. "The Control Operations of Consciousness". *Consciousness in Contemporary Science* ed. by A. Marcel & E. Bisiach , 334-356, Oxford: Clarendon Press.

van Brakel, J. 1992. "The Plasticity of Categories: The Case of Colour". *The British Journal for the Philosophy of Science* 43.

van Brakel, J. Forthcoming. "The *Ignis Fatuus* of Semantic Universalia: The Case of Colour". To appear in *The British Journal for the Philosophy of Science*.

Van Der Horst, G., C.M. de Weert, & M.A. Bouman. 1967. "Transfer of Spatial Chromaticity-Contrast at Threshold in the Human Eye". *Journal of the Optical Society of America* 57.1260-1266.

Van Essen, D.C. 1985. "Functional Organization of Primate Visual Cortex". *Cerebral Cortex*. ed. by A. Peters & E.G. Jones, 259-329, New York: Plenum Publishing.

Van Essen, D.C., C.H. Anderson, & D.J. Felleman. 1992. "Information Processing in the Primate Visual System: An Integrated Systems Perspective". *Science* 255.419-423.

van Fraassen, B. 1980. *The Scientific Image*. Cambridge, Massachusetts: The MIT Press.

Van Gulick, R. 1981. "Functionalism, Information, and Content". *Nature and System* 2.139-162.

Van Gulick, R. 1990. "Physicalism and the Subjectivity of the Mental". *Philosophical Topics* 13.51-70.

Van Gulick, R. 1993. "Understanding the Phenomenal Mind: Are We All Just Armadillos?". *Consciousness* ed. by M. Davies and G. Humphreys, 137-154, Oxford: Blackwell.

Velmans, M. 1992. "Is Human Information Processing Conscious?" *Brain and Behavioral Science*, 14.

Verfaellie, M., R.M. Bauer, & D. Bowers. 1991. "Autonomic and Behavioral Evidence of 'Implicit' Memory in Amnesia". *Brain and Cognition* 15.10-25.

Viana Di Prisco, G., & W.J. Freeman. 1985. "Odor-Related Bulbar EEG Spatial Pattern Analysis During Appetitive Conditioning in Rabbits". *Behavioral Neuroscience* 99.964-978.

von der Malsburg, C. 1982. *The Correlation Theory of Brain Function*. Göttengen, Germany: Max-Planck Institute for Biophysical Chemistry.

von der Malsburg, C. 1987. "Synaptic Plasticity as Basis of Brain Organization". *The Neural and Molecular Bases of Learning* ed. by J.-P. Changeux & M. Konishi , 411-432, New York: John Wiley & Sons, Limited.

von der Malsburg, C., & J. Buhman. 1992. "Sensory Segmentation with Coupled Neural Oscillators". *Biological Cybernetics* 67.233-242.

Von Senden, M. 1932/1960. *Space and Sight: The Perception of Space and Shape in the Congenitally Blind Before and After Operation* trans. P. Heath. London: Methuen.

Wang, J., T. Aigner,& M. Mishkin, M. 1992. "Effects of Neostriatal Lesions on Visual Habit Formation of Rhesus Monkeys". *Society for Neuroscience Abstracts* 16.67.

Warren, R.M. 1967. "Perceptual Restoration of Missing Speech Sounds". *Science* 167.392-393.

Warren, R.M., & R.P. Warren. 1970. "Auditory Illusions and Confusions". *Scientific American* 233.30-36.

Warrington, E.K., & L. Weiskrantz. 1970. "Amnesic Syndrome: Consolidation or Retrieval?" *Nature* 228.629-630.

Warrington, E.K., & L. Weiskrantz. 1974. "The Effect of Prior Learning on Subsequent Retention in Amnesic Patients". *Neuropsychologia* 12.419-428.

Warrington, E.K., & L. Weiskrantz. 1982. "Amnesia: A Disconnection Syndrome". *Neuropsychologia* 20.233-248.

Watkins, M. 1989. "The Knowledge Argument Against The Knowledge Argument". *Analysis* 49.158-160.

Weinstein, E.A. 1971. "Linguistic Aspects of Amnesia and Confabulation". *Journal of Psychiatric Research* 8.439-444.

Weiskrantz, L. 1984. "On Issues and Theories of the Human Amnesic Syndrome". *Memory Systems of the Brain: Animal and Human Cognitive Processes* ed. by N. Weinberger, J. McGaugh, & G. Lynch , 380-315, New York: Guilford Press.

Weiskrantz, L. 1988. "Some Contributions of Neuropsychology of Vision and Memory to the Problem of Consciousness". *Consciousness in Contemporary Science* ed. by A. Marcel & E. Bisiach , 183-199, Oxford: Clarendon Press.

Weiskrantz, L. 1992. "Unconscious Vision: The Strange Phenomenon of Blindsight". *Science* 32.22.

Weiskrantz, L., & E.K. Warrington. 1979. "Conditioning in Amnesic Patients". *Neuropsychologia* 17.187-194.

Weiskrantz, L., E.K. Warrington, & M. Saunders. 1974. "Visual Capacity in the Hemianopic Field Following a Restricted Occipital Ablation". *Brain* 97.709-728.

Wertheimer, M. 1912. "Experimental Studies of the Perception of Movement". *Zeitschrift fuer Psychologie* 61.161-265.

Wertheimer, M. 1967. "Gestalt Theories". *A Source Book of Gestalt Psychology* ed. by W.D. Ellis, 1-11, New York: Humanities Press.

Whishaw, I.Q. 1991. "Locale and Tason Systems: No Place for Neophrenology?" *Hippocampus* 1.272-274.

Wickelgren, W.A. 1979. "Chunking and Consolidation: A Theoretical Synthesis of Semantic Networks, Configuring in Conditioning, S-R Versus Cognitive Learning, Normal Forgetting, the Amnesic Syndrome, and the Hippocampal Arousal System". *Psychological Review* 86.44-60.

Wilkes, K. 1984. "Is Consciousness Important?" *British Journal for the Philosophy of Science* 35.223-243.

Wilkes, K. 1988. "_____, Yishi, Duh, Um, and Consciousness". *Consciousness in Contemporary Science* ed. by A. Marcel & E. Bisiach, 16-41, Oxford: Clarendon Press.

Wilson, M.A. & J.M. Bower. 1991. "Computer Simulation of Oscillatory Behavior in Cerebral Cortical Networks". *Advances in Neural Information Processing Systems 2* ed. by D. S. Touretzky, 84-91, San Mateo, California: Morgan Kaufman.

Wimsatt, W.C. 1976. "Reductionism, Levels of Organization, and the Mind-Body Problem". *Consciousness and the Brain* ed. by G. Globus, G. Maxwell, & I. Savodnik. New York: Plenum Press.

Winfree, A.T., & S.H. Strogatz. 1983. "Singular Filaments Organize Chemical Waves in Three Dimensions". *Physica* 8D.35.

Winnick, W.A., & S.A. Daniel. 1970. "Two Kinds of Response Priming in Tachistoscopic Recognition". *Journal of Experimental Psychology* 84.74-81.

Winocur, G., & L. Weiskrantz. 1976. "An Investigation of Paired-Associated Learning in Amnesic Patients". *Neuropsychologia* 14.97-110.

Winograd, T. 1975. "Frame Representations and the Declarative-Procedural Controversy". *Representations and Understanding: Studies in Cognitive Science* ed. by D.G. Bobrow & A.M. Collins. New York: Academic Press.

Winters, W.D., & M.B. Wallach. 1970. "During Induced States of CNS Excitation: A Theory of Hallucinosis". *Psychotomimetric Drugs* ed. by D.H. Efron, 193-214, New York: Raven Press.

Wisdom, J. 1952. *Other Minds*. New York: Philosophical Library.

Witherspoon, D., & M. Moscovitch. 1989. "Stochastic Independence between Two Implicit Memory Tasks". *Journal of Eperimental Psychology: Learning, Memory, and Cognition* 15.22-30.

Wittgenstein, L. 1953. *Philosophical Investigations*. Oxford: Blackwell.

Wittgenstein, L. 1968. "Notes for Lectures on 'Private Experience' and 'Sense Data'". ed. by R. Rhees. *Philosophical Review* LXXVII.275-320.

Wood, R., V. Ebert, & M. Kinsbourne. 1982. "The Episodic-Semantic Memory Distinction in Memory and Amnesia: Clinical and Experimental Observations". *Human Memory and Amnesia* ed. by L.S. Cermak. Hillsdale, New Jersey: Lawrence Erlbaum Associates.

Woodruff, G., & D. Premack. 1981. "Primitive Mathematical Concepts in the Chimpanzee: Proportionality and Numerosity". *Nature* 293.568-570.

Wundt, W. 1874. *Principles of Physiological Psychology*. Leipzig: Engelmann.

Wundt, W. 1896. *Outline of Psychology*. Leipzig: Engelmann.

Yao, Y., & W.J. Freeman. 1990. "Models of Biological Pattern Recognition with Spatially Chaotic Dynamics". *Neural Networks* 3.153-170.

Yorke, & T-Y. Li. 1975. "Period Three Implies Chaos". *American Mathematical Monthly* 82.985-992.

Young, M.P., K. Tanaka, & S. Yame. 1992. "On Oscillating Neuronal Responses in the Visual Cortex of the Monkey". *Journal of Neurophysiology* 67.1464-1474.

Zeki, S. 1992. "The Visual Image in Mind and Brain". *Scientific American* 267.68-77.

Zola-Morgan, S., & L.R. Squire. 1984. "Preserved Learning in Monkeys with Medial Temporal Lesions: Sparing of Motor and Cognitive Skills". *Journal of Neuroscience* 4.1072-1085.

Zucker, K.J. 1982. *The Development of Search for Mother During Brief Separation*. Ph.D. thesis, University of Toronto.

Index

What good is consciousness?
Must we put consciousness into
our robots?
Appearance and reality.